Geometric Origami

Robert Geretschläger

Shipley, United Kingdom

Geometric Origami

Copyright © Robert Geretschläger 2007

All rights reserved. No part of this publication may be reproduced or transmitted in any form or by any means, electronic or mechanical, including photocopy, recording, or any information storage and retrieval system, without permission in writing from the publisher.

Published by Arbelos.

PO Box 203, Shipley, BD17 5WT, United Kingdom
http://www.arbelos.co.uk

First published 2008.

Available in Japanese as "Mathematics of Origami", published by Morikita Publishing (2002).
1-4-11, Fujimi, Chiyoda-ku, Tokyo 102-0071, Japan
http://www.morikita.co.jp

Cover illustration and typographic design by Andrew Jobbings.
Typeset with LaTeX.

Printed in the UK for Arbelos by The Charlesworth Group, Wakefield.
http://www.charlesworth.com

ISBN 978-0-9555477-1-3

Contents

List of Models   v

Key for the Models   vii

Foreword   ix

Preface   xi

I   Some Theory   **1**

1   Euclidean and Origami Procedures   **3**
    1   Geometric constructions and where they come from 3
    2   Elementary Euclidean procedures 5
    3   Elementary geometric procedures of origami 7
    4   Reducing Euclidean procedures to origami 13
    5   Reducing origami procedures to Euclidean constructions 17

2   Origami Constructions and Algebra   **19**
    6   Linear equations 21
    7   Quadratic equations 23
    8   Folding cube roots 26
    9   Solving general cubic equations 30
    10   Trisecting angles 33
    11   Solving quartic equations 37

3   Properties of Origami Constructions   **53**
    12   Dividing line segments into sections of equal length 53
    13   Six problems from one fold 64
    14   Determining common folding methods for given creases 70
    15   Origami constructions on a parabola 96

4   The Maximum Polygon Problem   **103**

II   Some Practice   **113**

5   Triangles, Squares and More   **115**
    16   Triangles 115

17	The regular octagon and n-gons with $n = 2^k$	122
18	The regular hexagon and n-gons with $n = 3 \cdot 2^k$	125

6 The Regular Pentagon and its Cousins   129
19	Regular pentagons and the golden section	129
20	Some precise methods for folding a regular pentagon	133
21	The regular n-gon with $n = 5 \cdot 2^k \cdot 3^l$	139

7 The Regular Heptagon Family   145
22	The cubic equation	145
23	The "easy" regular heptagon and the regular 14-gon	148
24	The maximum regular heptagon	152

8 A Few More Polygons   159
25	The regular nonagon	159
26	The regular triskaidekagon	164
27	The regular 17-gon	172
28	The regular 19-gon	180

Some Final Remarks   **191**

Bibliography   **193**

List of Models

MODEL I	Maximum Equilateral Triangle	118
MODEL II	Regular Triangular Grid	120
MODEL III	Maximum Regular Octagon	122
MODEL IV	Maximum Regular 16-gon	124
MODEL V	Maximum Regular Hexagon	125
MODEL VI	Maximum Regular Dodecagon	128
MODEL VII	Easy Regular Pentagon	134
MODEL VIII	Maximum Regular Pentagon	136
MODEL IX	Maximum Regular Decagon	140
MODEL X	Easy Regular Heptagon	148
MODEL XI	Maximum Regular Heptagon	154
MODEL XII	Regular Nonagon	161
MODEL XIII	Regular Triskaidekagon	168
MODEL XIV	Regular 17-gon	175
MODEL XV	Regular 19-gon	184

Key for the Models

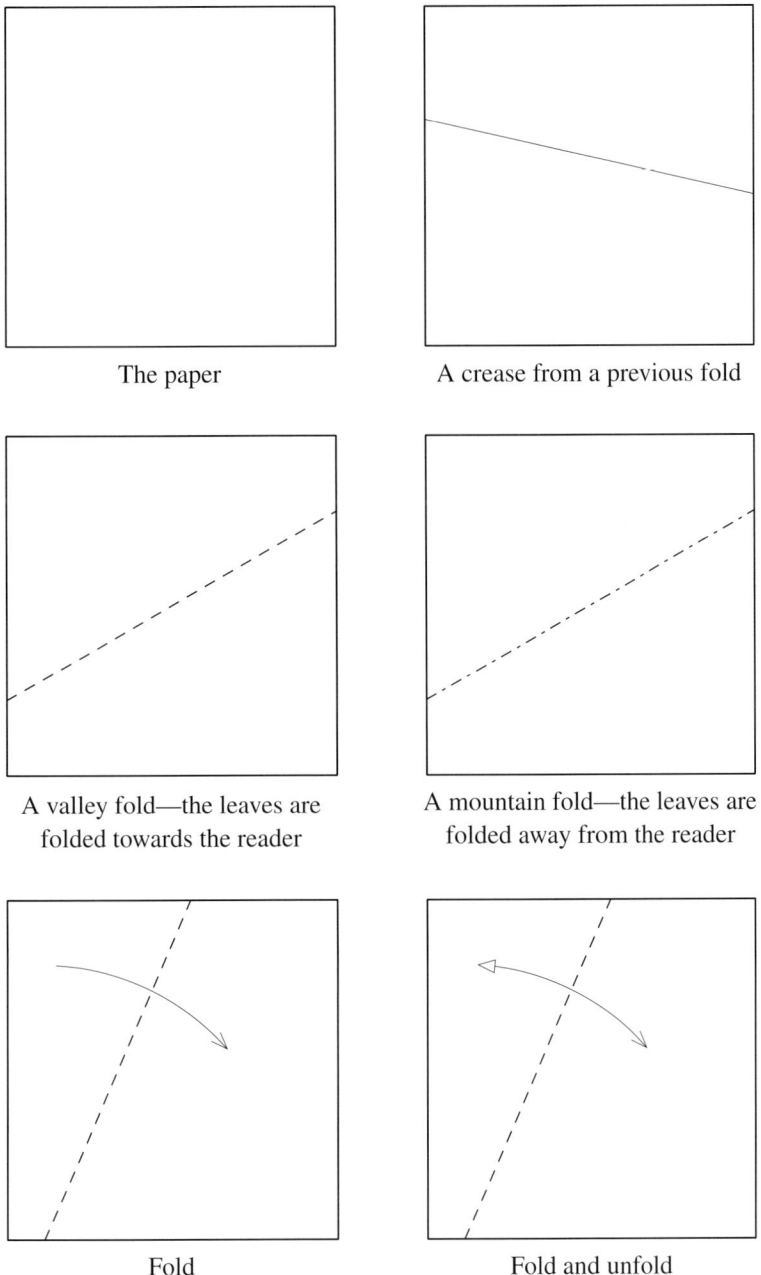

Foreword

Surely there is not much to be said about folding a sheet of paper? How wrong—there is very much that can be said, as is well known to anyone with more than a basic knowledge of origami, and to a few mathematicians.

Geometric Origami reveals some of the rich mathematics inherent in paper folding, and will help origamists, mathematicians and the interested general reader appreciate the value of studying the geometrical properties of folding a square of paper.

Robert Geretschläger and his family were kind and generous hosts during my stay in Graz in October 2007, and it gave me particular pleasure when Robert agreed for his book to be published in English[*] under the Arbelos imprint. I am sure it will become a classic in the field of mathematical origami.

The quality of the final book has been considerably improved by the work of two people. I am extremely grateful to Dennis Ward, who greatly assisted by copy-editing the text and mathematics with characteristic thoroughness. My special thanks are due to Daisy Gomersall, who put the step-by-step folding instructions to the test by carefully making all the Models with invaluable attention to detail. Of course, any remaining errors are the sole responsibility of the publisher and author.

Andrew Jobbings   Baildon, UK, September 2008

About the Author

Robert Geretschläger was born in Toronto, Canada in 1957. He moved to Austria in 1972, where he has been continuing his education ever since. Along the way he visited the Karl-Franzens University in Graz and the Graz University of Technology, picking up a Masters teaching degree in mathematics and descriptive geometry and a doctorate in mathematics. His doctoral thesis was in functional analysis, a subject area which he then immediately abandoned in favor of the more "pure" areas of geometry and problem mathematics.

---

[*]Though published in the United Kingdom, the author's original North American spelling has been retained.

Since 1981 he has been teaching in various schools, above all the Bundesrealgymnasium Keplerstrasse in Graz, and since 2003 he has also been teaching a geometry course at the Karl-Franzens University. During the course of his teaching activities, Robert became involved in the organization and preparation of student mathematics competitions; this has developed to a point where hardly a day goes by without some sort of competition related activity. He is one of the coaches of the Austrian team for the International Mathematical Olympiad, and was involved in the introduction in Austria of both the Kangourou des Mathématiques and the Tournament of the Towns.

His interest in origami goes back to childhood, and fond memories of struggling to fold a frog without its legs turning to mush are still very present. A number of his published mathematical papers are somehow related to this subject.

Robert has been happily married to Zita Geretschläger-Hauptmann since 1989, and they have one daughter, Lisa.

Preface

As you would probably expect, a book like this is not written in one sitting, but develops over an extended period of time. I first had the idea to combine my interests for geometry and origami somewhere around the early 1990s. At that time, I did not have any real notions of where this would lead, nor was I aware that any work in this area had already been published.

After a lot of puttering around with various notions of what could be considered "elementary" to the geometry involved in origami, I decided to settle on the intrinsic geometry of the creases created in the paper when folding it. This lead directly to many of the ideas presented here in the first few sections, and to my first paper on the subject, *"Euclidean Constructions and the Geometry of Origami"* [14].

At that time, I was well aware that there was a lot more that could still be said on the subject, but I was not yet sure how I should extend my approach. It seemed an obvious application of what I had already written to develop methods of folding some regular polygons, and my first impulse was to find folding methods for polygons that could not be constructed by Euclidean methods. The immediate results of this idea were two papers, [15] and [16], which were eventually to become the basis for sections 22, 23 and 25 of this book.

It was around the time I was working on these two papers (with the first about to be published) that I first gained access to a copy of the *Proceedings of the First International Meeting of Origami Science and Technology* [64], which finally gave me insight into what had already been done in the area. It was quite interesting to note that some of the ideas that I had come up with in the quiet of my own home had already been developed elsewhere in a slightly different way. (Needless to say, proper credit is given in the body of the text where ever I am aware that such parallel development has taken place.) Just as interesting, however, was the fact that the same fundamental concept had led people into radically different intellectual directions as well. It surprised me to see that there were profound connections to such diverse areas as map folding, fractal geometry and thermodynamics.

In January 1998 I had the opportunity to learn of more such things, as I was able to participate in the Joint Meetings of the AMS (American Mathematical Society), MAA (Mathematics Association of America) and SIAM (Society for Industrial and Applied Mathematics) in Baltimore. It was there that Tom Hull, who had already become something of a central figure in the origami and mathematics scene, despite the fact that he was just in the process of beginning his own academic career, had organised a special session on Paper Folding and Mathematics. This special session created quite a buzz at the meeting, and the room in which it was held was filled to overflowing at times. I had prepared three papers for this conference, [17], [18] and [19], which were eventually to develop into sections 26, 28, and 11 of this book, respectively.

It was while writing these papers that it became clear to me that I was already holding the skeleton of a book in my hands. This skeleton was then fleshed out to create the first version of the book you now hold in your hands. As I was looking for a publisher for my work, my good friend Hidetoshi Fukagawa decided that translating it into Japanese would make an interesting project. He went on to do this, and through his contact to Morikita Publishing, the Japanese version of the book was published in 2002. This original version has now been slightly updated, taking some recent developments into account.

The structure of the book

Part I of the book covers the mathematical theory of origami constructions. Chapter 1 discusses Euclidean and origami procedures for geometric constructions, and the relationship between them. Chapters 2 to 4 then build on Chapter 1 to consider the algebra behind origami constructions, the properties of origami constructions, and the problem of locating a maximum regular polygon in a square.

How does one fold regular polygons? Using the results in Part I methods for folding regular polygons of various types can be determined, and Part II gives step-by-step folding instructions for fifteen such models, from the equilateral triangle to the 19-gon. Where appropriate the mathematical derivation of each folding method, based on the work of Part I, is given after the instructions.

I suspect that no one reader will be equally interested in every part of this book, although I hope that every part will be of interest to someone. It was my intention to offer something on the subject for every possible interested reader, and so it was inevitable that there would be parts that any potential reader would find superfluous for their tastes. Some of the purely mathematical parts are highly elementary, and are certain to be skipped over by professional mathematicians. On the other hand, other parts are quite complex, and will go well beyond the scope of any readers with little or no mathematical background. The fifteen models are diagrammed such that they can be folded without bothering with the intrinsic mathematics at all—these parts are therefore accessible to origamists not interested in the scientific background. All told, I feel that readers only interested in the models, readers somewhat interested in the mathematical background but with little previous knowledge, and mathematicians interested in geometric constructions will all find approximately the same percentage of this work to suit their specific interests.

Acknowledgments

A great many people have assisted in the writing of this book in some way. Some helped with specific ideas or proofs, and these are duly noted in the text itself. A far greater number helped in more subtle ways, whether by pointing out relevant material to me, helping me get in touch with others, or just by being very supportive of my work. Some, I have never even had the pleasure of meeting in person, but I owe them all my gratitude, and I wish to thank them by naming them here.

Special thanks must go to Andrew Jobbings of Arbelos publishing, not only for taking the leap to publish the book in its original language, but also for doing the final polishing and making the raw LaTeX manuscript look like an actual book.

My profound thanks also go to: Gerd Baron, Erik Demaine, David Dureisseix, Peter-paul Forcher, Hidetoshi Fukagawa, Michael Hofer, Tom Hull, Stephen Keeling, Robert J. Lang, Vincent J. Matsko, Gottfried Perz, Gerhard Plattner, Douglas Rogers, Benedetto Scimemi and Andrei Storozhev.

Most importantly, I would like to thank my mother, Ingeborg Geretschläger, my daughter, Lisa Geretschläger, and my wife Zita Geretschläger-Hauptmann, for all their loving support and for providing the emotional stability needed to get through a project of this magnitude.

Robert Geretschläger   Graz, Austria, August 2008

Part I

Some Theory

Chapter 1

Euclidean and Origami Procedures

1 Geometric constructions and where they come from

Since well before the days of ancient Greece, mathematically inclined people have been thinking about methods of creating plane geometric figures. At first this was pretty much limited to sketching with a stick in the sand or doodling shapes on a cave wall with a piece of charcoal. Eventually, however, some clever people came up with better ways of doing this, going so far as to invent specific tools suited to the job, in particular the straight-edge (or ruler) and the compass. Soon they were giving a lot of thought to the problem of determining the limits of what exactly they could and couldn't draw using these tools.

One of the great intellectual achievements of humanity is Euclid's book *Elements*, which includes his method of deducing theorems by strictly applying rules of logic to certain definitions, axioms and postulates. This method led inevitably to similarly strict rules for creating geometric constructions with a straight-edge and compass, and the "Euclidean" constructions allowed by these rules have been the standard in plane geometry against which all else has been measured for over two thousand years. The simplicity of the rules describing what is "allowed" by these rules contrasts sharply with the seemingly unlimited possibilities they imply, and the precise inspection of what is and is not possible under these restrictions has been the motivation for discovering much of what makes up modern mathematics.

In the course of centuries of mathematical research, many alternatives to Euclid's rules have been considered. For instance, it is quite interesting to consider which constructions are possible when only either a straight-edge or a compass, but not both, is available. On the other hand, it is also quite interesting to consider the possibilities arising when constructions other than those defined by Euclid are allowed. The simple expedient of marking one point on the straight-edge yields a marked ruler, and using a marked ruler allows many additional constructions to be made which are not possible using only the basic Euclidean procedures. Similarly, many additional constructions become possible when new tools are introduced, such as a right-angle ruler or a three-legged compass. The same is true if a certain curve, such as a conic, is assumed to be given in the drawing plane. A great deal has been written about the possibilities offered by such extensions and their intrinsic rules, excellent examples being the books by J. Hjelmslev [28] and L. Bieberbach [3], or more recently the book by G. Martin [48].

Ever since paper was discovered (just a few centuries after the days of Euclid) people have been folding and unfolding it, and noting the fact that a crease pattern inevitably results. It is difficult to say who was the first to give any thought to the intrinsic geometry of these crease patterns, but it seems safe to say that the first published work on the subject was the famous book *Geometric Exercises in Paper Folding*, written by T. Sundara Row in 1893 [61]. This book might have been relegated to obscurity had it not come to the attention of Felix Klein (see [42] and [43]). The mention of Sundara Row's book in print by such a famous mathematician generated sufficient interest to warrant re-printings, and so this wonderful volume was made easily accessible to anyone who was interested.

This was certainly the starting point for many others who were to take up work in the field. Remarkable papers were published by C. A. Rupp [58] in 1924 and by Margherita Piazzolla Beloch, [56] and [57], in 1935 and 1936. Piazzolla Beloch's work seems to be the first specifically comparing the geometry of paper-folding creases with the geometry of Euclidean constructions. She was almost certainly the first to note the fact that paper-folding, if defined correctly, allows more than Euclidean constructions do, specifically the solution of cubic and quartic equations (although she did not describe specific methods of doing so).

Many decades have passed since then. During the last twenty years or so, interest in the geometry of paper-folding has grown immensely. The starting point for this very recent explosion was certainly a conference — the First International Meeting of Origami Science and Technology held in Ferrara, Italy in December 1989 — the proceedings of which have become the standard work commonly cited in modern papers on the subject. More specifically the work of Humiaki Huzita as editor of the proceedings and author in his own right together with Benedetto Scimemi was ground-breaking. Since then, there have been three more such meetings, held in Otsu, Japan in 1994, in Asilomar, California in 2002 and in Pasadena, California in 2006. Also, the Joint Meetings of the American Mathematical Society and the Mathematical Association of America in Baltimore in January 1998 saw a remarkable special session on Mathematical Methods in Paper Folding that surely did a great deal toward popularizing the subject.

Having taken this short side trip to the historical roots of our subject, we will now go on to look at the geometric constructions elementary to paper folding (including a definition of what we will consider to be "elementary"), and compare these to the constructions resulting from classical Euclidean methods. Once we have established what is possible, we will be able to apply this knowledge toward the solution of specific problems in further sections.

2 Elementary Euclidean procedures

When considering Euclidean constructions, it is assumed that specific points are known a priori in an infinite Euclidean plane. This is in sharp contrast to drawings that are actually constructed on paper or a blackboard. Any actual drawing surface is always finite. (A scrolling computer screen may seem infinite superficially, but the capacity of the computer doing the requisite calculations is also certainly finite.) It is not actually possible to draw points, since points in the Euclidean sense have position, but not magnitude, whereas any kind of a real visible marking always has some magnitude, no matter how small. These conceptual niceties will be mirrored by similar considerations in the case of origami constructions.

If needed, random points can be marked in addition to those already known. The reason that points are considered primal in this sense has to do with the way we create geometric drawings with straight-edge and compass. Whether we are drawing with a pencil on paper or with chalk on a blackboard or with a stick in the sand, merely touching the drawing implement lightly to the drawing surface creates a small blob, which can be abstracted to a point. Using straight-edge and compass as tools, we can then create lines and circles in accordance with specific set procedures. Since lines and circles are produced by moving the drawing implement on the drawing surface, they can be considered to be "made up" of points in a very real way. This idea means that we will think of lines and circles as sets of points as well as thinking of them as geometric entities in their own right. (It is also possible to think of a point as the set of all lines passing through it, of course. This "dual" way of thinking will be necessary for our considerations on origami constructions, as we shall soon see. Going back and forth between dual concepts is an essential basic concept of projective geometry, and this way of thinking will be mirrored in what follows.)

The following procedures are defined as being "allowed":

(E1) Given two non-identical points P and Q, one can draw the unique straight line $\ell = PQ$ containing both points, using the straight-edge.

(E2) Given a point M and the length of a line segment $r > 0$, one can draw the unique circle $c = \{M; r\}$ with M as center and r as radius, using the compass.

Specifically, the radius r has to be given as the length of a line segment connecting two known points P and Q, one of which may be M, in which case the other is a point on the circle (Figure 1.1).

A few important but subtle points must be included here that are often not mentioned in texts on Euclidean constructions, although they are always implicitly assumed. Just as we can mark random points in the plane and thereafter assume them to be "known" for the purpose of further constructions, we can do the same with points on a line or a circle once the line or circle has been determined by virtue of (E1) or (E2). We assume, as stated earlier, that lines and circles can be thought of as point sets, and that knowledge of the entire set therefore implies knowledge of each element of the set. Thinking of lines and circles as point sets means that it is not necessary to include (as Euclid himself did)

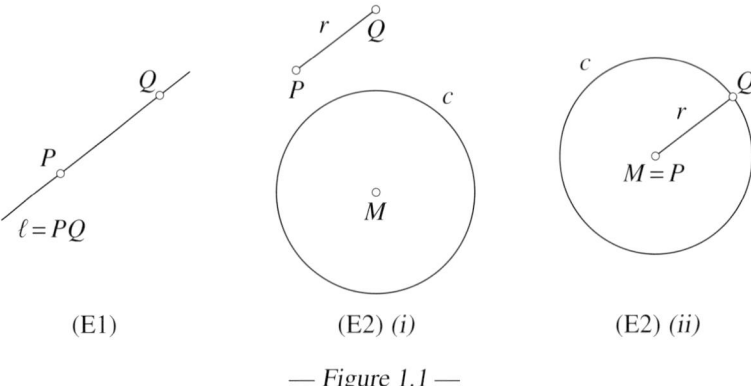

(E1) (E2) (i) (E2) (ii)

— Figure 1.1 —

the possibility of extending a known line segment indefinitely as a separate procedure. Knowledge of a line segment implies knowledge of its end-points, and so the complete (infinite) line is assumed to be constructible by virtue of (E1) if we are given these two points.

Also, random lines or circles can be introduced, since their generation can always be understood as an application of (E1) and (E2) to random points. This is done routinely in the course of geometric constructions with straight-edge and compass, but the justification of these actions is actually a rather fine point.

Application of (E1) and (E2) to the points known a priori leads to specific straight lines and circles. Knowledge of these then leads to further points by virtue of the following procedures of intersection, which are also defined as being "allowed" (Figure 1.2):

(E3) Given two non-parallel straight lines ℓ_1 and ℓ_2, one can determine their unique point of intersection $P = \ell_1 \cap \ell_2$.

(E4) Given a circle $c = \{M; r\}$ and a straight line ℓ, such that the distance between M and ℓ is not greater than r, one can determine the point(s) of intersection of c and ℓ.

(E5) Given two circles $c_1 = \{M_1; r_1\}$ and $c_2 = \{M_2; r_2\}$, such that either

(i) neither circle contains the center of the other in its interior, and the distance between the centers is not greater than the sum of the radii, or

(ii) one circle contains the center of the other in its interior, and the distance between the centers is not less than the difference of the radii,

one can determine the point(s) of intersection of c_1 and c_2.

(In practical applications, the locations of these points of intersection may not be known with sufficient precision to be of any use. The angle of intersection may be very small, or the relative positions of intersecting straight lines or circles may be inconvenient in other ways, so that the points of intersection may not be practically accessible. They are nevertheless assumed to be known in theory.)

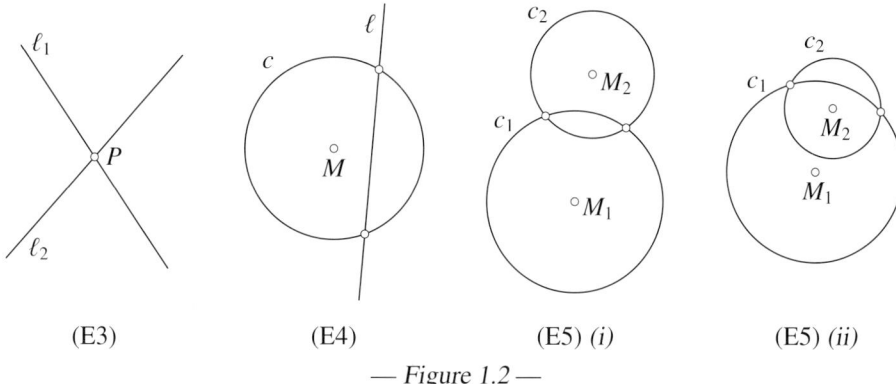

(E3)　　(E4)　　(E5) *(i)*　　(E5) *(ii)*

— *Figure 1.2* —

Iterated applications of (E1) to (E5) lead from a priori knowledge of specific points to specific straight lines and circles, then to further points, and so on. (Note that the tangent cases — line tangent to a circle or two touching circles — are usually assumed to require constructions in order to precisely determine the points of tangency. These cases are assumed to be included in (E4) and (E5).) A geometric construction problem is said to be "solvable" by Euclidean methods, if it can be shown that iterated application exclusively of (E1) to (E5) leads from certain given points to those points and/or straight lines and/or circles that have whatever geometric property is required.

3 Elementary geometric procedures of origami

Origami is, of course, the art of paper folding. (*Kami* is the Japanese word for paper, and *ori* the Japanese for folding; thus ori-kami, or origami.) As anyone who has ever put a crease in a piece of paper knows, there are certain procedures in paper folding that seem natural and basic. It is natural to fold a straight line, for instance, whereas folding a curve is possible, but difficult to control. (Although there are models in practical origami utilizing curved folds, for the moment we shall exclude these as non-elementary.) Folding a plane sheet of paper in such a way that a crease in the form of a line segment is created can be said to correspond to dividing a plane into two half-planes by a straight line and rotating one half-plane onto the other with the delineating line as the axis of rotation. It is very difficult to imagine a similar interpretation of folding curved creases, and in fact it requires concepts from calculus to do so. In this book, we shall restrict our considerations to straight folds exclusively.

As an origami model develops, its increasing complexity creates an increasingly complex analogous geometric pattern composed of straight lines (or, more precisely, line segments) on the paper used in producing the model. In most origami models, the result is in some way three-dimensional (although folding 2-dimensional forms such as regular polygons or stars is also sometimes considered), but every model can be opened up, and what we are considering in this book is essentially the geometry of the folds on the opened paper. Some abstraction is necessary, of course. Although most origami is done with squares (or rectangles), and certainly all with finite pieces of paper, for theoretical purposes we will consider folding an infinite Euclidean plane, with each fold creating an infinite straight line as a crease. This corresponds to the abstraction we agreed upon in defining Euclidean constructions, where we also consider our medium to be the infinite Euclidean plane, despite the fact that actual drawing is always done on a finite surface.

Folding multiple layers of paper also leads to some interesting phenomena. For instance, the result of a multi-level fold may be a finite line segment. We will consider such a line segment as automatically defining the infinite straight line of which it is a part. This is legitimized by the fact that every line segment has a unique pair of end-points, which lead to a whole line by folding the infinite paper through these points (a procedure we will define as being allowed). This is, of course, reminiscent of the idea used in the previous section to include the extension of a line-segment to an infinite line by virtue of (E1). Also, folding multiple layers allows points to be "marked" through the paper. That is, if a specific point comes to lie over another through folding, the multi-layered model can be folded (at least twice) along folds containing that specific point, thus "marking" the points on the other layers of paper immediately above or below that point. It therefore seems natural to assume that a known point, which is brought to lie over another through folding, defines the point in the other layer as equally well known. The same can be said to hold for a line which is brought into another position through folding; it too defines the overlying and underlying lines in the other layers of paper. The concept of reflection is therefore highly elementary to the theory of origami constructions, much more so than in the Euclidean case, since each folding procedure is essentially equivalent to a reflection on the crease line.

If we wish to compare Euclidean procedures to those used in origami, we must define "allowed" procedures, just as we did in the Euclidean case. As we have just seen, the basic geometric entity of origami is the straight line, in the form of a crease. There is no drawing utensil used in creating the creases in paper folding, and so points are not primal in the same sense that they are in the case of Euclidean constructions. There, the basic entity is the point, knowledge of points then leading to straight lines and circles, and so on. Here, the basic entity is the line, and points will be defined by means of certain lines on which they lie. This is an essential difference between the two types of constructions which cannot be overemphasized at this point. The dichotomy of primal entities — Euclidean points and origami lines — will have far-reaching consequences, not only for elementary considerations, but especially for the algebraic calculations to follow.

It seems reasonable to assume that a straight line can be folded randomly anywhere on the plane, just as a point can be drawn randomly anywhere in the plane. (We shall use the short form verbs "draw" for Euclidean constructions and "fold" for origami constructions.) Given this, it seems reasonable to first define the following as "allowed":

(O1) Given two non-parallel straight lines ℓ_1 and ℓ_2, one can determine their unique point of intersection $P = \ell_1 \cap \ell_2$.

(This is, of course, precisely the same as (E3), but in the origami case it defines how points can be considered to be known as secondary geometric entities, whereas in the Euclidean sense it is a posteriori in the sense that points are primal, but straight lines secondary, in that they have to be constructed with a straight-edge in order to exist in the construction at all.) Two non-parallel straight lines are thus considered to define their point of intersection.

When two parallel straight lines are given, one can always fold one onto the other in a unique way. The resulting fold is the straight line parallel to both, and equidistant from them. When two intersecting straight lines are given, they can be folded onto each other in two ways, the resulting folds being the angle bisectors of the given lines. It therefore seems reasonable to assume the following as "allowed":

(**O2**) Given two parallel straight lines ℓ_1 and ℓ_2, one can fold the line m parallel to and equidistant from them ("mid-parallel").

(**O3**) Given two intersecting straight lines ℓ_1 and ℓ_2, one can fold their angle bisectors a and a'.

Of course, (O3) includes the case where $\ell_1 = \ell_2$. In this case, the point of intersection can be assumed anywhere on the line $\ell_1 = \ell_2$, and for any such point, one "angle bisector" is the line itself (which does not actually need to be folded), and the other is the line through this point of intersection and orthogonal to $\ell_1 = \ell_2$.

By virtue of the fact that folding a point or a line onto another spot implies knowledge of points and lines in the other layers immediately above or below, these two procedures include the transferring of a known angle to another line. (O2) is the transfer of a line to a parallel line and (O3) that to an intersecting line (Figure 1.3). Also, (O3) includes the rotation of a given line-segment PQ, with one end-point in the point of intersection P of the two lines, from one line to the other.

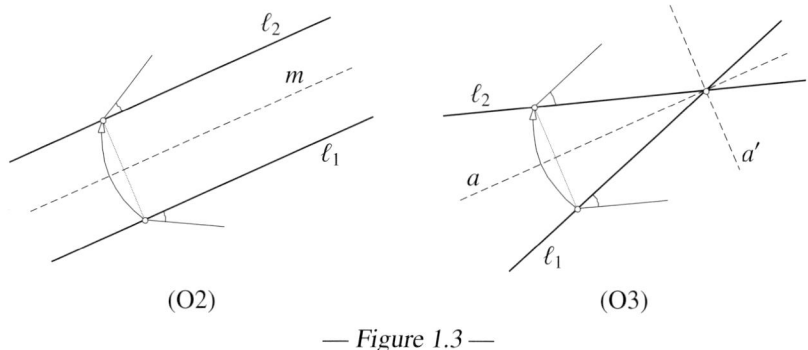

— Figure 1.3 —

Given two points on a piece of paper, it is straightforward to fold the unique straight line joining the two points (Figure 1.4). Equally straightforward, however, is the folding of one given point onto the other. The resulting fold is perpendicular to the line connecting the given points, and these points are equidistant from it. It is therefore the perpendicular bisector of the line segment defined by the two points. Further reasonable "allowed" procedures are therefore:

(O4) Given two non-identical points P and Q, one can fold the unique straight line $\ell = PQ$ connecting both points.

(O5) Given two non-identical points P and Q, one can fold the unique perpendicular bisector b of the line segment PQ.

Procedure (O4) is, of course, identical to (E1).

As with the rotation of a line segment in (O3), procedure (O5) includes transferring one end-point of a line segment of known length to another point (Figure 1.4). Together, (O5) and (O3) mean that one can transfer a line segment of known length to any spot on the paper, as any transfer can be achieved by combining reflections and rotations.

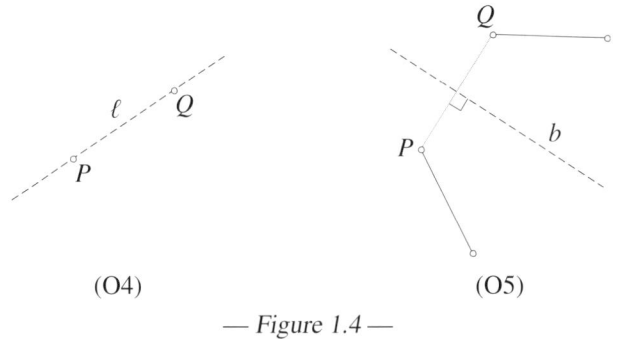

(O4) (O5)

— Figure 1.4 —

Given a point P and a straight line ℓ, it is straightforward to fold the line onto itself, such that the given point lies on the fold. Since the given line is folded onto itself, the fold has to be perpendicular to it, as described in (O3). If P is a point on ℓ, this is in fact the same as (O3) in the special case $\ell_1 = \ell_2$ (Figure 1.5). A further "allowed" procedure is thus:

(O6) Given a point P and a straight line ℓ, one can fold the unique line ℓ' perpendicular to ℓ and containing P.

Note that a fold of this type can also be interpreted as joining the point P with the point at infinity orthogonal to ℓ. In this sense, (O6) is not a separate procedure at all, but rather a special case of (O4).

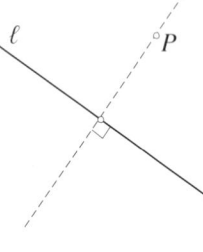

— Figure 1.5 —

Finally, given a straight line ℓ and a point P not on the line, it is straightforward to fold P onto any point on the line. The resulting (infinitely many) folds are the elements of the set of perpendicular bisectors of all line segments with the given point P at one end, and a point on the line ℓ at the other. This is precisely the set of tangents of the parabola with P as its focus and ℓ as its directrix (Figure 1.6a).

Why is this the case? A parabola is, of course, defined as the set of all points in the plane equidistant from a point P and a line ℓ. Folding P onto a point P' on ℓ yields a crease c, and the point X on c obtained by intersecting c with the line through P' orthogonal to ℓ

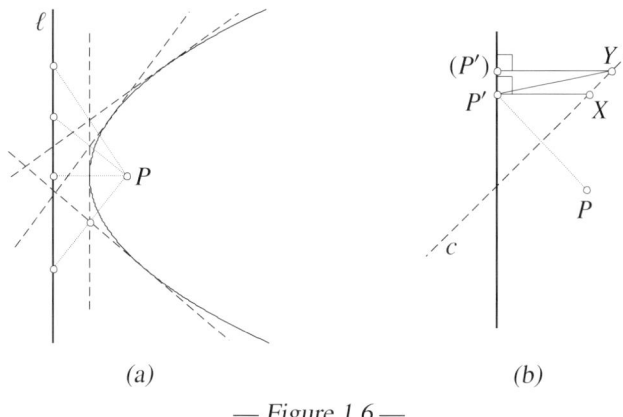

— *Figure 1.6* —

certainly has the property of equidistance from P and ℓ (Figure 1.6b). In order to show that c is a tangent of this parabola, we must show that there is no further point of the parabola on c.

If we assume the existence of a further such point $Y \neq X$ on c, we note that $YP = YP'$, since Y is a point of the perpendicular bisector c of PP'. On the other hand, if we designate the foot of Y on ℓ as (P'), we see that $Y(P') < YP' = YP$, since the side $Y(P')$ of the right triangle $\triangle Y(P')P'$ is shorter than its hypotenuse YP'. It is therefore impossible for Y to be equidistant from P and ℓ, and we see that X is the only point of the parabola on c. The crease c is therefore a tangent of the parabola.

We see that parabolas, or rather the sets of tangents of parabolas, play an elementary role in the geometry of paper folding. The role played by parabolas in the intrinsic geometry of paper folding is comparable to the role played by circles in the intrinsic geometry of Euclidean constructions. Here, we are dealing with line conics (that is, the sets of tangents of the parabolas), whereas in the case of the circles in Euclidean constructions, we are dealing with point conics (that is, the sets of points of the circles), again an indication of the dichotomy Euclidean points – origami lines.

Given P and ℓ and a further point Q, it is also straightforward to fold P onto ℓ such that Q lies on the fold. The fold is therefore a tangent of the parabola, containing Q (Figure 1.7a on the following page). If the point Q is a point at infinity, this means that we can also fold P onto ℓ such that a line q is folded onto itself (Figure 1.7b). (This possibility was not expressly mentioned in previous versions of this description of origami constructions, such as in [14], a fundamental omission pointed out by Koshiro Hatori in 2002.)

A further "allowed" procedure is therefore:

(O7) Given a point P and a straight line ℓ, one can fold any tangent of the parabola with focus P and directrix ℓ. Specifically, given a further point Q, one can fold the tangents of the parabola containing Q (when they exist), and given a line q not parallel to ℓ, one can fold the tangent of the parabola perpendicular to q. If $P \in \ell$, folding P onto the points of ℓ yields all lines orthogonal to ℓ, except that one passing through P.

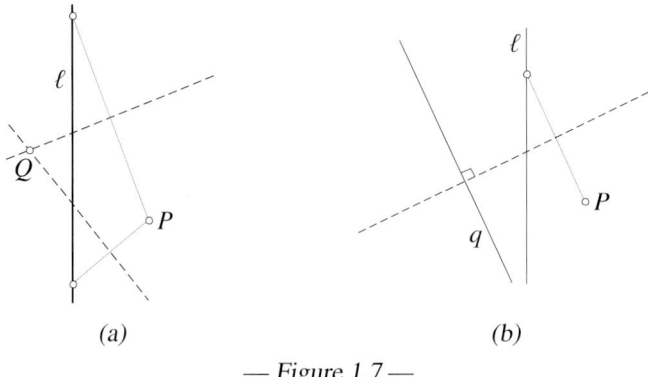

(a) (b)

— *Figure 1.7* —

As with (O3) and (O5), this includes the fact that one can find the points X and $\overline{X}$ on a given line ℓ having the same distance from a given point Q as another given point P. This is slightly more specific than (O3). Procedure (O3) merely means that the points of a circle can be found by folding (see 4.2), whereas (O7) implies that the points of intersection of a line and a circle can be found immediately (see 4.4 and Figure 1.9).

Given two points P_1 and P_2 and two lines ℓ_1 and ℓ_2, it is still straightforward to fold P_1 onto ℓ_1 and P_2 onto ℓ_2 with the same fold (Figure 1.8). (The word "onto" has to be understood in a wide sense here, as the points can come to lie above the lines, or the lines above the points, or one of each.) In any case, the resulting fold is a common tangent of the two parabolas with foci P_1 and P_2 and directrices ℓ_1 and ℓ_2 respectively.

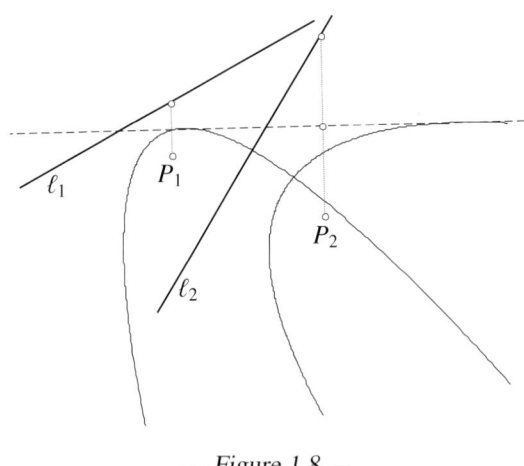

— *Figure 1.8* —

A final "allowed" procedure is thus:

(O7*) Given (possibly identical) points P_1 and P_2 and (possibly identical) lines ℓ_1 and ℓ_2, one can fold the common tangents of the parabolas p_1 and p_2 with foci P_1 and P_2 and directrices ℓ_1 and ℓ_2.

It is the existence of procedure (O7*) that makes the geometry of origami constructions fundamentally different from that of Euclidean constructions. As we shall see in the next two sections, Euclidean constructions are equivalent to that part of origami constructions utilizing (O1)–(O7). Procedure (O7*), however, allows constructions not accessible by Euclidean methods, similar to those utilizing a marked ruler, the theory of which is well established (see [3] pp. 74–78). It is not surprising that (O7*) goes beyond Euclidean constructions, if one considers what it means analytically. It is known that two conics in general have four common tangents. If both are parabolas, one of these common tangents is the line at infinity. This leaves three common tangents to determine, and it is thus a cubic problem to find the common tangents of two parabolas. In general, it is not to be expected that any cubic problem can be solved by Euclidean methods.

If the foci P_1 and P_2 are identical, the only common tangent is found by folding this point onto the point of intersection of ℓ_1 and ℓ_2. It is not surprising that there is only one further common tangent of p_1 and p_2 to be found, since it is known from projective geometry that the common focus is equivalent to a pair of common complex tangents.

If the directrices are identical, p_1 and p_2 not only have the line at infinity as a common tangent, but they also have a common point at infinity where the line at infinity is tangent. The line at infinity therefore counts as a double common tangent, and there are only two further common tangents to be found. These are then, of course, the angle bisectors of the common directrix and the line joining the two foci. In these two special cases, finding the common tangents can be solved by Euclidean methods, as the problem is reduced to a linear or quadratic one.

4 Reducing Euclidean procedures to origami

In this section, we shall show that each of the elementary Euclidean procedures (E1)–(E5) can be replaced by combinations of (O1)–(O7).

4.1 Reducing (E1) to origami

Procedure (E1) is identical to (O4).

4.2 Reducing (E2) to origami

A circle cannot be "drawn" by origami procedures in the same sense as is possible with a compass. By virtue of (E2), it is assumed that the entire infinite set of points, whose distance from a certain point M is a constant value r, can be determined in its entirety using the compass. This is certainly not possible by origami methods, since every step as defined from (O1) through (O7*) creates either one or more straight lines as creases or one or more discrete points as points of intersection of creases. Each step creates a finite number of points of a specific circle at most. The infinitely many points of a circle are therefore not "foldable".

Nevertheless, a circle can still be considered to be well-determined if one knows its center

M and radius r, as one can determine any number of points and tangents of the circle. This can be achieved in the following manner (Figure 1.9):

(a) If the center M and radius $r = AB$ of a circle are known, it is possible to fold A to M by virtue of (O5) (folding the perpendicular bisector of MA). This brings B to a point B', and we have $r = MB'$.

(b) If a specific line ℓ through M is given, the radius $r = MB'$ can be folded onto it by virtue of (O3) (folding an angle bisector of $\angle MB', \ell$). This yields the point P as a point on the circle on the diameter ℓ. (The other angle bisector yields the diametrically opposite point of the circle.)

(c) Folding ℓ onto itself through P by virtue of (O6) yields the line perpendicular to the diameter containing P, which is precisely the tangent of the circle in P.

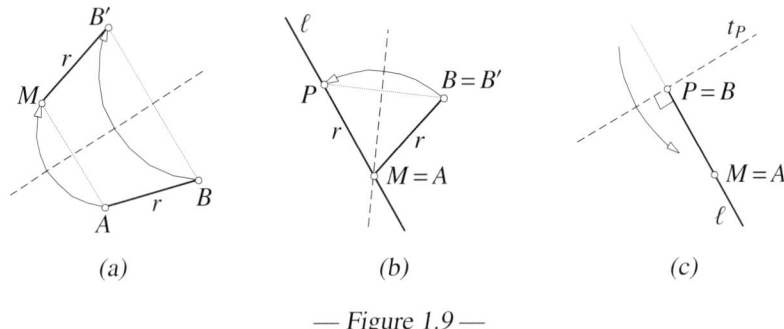

— Figure 1.9 —

While we may not be able to determine the sets of points or tangents of a circle in their entirety, we see that we can determine all points and tangents of any circle individually. Since it is also possible to determine the points of intersection of a circle and a line, as well as those of two circles (as we shall see momentarily), we are quite justified in saying that the drawing of a circle as defined in (E2) can be replaced by a combination of origami procedures.

4.3 Reducing (E3) to origami

Procedure (E3) is identical to (O1).

4.4 Reducing (E4) to origami

If a circle is known by its center M and a point P on its circumference, and a line ℓ is given, the points of intersection of the circle and ℓ can be found by folding P onto ℓ such that the fold contains M. This is possible by virtue of (O7) (Figure 1.10). In doing this, finding the points of intersection of a circle and a straight line is seen to be equivalent to finding the tangents of a specific parabola (with focus P and directrix ℓ) containing a specific point (M).

4 Reducing Euclidean procedures to origami

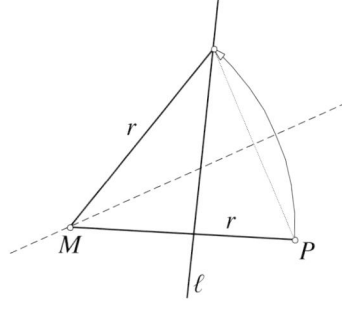

— Figure 1.10 —

4.5 Reducing (E5) to origami

Since circles are only accessible in origami through knowledge of specific points and tangents, it is obviously not possible to find the common points of two circles directly. It is, however, possible to find the common chord of intersecting circles, thus reducing (E5) to (E4). This can be achieved in the following manner.

We assume that two circles, whose points of intersection we wish to determine, are given. Let the distance between their centers be a, and let the radii be b and c respectively. Assuming (in Figure 1.11) the center of one circle in the origin of a cartesian coordinate system, and the center of the other on the x-axis, their equations are $x^2 + y^2 = c^2$ and $(x - a)^2 + y^2 = b^2$ respectively.

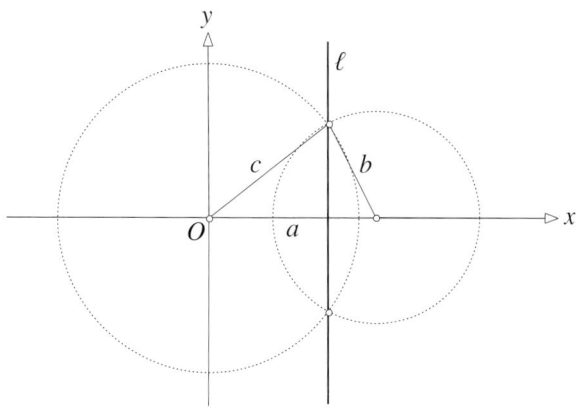

— Figure 1.11 —

Their common chord is therefore the line represented by the equation

$$x^2 + y^2 - c^2 = x^2 - 2xa + a^2 + y^2 - b^2$$

$$\Leftrightarrow \quad x = \frac{a^2 - b^2 + c^2}{2a}.$$

The common points of the two circles thus lie on the line which is perpendicular to the line connecting their centers, and whose distance to the center of the circle with radius

Chapter 1   Euclidean and Origami Procedures

c is $\frac{a^2-b^2+c^2}{2a}$ (or equivalently, whose distance to the center of the circle with radius b is $\frac{a^2+b^2-c^2}{2a}$). This line can readily be found by origami procedures. One way of doing this is described in the following four steps.

Step 1   Since the distances a and c are known, it is possible to fold a right triangle with sides a and c ((O3), (O5), (O6)).

The length of the hypotenuse is then $\sqrt{a^2 + c^2}$.

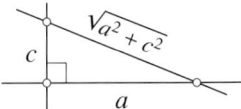

Step 2   The distances b and $\sqrt{a^2 + c^2}$ are known.

Therefore it is possible to fold a right triangle with side b and hypotenuse $\sqrt{a^2 + c^2}$ ((O3), (O5), (O6), (O7)).

The length of the second side is then $\sqrt{a^2 - b^2 + c^2}$.

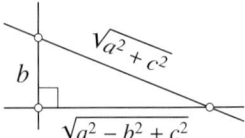

Step 3   A triangle can be folded with one side of unit length 1 and one side of length $\sqrt{a^2 - b^2 + c^2}$.

A similar triangle can then be folded ((O2), (O3)) with a side of length $\sqrt{a^2 - b^2 + c^2}$ corresponding to that side of the first triangle with length 1.

Then the side of the second triangle corresponding to that side of the first triangle with length $\sqrt{a^2 - b^2 + c^2}$ has length $a^2 - b^2 + c^2$.

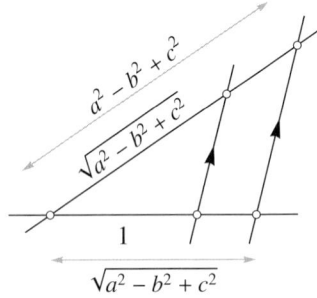

Step 4   A triangle can be folded with one side of length $2a$ and another of length $a^2 - b^2 + c^2$ ((O2), (O3)).

A similar triangle can be folded with a side of length 1 corresponding to the side of the first triangle with length $2a$ ((O2), (O3), (O5)).

Then the side corresponding to the side of the first triangle with length $a^2 - b^2 + c^2$ has length $\frac{a^2-b^2+c^2}{2a}$.

This is precisely the length we set out to produce.

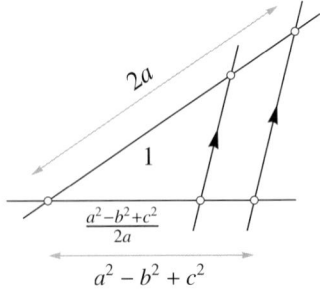

Procedure (E5) is thus reduced to (E4), as we need only find the points of intersection of the common chord with either circle.

In summary, we have the following

Theorem 1
Every construction that can be done using Euclidean methods can also be achieved by elementary methods of origami. Specifically, the Euclidean procedures (E1)–(E5) can all be replaced by combinations of the origami procedures (O1)–(O7).

5 Reducing origami procedures to Euclidean constructions

In this section we shall show that each of the elementary origami procedures (O1)–(O7) can be replaced by combinations of (E1)–(E5). That this is not to be expected for (O7*) has already been explained at the end of section 3 on pages 12–13.

5.1 Identical procedures

As already mentioned in sections 4.1 and 4.3 on pages 13–14, (O1) is identical to (E3), and (O4) is identical to (E1).

5.2 The basic procedures (O2), (O3), (O5) and (O6)

The origami procedures (O2), (O3), (O5) and (O6) are the constructions of, respectively: the mid-parallel of two parallel lines; the angle bisectors of two intersecting lines; the perpendicular bisector of a line segment; and a line through a given point and perpendicular to a given line. All of these constructions are known to be possible using Euclidean methods.

5.3 Reducing (O7) to Euclidean constructions

Determining the tangents of a parabola given by its focus P and directrix ℓ through a given point A or perpendicular to a given line q by Euclidean methods is not difficult, but the methods are perhaps not as well-known as those in 5.2. A review of some elementary properties of the parabola seems in order here (Figure 1.12 on the next page).

If a specific point X of a parabola with focus P and directrix ℓ is known, we have $XP = X\ell$ by definition of a parabola. The axis a of the parabola contains P and is perpendicular to ℓ. The line parallel to a passing through X intersects ℓ in a point P'. Obviously $XP' = X\ell = XP$. As we saw in section 3 (Figure 1.6b on page 11), the perpendicular bisector of PP' is the tangent of the parabola in X. It therefore follows that all points of this tangent are equidistant from P and P'.

If we are given a point A not on the parabola (Figure 1.12a), and wish to determine the tangents of the parabola passing through A, we can therefore apply the following method.

Since a tangent t containing A is the perpendicular bisector of the line segment PP', where P' is the point on ℓ corresponding to that point X where t is tangent to the parabola, the distance from A to P is equal to the distance from A to P'. Using the compass, we can find the two possible points P' (if they exist), and can thus find the tangents t along with the points X by first determining the perpendicular bisectors of the resulting line segments PP' and then determining the points of intersection of each of the tangents t with the respective lines parallel to a passing through the respective points P'.

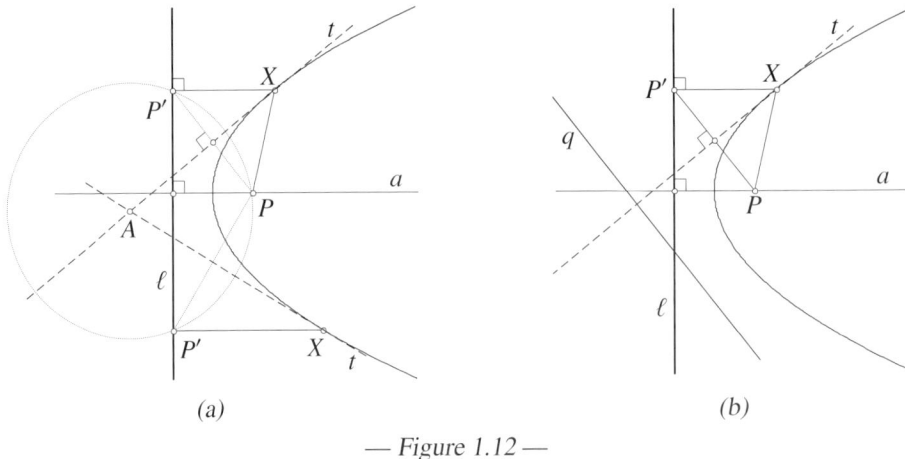

— Figure 1.12 —

If we are given a line q not parallel to ℓ (Figure 1.12b), and wish to determine the tangent of the parabola perpendicular to q, we need only note that PP' is perpendicular to the tangent in question, and therefore parallel to q. The point P' is therefore the point in which ℓ intersects the line parallel to q and passing through P, and the tangent we wish to determine is the bisector of PP'.

We see that (O7) is also replaceable by Euclidean methods. In summary, we therefore have the following

Theorem 2
Every construction that can be done using the origami methods (O1)–(O7) exclusively can also be achieved by Euclidean methods.

Together with Theorem 1 this means that every geometric construction that is possible using the origami methods (O1)–(O7) can also be achieved by the Euclidean methods (E1)–(E5) and vice versa. The two sets of constructions are thus equivalent. As we have already seen, the procedure (O7*) adds additional geometric constructions to the set of possible constructions generated by these equivalent sets. We therefore see that the set of constructions that can be generated by Euclidean methods is a true subset of the set that can be generated by origami methods. It will be of special interest in the following sections to find solutions to construction problems using origami methods that are known to be impossible by Euclidean methods.

Chapter 2

Origami Constructions and Algebra

When Euclidean constructions are analyzed from an algebraic view-point, it is assumed that a system of cartesian coordinates is embedded in the drawing plane. As points are constructed, their coordinates can be calculated, and so constructions can be simulated by parallel algebraic "constructions". The straight lines produced by the straight-edge by virtue of (E1) are considered equivalent to the set of all points represented by ordered pairs of coordinates (x, y) in $\mathbb{R}^2$ solving a linear equation in two variables. The equations are of the form

$$px + qy = r,$$

with real coefficients p, q and r and $(p, q) \neq (0, 0)$.

Similarly, the circles produced by the compass by virtue of (E2) are considered equivalent to the set of all points represented by ordered pairs of coordinates (x, y) in $\mathbb{R}^2$ solving a quadratic equation in two variables of the form

$$(x - m)^2 + (y - n)^2 = r^2.$$

The mid-point of the circle is the point with coordinates (m, n), and the radius of the circle is r.

Procedures (E3), (E4) and (E5) can then all be thought of as determining the solution(s) of systems of equations in two variables, whereby (E3) is the solution of a system of two linear equations, (E4) is the solution of a system consisting of a linear and a quadratic equation, and (E5) is the solution of a system of two quadratic equations.

If we now wish to turn our attention to the algebraic analysis of origami constructions, one option is to consider point coordinates as variable as we did for Euclidean constructions. Each crease is then a straight line and can be considered as a set of points represented by ordered pairs of coordinates (x, y) as in the Euclidean case. We will be considering a few applications of this idea in the next two sections.

Another option can be derived from the primality of lines in origami constructions (in contrast to the primality of points in Euclidean constructions). As we shall see in the next few sections, this can be a better option, yielding simpler calculations and methods.

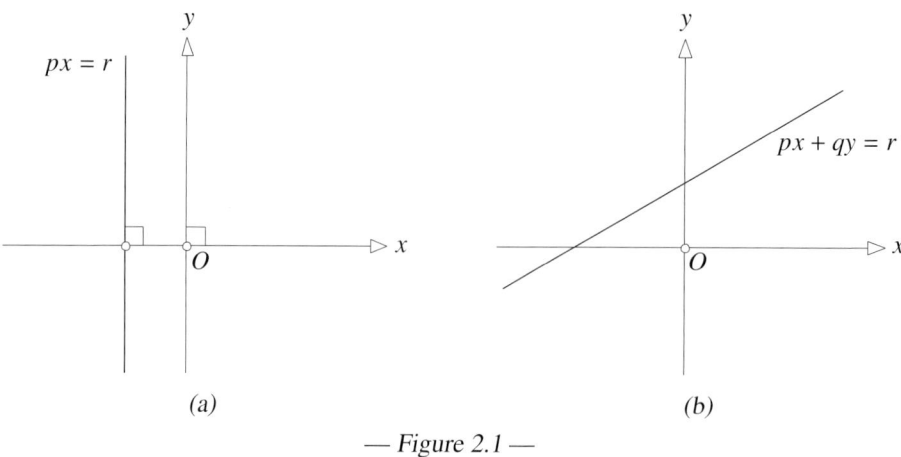

— Figure 2.1 —

In this case, as before, we assume a system of cartesian coordinates embedded in the folding plane. In the sense described above, the line is represented by a linear equation of the form $px + qy = r$, with $(p, q) \neq (0, 0)$. If $q = 0$ (Figure 2.1a), the line is parallel to the y-axis and intersects the x-axis in $\left(\frac{r}{p}, 0\right)$.

If $q \neq 0$ (Figure 2.1b), we can divide the equation by q, which (by subtracting $\frac{p}{q} \cdot x$) yields the equivalent equation

$$y = -\frac{p}{q} \cdot x + \frac{r}{q}.$$

Renaming $-\frac{p}{q} =: m$ and $\frac{r}{q} =: b$, this yields the equation

$$y = mx + b.$$

m is called the "slope" of the line, and b the "y-intercept" (because the common point of the line and the y-axis has the coordinates $(0, b)$).

In a sense, we can say that a line not parallel to the y-axis is equivalent to the ordered pair of numbers $(m; b)$, and the slope m by itself is equivalent to the set of all parallel lines with equations $y = mx + b$ and variable b. By defining the slope of lines parallel to the y-axis as infinite, we can therefore represent each set of parallel lines by a unique number $m \in \mathbb{R} \cup \{\infty\}$, which we again name the "slope" of the set of lines.

The slope has an immediate connection to point coordinates, which is standard knowledge from Euclidean constructions, and which will prove to be quite practical for origami constructions (Figure 2.2).

If (x_0, y_0) is a point on the line $y = mx + b$, so is the point $(x_0 + 1, y_0 + m)$, since

$$y_0 + m = m \cdot (x_0 + 1) + b$$

and

$$y_0 = mx_0 + b$$

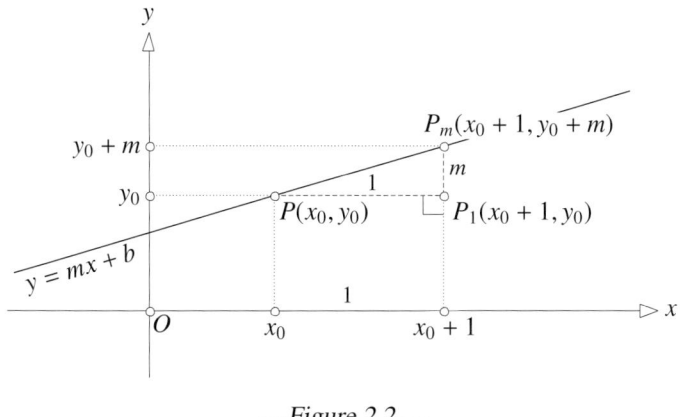

— Figure 2.2 —

are equivalent equations. Determining the slope m of a line as the length of a line segment therefore simply involves choosing any point P on the given line, then determining the point P_1 which results by transferring P by the unit length in the direction of the positive x-axis, and finally determining the point P_m, which lies on the given line such that $P_1 P_m$ is parallel to the y-axis. The line segment $P_1 P_m$ then has length m.

As we now turn our attentions to specific methods of solving equations, we shall see that the concept of slope will come in very handy. Although we shall assume that all coefficients of equations to be solved are given as lengths of line segments, actually solving the equations will be simpler if we consider slopes of lines as representing the solutions than is the case if we attempt to find the solutions directly as lengths of line segments.

6 Linear equations

Our object in this section is to describe a method of determining line segments whose lengths are solutions of the equation

$$ax = b$$

if a and b are given as oriented lengths of line segments with $a \neq 0$ (we shall ignore the trivial case $b = 0$ as well). This is, of course, equivalent to finding line segments whose length is $\frac{b}{a}$.

One way of doing this is by exploiting some elementary properties of similar triangles (Figure 2.3 on the following page).

We assume that XAB is a triangle with $XA = a$ and $XB = b$. (Here we are considering the case of non-oriented line segments, and therefore assuming for the moment that a and b are both positive. If this is not the case, we can replace them by their absolute values.) We let U be a point on XA such that the length of XU is the unit length 1 (if $a < 1$, choose U beyond A on the ray $\overrightarrow{XA}$), and determine UP parallel to AB with P on the line XB.

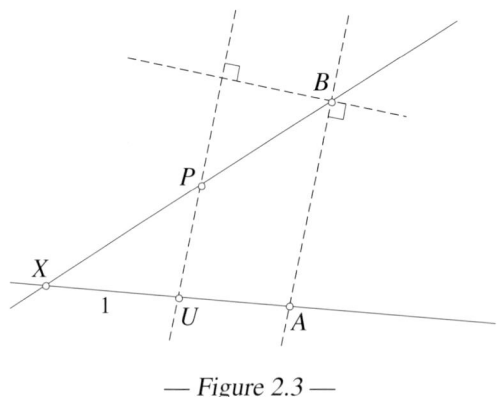

— Figure 2.3 —

Since the triangles $\triangle XUP$ and $\triangle XAB$ are similar, we have

$$XP : XU = XB : XA$$

or $$XP : 1 = b : a,$$

which means that $$XP = \frac{b}{a}.$$

If a and b are both positive or both negative, $\frac{b}{a}$ is positive. If one number is positive and the other negative, the quotient is negative, and this determines the orientation of the line segment.

A special case of this method is given if we assume a right angle in X (Figure 2.4).

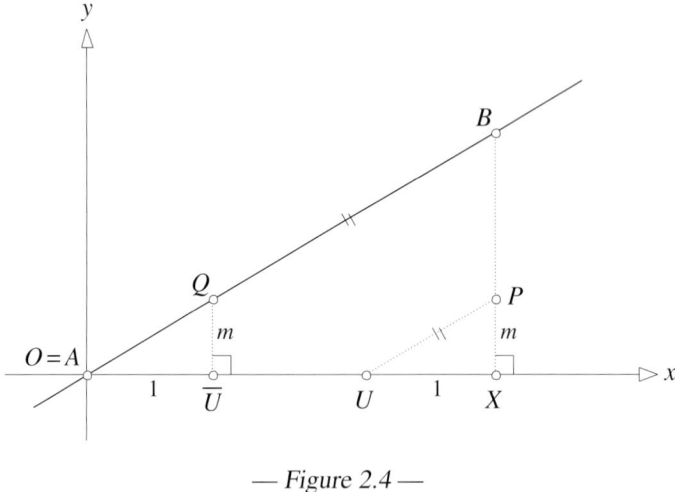

— Figure 2.4 —

Here, we assume that a and b are oriented line segments. (In the figure, both are positive, but the method works no matter how a and b are oriented.) We have chosen A in the origin O, X on the x-axis such that $\overrightarrow{AX} = a$ and B such that $\overrightarrow{XB} = b$ is parallel to the y-axis. Furthermore, U is chosen on the x-axis such that $\overrightarrow{UX} = 1$. As before, it follows that $\overrightarrow{XP} = \frac{b}{a}$.

If $\overline{U}$ is the point on the x-axis with $\overrightarrow{AU} = 1$, and Q is the point on the line AB with $\overline{QU}$ parallel to the y-axis, triangles $\triangle AQ\overline{U}$ and $\triangle UPX$ are congruent by the angle-side-angle theorem, and we have $\overrightarrow{\overline{U}Q} = \overrightarrow{XP} = \frac{b}{a}$.

At the same time, $\overrightarrow{\overline{U}Q}$ is the slope m of the line AB as discussed on pages 20–21 (Figure 2.2). Since A was chosen in O, B has the coordinates (a, b), and we see that the solution x of the linear equation $ax = b$ is simply the slope of the line connecting $O = A$ and B. If a and b are given, this means that we must simply determine the point with coordinates (a, b), and the line connecting this point with the origin has a slope solving the associated linear equation. Since this only involves making a single crease OB (by virtue of (O4)), this is about as simple an origami construction as there can be.

In the next section, we shall compare methods for solving quadratic equations derived from point coordinates and slopes respectively, and the advantages of the slope method will be even more pronounced. So much so in fact, that we shall only be considering slope methods for solving cubic and quartic equations in the following sections.

7 Quadratic equations

In this section, we develop methods of solving quadratic equations of the form

$$ax^2 + bx + c = 0,$$

with $a \neq 0$. In order to keep things a bit simpler, we divide the equation by a and consider the normalized equation

$$x^2 + px + q = 0$$

resulting from the substitutions $\frac{b}{a} =: p$ and $\frac{c}{a} =: q$. (These divisions can, if necessary, be performed as shown in the previous section.)

First of all, we consider a method derived from Euclidean constructions. (This method is also described in [53].)

As we see in Figure 2.5a on the next page, we assume a system of cartesian coordinates as given in the plane. The point U lies on the y-axis, one unit above the origin (that is, U has the coordinates $(0, 1)$). X is the point with coordinates $(-p, q)$ with p and q as determined by the coefficients of the quadratic equation.

M is the mid-point of XU, and R and S are the points in which the circle with diameter XU (and therefore mid-point M) intersect the x-axis. What are the coordinates of R and S?

(a) (b)

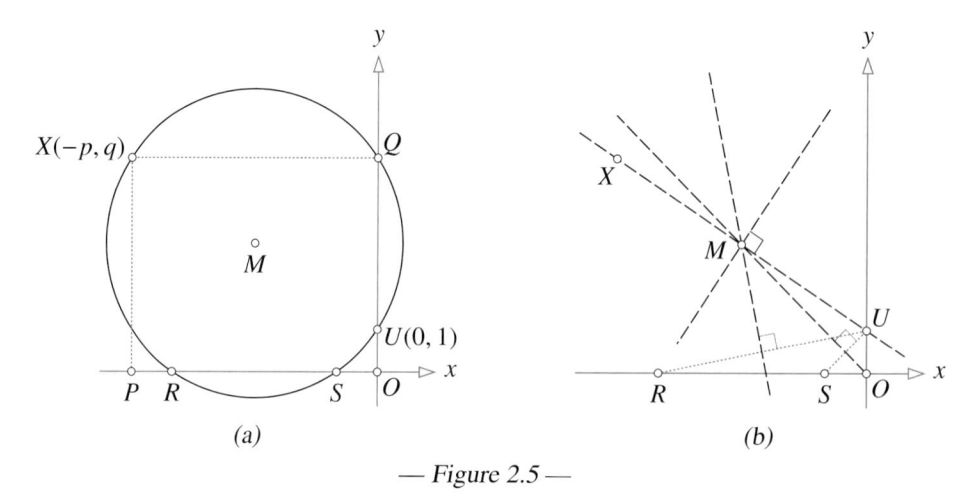

— Figure 2.5 —

Since they are points of the x-axis, their y-coordinates are obviously each equal to 0. In order to determine their x-coordinates, we note that M is equidistant from R, S and U. Since M is the mid-point of XU, its coordinates are

$$M\left(-\frac{p}{2}, \frac{q+1}{2}\right).$$

If we now assume that the x-coordinates of R and S are represented by a variable x_0, the fact that

$$|MR| = |MS| = |MU|$$

means

$$\sqrt{\left(x_0 + \frac{p}{2}\right)^2 + \left(\frac{q+1}{2}\right)^2} = \sqrt{\left(\frac{p}{2}\right)^2 + \left(\frac{1-q}{2}\right)^2}$$

or

$$x_0^2 + px_0 + \frac{p^2}{4} + \frac{q^2 + 2q + 1}{4} = \frac{p^2}{4} + \frac{1 - 2q + q^2}{4},$$

that is,

$$x_0^2 + px_0 + q = 0.$$

We see that the x-coordinates of R and S are precisely the solutions of the given quadratic equation. The circle with diameter XU intersects the x-axis if and only if the equation has real solutions.

In order to apply this idea to an origami construction (Figure 2.5b), we assume that the x-axis and the points U and X are given. (Note that the direction of the x-axis as well as the unit length can be chosen freely. The values of p and q are then specific multiples of the unit length.) Folding the crease joining X and U (by (O4)) and the perpendicular bisector of XU (by (O5)) determines M as the mid-point of XU. Folding U onto the x-axis such that the crease passes through M transfers U to R (and S) by (O7).

This method involves a circle, which is quite elementary from a Euclidean viewpoint, but not so when using origami methods. It is to be expected that a slightly simpler method

7 Quadratic equations

could be derived by somehow "replacing" the circle by a parabola. In order to do this, we assume the following situation as given.

Consider a parabola with the equation

$$p_0 : x^2 = 2u \cdot y$$

(where u is the parameter of p_0), and the point $P_0(v, w)$, as in Figure 2.6.

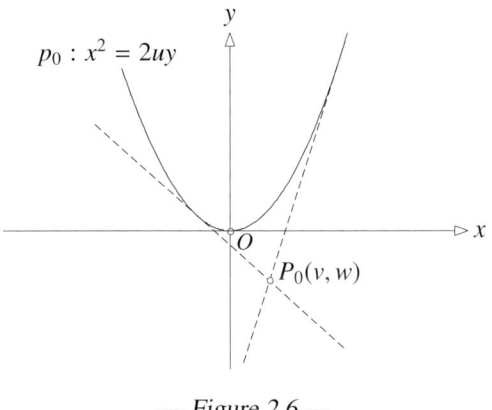

— Figure 2.6 —

The line containing P_0 and with slope s is described by the equation

$$y = s(x - v) + w.$$

If such a line is to be a tangent of the parabola p_0, the equation

$$x^2 = 2u(s(x - v) + w) \quad \Leftrightarrow \quad x^2 - 2usx + 2uvs - 2uw = 0$$

will have a discriminant equal to 0. This means

$$u^2 s^2 - 2uvs + 2uw = 0$$

$$\Leftrightarrow \quad s^2 - \frac{2v}{u} \cdot s + \frac{2w}{u} = 0,$$

and we see that the slopes of the tangents of p_0 containing P_0 are the solutions of the equation

$$x^2 + px + q = 0$$

if

$$p = -\frac{2v}{u} \quad \text{and} \quad q = \frac{2w}{u}$$

hold. If we therefore wish to determine the solutions of a given quadratic equation

$$x^2 + px + q = 0,$$

25

we can choose $u = 2$, $v = -p$ and $w = q$, and thus obtain the solutions as the slopes of the tangents of the parabola

$$p_0 : x^2 = 4y$$

containing the point $P_0(-p, q)$.

These tangents are simply the creases obtained by folding the focus $F(0, 1)$ onto directrix $\ell : y = -1$, such that the fold contains $P_0(-p, q)$.

We note that this method requires only half the number of steps of the previous one, as the preparatory folds determining M are not needed here. We are starting to appreciate the advantages of considering slopes, and these will become even more obvious in the coming sections.

8 Folding cube roots

As already mentioned in section 3, on page 13, finding the common tangents of two parabolas is, analytically, a cubic problem. Since (O7*) makes it possible to fold the common tangents of two parabolas, it is not unreasonable to expect that it should be possible to find cube roots utilizing (O7*), which is, of course, not possible by Euclidean methods. In this section, we shall become acquainted with a simple method of folding the cube root of the quotient of the lengths of any two given line segments as well as a very elegant method of folding the cube root of 2.

First, we consider two parabolas with a common vertex and perpendicular axes. That such parabolas intersect in points whose coordinates solve simple cubic equations was already known to Descartes, and that such parabolas have something to do with finding cube roots was even known in antiquity (see [28] p 12, or [2] pp 342–344). Since folding does not allow us to work with points of intersection, but rather with common tangents, we must deal with these. As we have been arguing in the last two sections, working with the slopes of these common tangents will be the easiest way of dealing with this situation.

We consider the parabolas (Figure 2.7) with the equations

$$p_1 : y^2 = 2ax \quad \text{and} \quad p_2 : x^2 = 2by.$$

Since these parabolas intersect in two points with real coordinates, they have only one real common tangent. We assume this tangent (which cannot be parallel to either axis) to be

$$t : y = cx + d.$$

We assume further that $P_1(x_1, y_1)$ is the point at which t is tangent to p_1, so that t then also has the equation

$$yy_1 = ax + ax_1 \quad \Leftrightarrow \quad y = \frac{a}{y_1} \cdot x + \frac{ax_1}{y_1}.$$

8 Folding cube roots

— Figure 2.7 —

Therefore $\quad c = \dfrac{a}{y_1} \quad$ and $\quad d = \dfrac{ax_1}{y_1} = cx_1$

$\Rightarrow \quad y_1 = \dfrac{a}{c} \quad$ and $\quad x_1 = \dfrac{d}{c}$

$\Rightarrow \quad \dfrac{a^2}{c^2} = 2a \cdot \dfrac{d}{c}$

$\Rightarrow \quad a = 2cd.$

We further assume that $P_2(x_2, y_2)$ is the point in which t is tangent to p_2, so that t then also has the equation

$$xx_2 = by + by_2 \quad \Leftrightarrow \quad y = \dfrac{x_2}{b} \cdot x - y_2.$$

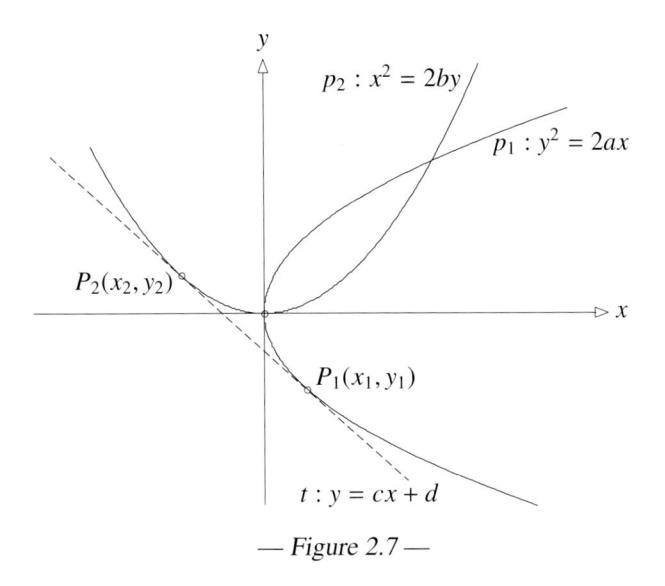

Therefore $\quad c = \dfrac{x_2}{b} \quad$ and $\quad d = -y_2$

$\Rightarrow \quad x_2 = bc \quad$ and $\quad y_2 = -d$

$\Rightarrow \quad b^2c^2 = -2bd$

$\Rightarrow \quad d = -\dfrac{bc^2}{2},$

and we have $\quad a = 2cd \quad$ and $\quad d = -\dfrac{bc^2}{2}$

$\Rightarrow \quad a = -bc^3$

$\Rightarrow \quad c = -\sqrt[3]{\dfrac{a}{b}}.$

27

We see that the slope of the common tangent is the (negative) cube root of the quotient of the parameters of the parabolas.

If b is equal to the unit length, the slope of the common tangent is the cube root of the parameter of p_1.

A cube root can therefore be folded in the following manner (Figure 2.8).

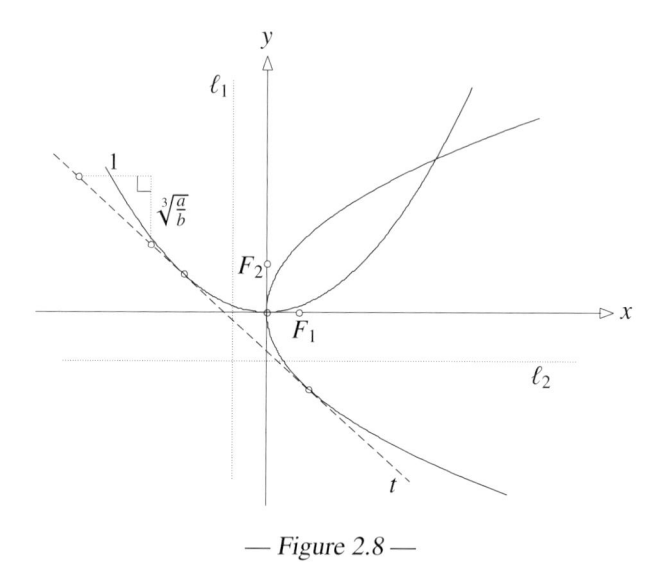

— Figure 2.8 —

If a and b are given, we fold a right angle anywhere to represent the parabola axes. We fold $\frac{a}{2}$ to the left and right of the origin to obtain the directrix ℓ_1 and the focus F_1 of p_1 respectively, and $\frac{b}{2}$ to the top and bottom to similarly obtain the directrix ℓ_2 and the focus F_2 of p_2. (Since $\frac{a}{b} = \frac{2a}{2b}$, we can also use a and b rather than $\frac{a}{2}$ and $\frac{b}{2}$.) Folding F_1 onto ℓ_1 and F_2 onto ℓ_2 simultaneously by virtue of (O7*) gives us the common tangent t, whose slope is then $-\sqrt[3]{\frac{a}{b}}$. Folding the unit length from any point on t parallel to the x-axis and completing the right triangle with hypotenuse on t thus yields a line segment of length $\sqrt[3]{\frac{a}{b}}$ as the second side of the triangle.

Choosing $a = 2b$ in this construction yields a common tangent t of the parabolas p_1 and p_2 with slope $-\sqrt[3]{2}$. Ignoring the sign of the slope, this means that we have described a solution to the classical "Delian Problem".

Legend has it, that the oracle at Delos foretold the ancient Athenians that they would have to double the size of the cubic altar of Apollo in order to rid themselves of the raging plague. Since doubling the volume of a cube is equivalent to increasing the lengths of its edges by a factor of $\sqrt[3]{2}$, the problem of constructing a line segment whose length is $\sqrt[3]{2}$ times the length of a given line segment became attached to the Delian oracle. Finding such a construction by Euclidean methods was one of the great unsolved problems of Greek antiquity (together with the problems of trisecting an angle, which we shall consider in section 10 on page 33, and squaring the circle, which is equally impossible

8 Folding cube roots

to solve by Euclidean or origami methods), and it took hundreds of years of research to finally prove the impossibility of such a construction.

A very elegant solution to this problem using origami methods was proposed by Peter Messer in [50] (Figure 2.9).

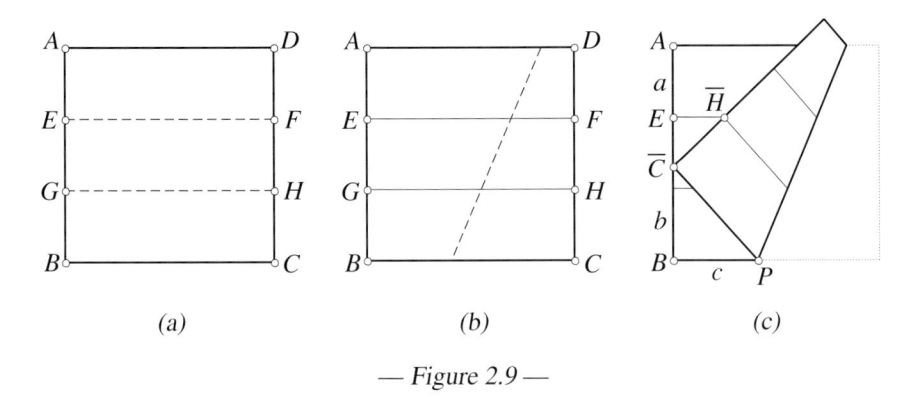

Figure 2.9

First of all, in Figure 2.9a a square is folded into three equal sections, such that

$$AE = EG = GB = DF = FH = HC.$$

(Methods of doing this are presented in section 12 of Chapter 3, page 53)

In Figures 2.9b and 2.9c, the square is folded such that C comes to lie on a point $\overline{C}$ on AB, and H simultaneously comes to lie on a point $\overline{H}$ on EF (by virtue of (O7*)). It then turns out that the length of $A\overline{C}$ is $\sqrt[3]{2}$ times the length of $\overline{C}B$.

Proof If we let a denote the length of $A\overline{C}$ and b denote the length of $\overline{C}B$, the folding square has sides of length $a + b$. We use P to denote the end-point of the crease created in Figure 2.9b on BC, and c to denote the length of BP.

Since
$$P\overline{C} = PC,$$
we have
$$P\overline{C} = (a + b) - c,$$
and since $\triangle BP\overline{C}$ is a right triangle, we have
$$b^2 + c^2 = (a + b - c)^2$$
or
$$0 = a^2 + 2ab - 2c(a + b),$$
and therefore
$$c = \frac{a^2 + 2ab}{2(a + b)}.$$

Triangles $\triangle BP\overline{C}$ and $\triangle E\overline{C}\overline{H}$ are similar, since
$$\angle \overline{C}BP = \angle \overline{H}E\overline{C} = 90°$$
and
$$\angle \overline{C}PB = 180° - \angle \overline{C}BP - \angle B\overline{C}P$$
$$= 90° - \angle B\overline{C}P$$

$$= 90° - (180° - \angle\overline{EC}\overline{H} - \angle\overline{HC}P)$$
$$= \angle\overline{EC}\overline{H}.$$

In $\triangle E\overline{CH}$ we have
$$\overline{CH} = \frac{a+b}{3}$$

and
$$\overline{EC} = a - \frac{a+b}{3}$$
$$= \frac{2a-b}{3},$$

and since
$$\frac{\overline{CH}}{\overline{EC}} = \frac{\overline{PC}}{\overline{BP}}$$

holds, we have
$$\frac{\frac{a+b}{3}}{\frac{2a-b}{3}} = \frac{a+b - \frac{a^2+2ab}{2(a+b)}}{\frac{a^2+2ab}{2(a+b)}}$$

$\Leftrightarrow \quad \dfrac{a+b}{2a-b} = \dfrac{a^2+2ab+2b^2}{a^2+2ab}$

$\Leftrightarrow \quad a^3 + 2a^2b + a^2b + 2ab^2 = 2a^3 + 4a^2b + 4ab^2 - a^2b - 2ab^2 - 2b^3$

$\Leftrightarrow \quad a^3 = 2b^3,$

and taking the cube root yields
$$a = \sqrt[3]{2} \cdot b.$$

We therefore have two line segments, namely $\overline{AC}$ and $\overline{CB}$, the ratio of whose lengths is $\sqrt[3]{2}$, and the problem is solved. ■

Note that we can now divide the length of any given line segment by $\sqrt[3]{2}$ as described in section 6 on page 21.

9 Solving general cubic equations

A slight generalization of the first method presented in the preceding section allows us to solve general cubic equations. We can see this in the following manner.

In Figure 2.10, we consider the parabolas with the equations

$$p_1 : (y-n)^2 = 2a(x-m) \quad \text{and} \quad p_2 : x^2 = 2by.$$

9 Solving general cubic equations

― Figure 2.10 ―

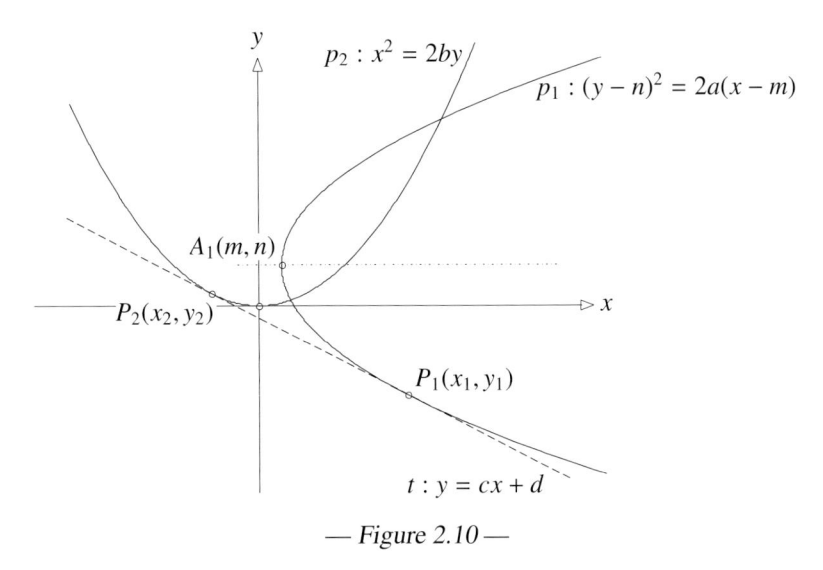

As before, we assume that the equation describing a common tangent of p_1 and p_2 (which need not be unique in this case), is

$$t : y = cx + d.$$

Again, such a common tangent cannot be parallel to either axis. We assume, as before, that $P_1(x_1, y_1)$ is the point in which t is tangent to p_1 so that t is then also represented by the equation

$$(y - n)(y_1 - n) = a(x - m) + a(x_1 - m)$$

$$\Leftrightarrow \quad y = \frac{a}{y_1 - n} \cdot x + n + \frac{ax_1 - 2am}{y_1 - n}.$$

Therefore

$$c = \frac{a}{y_1 - n} \quad \text{and} \quad d = n + \frac{ax_1 - 2am}{y_1 - n}$$

$$\Rightarrow \quad y_1 = \frac{a + nc}{c} \quad \text{and} \quad x_1 = \frac{d - n}{c} + 2m,$$

and

$$(y_1 - n)^2 = 2a(x_1 - m)$$

$$\Rightarrow \quad \frac{a^2}{c^2} = 2a\left(\frac{d - n}{c} + m\right)$$

$$\Rightarrow \quad a = 2c(d - n + cm).$$

As in the preceding section, assuming $P_2(x_2, y_2)$ to be the point in which t is tangent to p_2, we find that t is also represented by the equation

$$y = \frac{x_2}{b} \cdot x - y_2,$$

which again leads to
$$d = -\frac{bc^2}{2}.$$

Substituting for d, we obtain

$$a = 2c\left(-\frac{bc^2}{2} - n + cm\right) \iff bc^3 - 2mc^2 + 2nc + a = 0$$

$$\iff c^3 - \frac{2m}{b}\cdot c^2 + \frac{2n}{b}\cdot c + \frac{a}{b} = 0.$$

The slope of the common tangent is therefore a solution c of the cubic equation

$$c^3 - \frac{2m}{b}\cdot c^2 + \frac{2n}{b}\cdot c + \frac{a}{b} = 0.$$

This equation can have either one real solution and a pair of complex solutions, or three real solutions, of which two or all three can be equal. This corresponds to parabolas which intersect, and parabolas which do not, respectively. Two solutions are equal if and only if two tangents are equal (that is, if the parabolas are tangent), and all three are equal if and only if the parabolas osculate (that is, if they have contact of third order).

Given a cubic equation, one can therefore fold the roots of the equation by the following method.

Say the given equation is
$$x^3 + px^2 + qx + r = 0.$$

Assuming that the parameter b of p_2 is equal to the unit length 1, we have

$$p = -2m, \quad q = 2n \quad \text{and} \quad r = a$$

or

$$m = -\frac{p}{2}, \quad n = \frac{q}{2} \quad \text{and} \quad a = r.$$

We need therefore only find the point with coordinates

$$F_1\left(-\frac{p}{2} + \frac{r}{2}, \frac{q}{2}\right)$$

and the line ℓ_1 represented by the equation

$$x = -\frac{p}{2} - \frac{r}{2}.$$

These are then the focus and directrix of p_1 respectively. The focus F_2 of p_2 is $\left(0, \frac{1}{2}\right)$, and its directrix ℓ_2 is represented by the equation $y = -\frac{1}{2}$. Folding F_1 onto ℓ_1 and F_2 onto ℓ_2 simultaneously by virtue of (O7*) then yields the common tangent (or tangents) of p_1 and p_2, whose slope(s) solve(s) the given cubic equation.

10 Trisecting angles

As mentioned in section 8 on page 28, the problem of trisecting angles by Euclidean methods was another of the great unsolved problems of Greek antiquity. Today, we know that this problem cannot be solved in this way, but as for the Delian problem, origami methods put more powerful tools at our disposal.

If we wish to trisect an angle using origami methods, we find that the preceding result gives us a straightforward method of doing so. It is known that the equation

$$\cos 3\alpha = 4\cos^3 \alpha - 3\cos \alpha$$

holds for any angle α. (This is a highly elementary result that can be found in almost any high school trigonometry text book.) Assuming knowledge of $\cos 3\alpha$, finding $\cos \alpha$ is therefore merely a matter of solving the cubic equation

$$x^3 - \frac{3}{4} \cdot x - \frac{1}{4} \cdot \cos 3\alpha = 0.$$

As previously shown, this can be done by utilizing the parabola p_1 with the focus

$$F_1\left(-\frac{1}{8}\cos 3\alpha, -\frac{3}{8}\right)$$

and the directrix

$$\ell_1 : x = \frac{1}{8}\cos 3\alpha$$

(since a is negative, the parabola is open to the left in this case), as well as the "unit parabola" p_2 with focus $F_2\left(0, \frac{1}{2}\right)$ and directrix $\ell_2 : y = -\frac{1}{2}$. The slope of the common tangent of these parabolas solves the cubic equation, yielding $\cos \alpha$, which immediately leads to α itself.

While this result is quite nice, it is not as elegant as the following method of angle trisection found by H. Abe (see [31]) (Figure 2.11 on the following page).

As we can see in Figure 2.11a, we assume that $ABCD$ is a folding square, and the acute angle θ has been transferred such that $\theta = \angle EAB$, whereby E is a point either on BC or CD with $E \neq B$ and $E \neq D$. We fold creases $\overline{FF}$ and $\overline{GG}$ parallel to sides AB and CD ($F \neq A$) such that F and G lie on AD, $\overline{F}$ and $\overline{G}$ lie on BC, and G is the mid-point of AF (and therefore $\overline{G}$ the mid-point of $B\overline{F}$).

We now (by virtue of (O7*)) fold the square such that F comes to lie on a point F' on AE and A simultaneously comes to lie on a point A' on $\overline{GG}$ (Figure 2.11b). If G' is the point onto which G is folded by this process, we see that the lines AA' and AG' are the trisectors of $\angle EAB$.

Proof We first note that the crease resulting from this fold cannot be parallel to AB, since F' would otherwise lie on AD, which contradicts the assumption $E \neq D$. Similarly, the crease cannot be parallel to AD, since A' would otherwise lie on AB, which would mean

— Figure 2.11 —

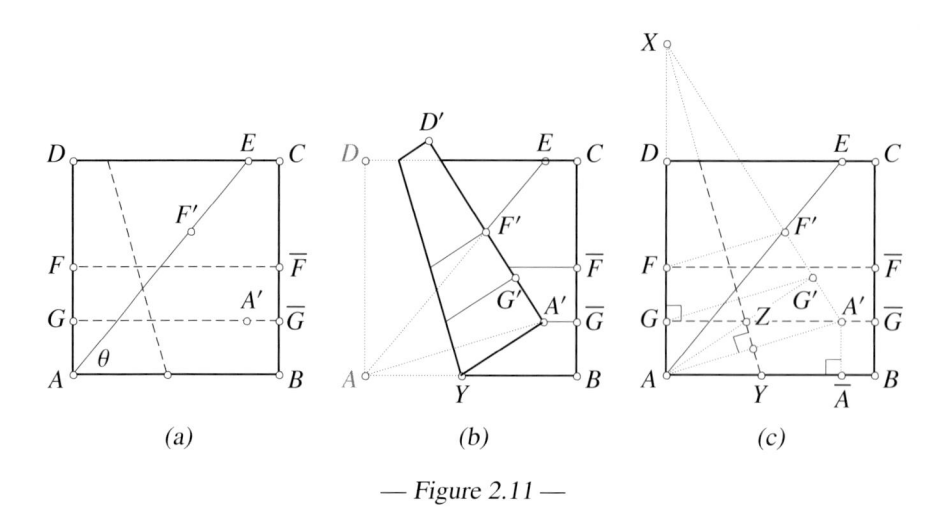

$AB = G\overline{G}$ and therefore $AB = F\overline{F}$, which contradicts $F \neq A$. We let X denote the point of intersection of the crease with the line AD (which may or may not be between A and D, see Figure 2.11c), and Y denote the point of intersection of the crease with the line AB.

If Z denotes the point of intersection of the crease with $G\overline{G}$, we note that Z is the orthocenter of triangle $\triangle AA'X$, since the line $A'G = G\overline{G}$ is orthogonal to AX, and AA' is orthogonal to the crease XY due to the definition of the fold. Since GA' folds to $G'A$ (and XA folds to XA'), it follows that AG' is the third altitude of $\triangle AA'X$, and therefore passes through Z.

If we name the angle $\angle AXY = \angle A'XY = \alpha$, we note that AG' is orthogonal to $A'X$ and AB is orthogonal to AX. We therefore have $\angle G'AB = \angle A'XA = 2\alpha$.

Letting $\overline{A}$ denote the foot of A' on AB, we see that triangles $\triangle AA'\overline{A}$ and $\triangle AA'G'$ are congruent, since both are right triangles with a common hypotenuse AA', and both $A'\overline{A}$ and $A'G'$ are equal in length to GA. We therefore have

$$\angle G'AA' = \angle A'A\overline{A} = \alpha.$$

Similarly, triangles $\triangle AA'G'$ and $\triangle AF'G'$ are also congruent. Both are again right triangles, they share side AG', and we have

$$F'G' = FG = GA = G'A'.$$

It therefore also follows that

$$\angle F'AG' = \angle G'AA' = \angle A'A\overline{A} = \alpha,$$

and the lines AG' and AA' are shown to be the trisectors of $\angle EAB$, as claimed. ∎

It is interesting to note that $\theta = 3\alpha$, and the angle $\angle YXA$ between the crease and the side of the folding square is one third of the given angle. In fact, we can generalize this result slightly (Figure 2.12).

34

10 Trisecting angles

Theorem 3
Given two parabolas p_1 (with focus F_1 and directrix ℓ_1) and p_2 (with focus F_2 and directrix ℓ_2) such that

(a) $F_1 \in \ell_2$,
(b) F_2 is symmetric to F_1 with respect to ℓ_1, and
(c) $\angle \ell_1 \ell_2 = \theta$ with $0° < \theta < 90°$,

then the parabolas have three real common tangents t_1, t_2 and t_3 with $\angle t_1, F_1 F_2 = \frac{\theta}{3}$, $\angle t_2, F_1 F_2 = 60° + \frac{\theta}{3}$ and $\angle t_3, F_1 F_2 = 120° + \frac{\theta}{3}$. Therefore t_1, t_2 and t_3 are the sides of an equilateral triangle.

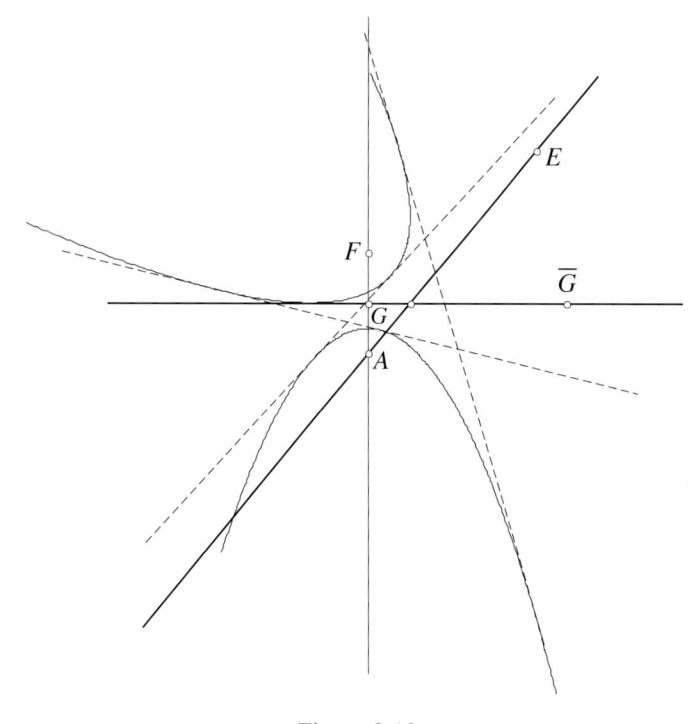

— Figure 2.12 —

Proof As we saw in Figure 2.11c, taking $A = F_1$, $\overline{GG} = \ell_1$, $F = F_2$ and $AE = \ell_2$, we have $XY = t_1$, with $\angle YXA = \frac{1}{3} \cdot \angle EAB = \frac{\theta}{3}$.

Since ℓ_1 is the perpendicular bisector of $F_1 F_2$ and $F_1 \in \ell_2$, ℓ_1 is a tangent of p_2, and since F_1 and F_2 lie on opposite sides of ℓ_1, the parabolas p_1 and p_2 certainly have three common real tangents.

As can be seen in Figure 2.13a on the next page, analogous arguments to those used for Figure 2.11c hold for t_2, since the triangles $\triangle AA'\overline{A}$, $\triangle AA'G'$ and $\triangle AF'G'$ are again congruent and we have

$$\angle t_2, AF = \angle A'A\overline{A} = \frac{1}{3} \cdot (180° + \theta) = 60° + \frac{\theta}{3}.$$

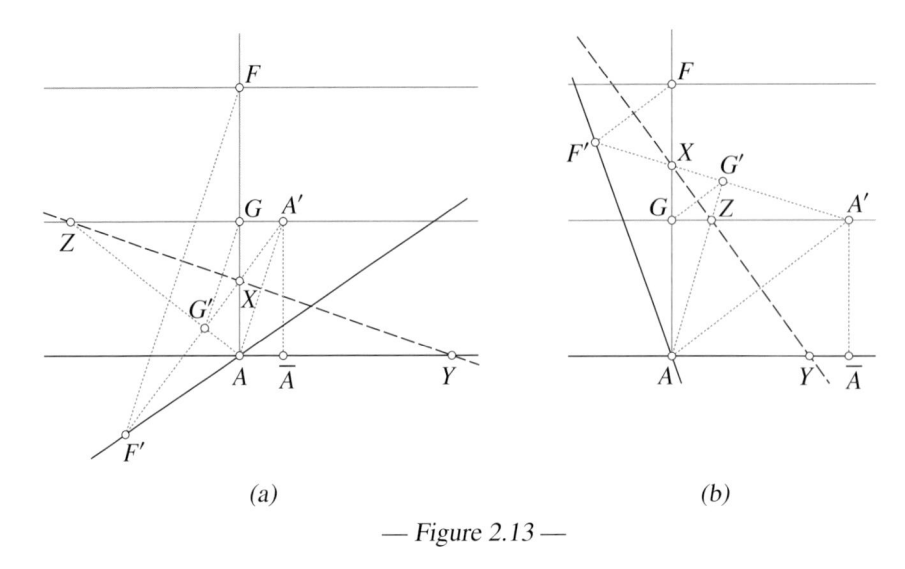

— Figure 2.13 —

In Figure 2.13b (where θ is chosen slightly larger than in Figure 2.13a in order to improve the clarity of the diagram), the same three triangles are again congruent for the same reasons, and we have

$$\angle A'A\overline{A} = \frac{1}{3} \cdot (180° - \theta) = 60° - \frac{\theta}{3}.$$

As before, we have

$$\angle t_3, AF = \angle A'A\overline{A} = 60° - \frac{\theta}{3},$$

and the other (supplementary) angle

$$\angle t_3, AF = 180° - \left(60° - \frac{\theta}{3}\right) = 120° + \frac{\theta}{3}$$

is therefore as claimed. ∎

All this gives us an easy and elegant method of trisecting any acute angle. A right angle is trisected by folding 30° and 60°, and easy methods of doing this will be described in section 16 (page 115).

Finally, a very nice method of trisecting obtuse angles was presented by Jacques Justin in [34] (Figure 2.14).

As we see in Figure 2.14a, we are given an obtuse angle $\alpha = \angle XOY$. We first determine a point A on OY and the point B symmetric to A with respect to O, as well as the line perpendicular to OX through O. Folding such that A comes to lie on the extension of OX and B on the line perpendicular to OX through O produces a preliminary crease. Folding this crease onto itself such that the resulting crease passes through O results in a crease OZ that trisects the original angle $\angle XOY$.

11 Solving quartic equations

(a)   *(b)*

— *Figure 2.14* —

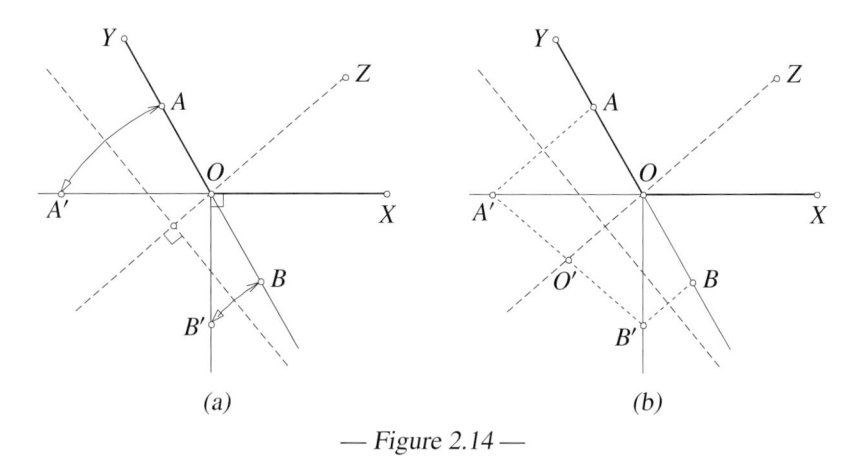

Proof As we see in Figure 2.14b, the point O', which lies under O after the first fold, is a point on the second crease, since both OO' and OZ are perpendicular to the first crease. Since both AA' and OO' are perpendicular to the first crease, $AA'O'O$ is a trapezium, and since AO and $A'O'$ are of equal length, it is isosceles. Naming $\beta = \angle XOZ$, we have $\angle A'OO' = \angle XOZ = \beta$, and

$$\angle A'O'O = \angle AOO' = 180° - \angle YOZ = 180° - (\alpha - \beta).$$

We note that all line segments OA, OB, $O'A'$ and $O'B'$ are of equal length. We name this length a. Since the triangle $\triangle A'B'O$ is right-angled in O, its circumcenter is the midpoint of its hypotenuse, which is O'. This means that the distance from O' to O is equal to its distance to A' and B', that is, to a. This means that $O'O$ and $O'A$ are of equal length, and $\triangle A'OO'$ is therefore isosceles. We therefore have $\angle OA'O' = \angle A'OO' = \beta$, and considering the angles in $\triangle A'OO'$ yields

$$\angle A'OO' + \angle OA'O' + \angle A'O'O = 180°$$
$$\Leftrightarrow \quad \beta + \beta + 180° - (\alpha - \beta) = 180°$$
$$\Leftrightarrow \quad 3 \cdot \beta = \alpha,$$

and we see that OZ trisects $\angle XOZ$ as claimed. ∎

11 Solving quartic equations

fourth-degree equation

11.1 How do we usually solve a fourth-degree equation?

In the sixteenth century, Ludovico Ferrari discovered a method of solving the general quartic (that is, fourth-degree) equation

(2.1) $$x^4 + ax^3 + bx^2 + cx + d = 0.$$

His method ingeniously introduces a second variable y, with $y = x^2$. The solutions of the fourth-degree equation (2.1) can then be thought of as the solutions of the system of equations given by

(I) $$y^2 + axy + by + cx + d = 0$$
(II) $$x^2 - y = 0.$$

These expressions can be thought of as equations of conics, whose points of intersection have coordinates corresponding to the the solutions of (2.1). Not only do these points lie on the curves represented by equations (I) and (II), however. They also lie on all curves represented by equations of the form

$$\lambda \cdot (x^2 - y) + y^2 + axy + by + cx + d = 0.$$

Among these expressions, we can therefore search for those that do not represent true conics, but rather degenerate conics, that is, pairs of (possibly identical) straight lines. It turns out that this involves solving a cubic equation in λ, a method for which was already known to Ferarri, due to his connections to Girolamo Cardano, who had learned about this method from Niccolò Tartaglia. (The complete story of these three men and their roles in the discovery and eventual publication of the solutions of cubic and quartic equations can be found in many books on the history of mathematics, such as [54] or [62].)

This means that the solutions of (2.1) can then be determined by calculating the points of intersection of a conic (either (I) or (II)) with two straight lines, which simply involves the solving of two quadratic equations. A fully detailed description of Ferarri's method can be found in many basic textbooks on elementary algebra, such as [63].

11.2 Applying Ferrari's ideas to origami

The ideas behind Ferarri's solution of the general quartic equation can be applied to origami constructions. This will involve applying the methods established in sections 7 and 9, on pages 23 and 30, for solving quadratic and cubic equations.

Taking a close look at Ferarri's method, we see that it involves the conic with the equation

$$y = x^2.$$

This is, of course, a parabola, and since we know from section 3 on page 7 that parabolas are highly elementary to the geometry of origami, we can reasonably expect this idea to translate quite readily. Of course, the variables x and y in the equation $y = x^2$ as used in Ferarri's method are cartesian point coordinates, whereas we require the slopes of tangents to be represented by a variable. This is not difficult to achieve.

We consider a parabola with the equation

$$x^2 = 2py,$$

where p is the parameter of the parabola.

11 Solving quartic equations

Let us assume that the line represented by the equation

$$y = qx + r$$

is a tangent of the parabola. This is the case if and only if the equation

$$x^2 = 2p(qx + r) \quad \Leftrightarrow \quad x^2 - 2pqx - 2pr = 0$$

has the discriminant 0, and this is equivalent to

$$p^2 q^2 = -2pr$$

or
$$pq^2 = -2r,$$

since $p \neq 0$. Taking $p = -2$ yields

$$q^2 = r,$$

and we see that the tangents of the parabola with the equation $p : x^2 = -4y$ (whose focus is $F(0, -1)$ and whose directrix is the line $d : y = 1$) are precisely those lines of the form $y = qx + r$ whose coefficients solve the equation $q^2 = r$ (Figure 2.15).

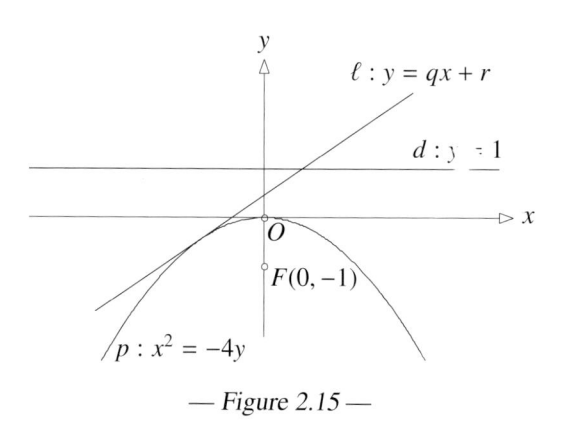

— Figure 2.15 —

We are now ready to formulate a dual version of the Ferarri approach, which will yield a method for solving the general quartic equation.

Let us assume as given a (monic) quartic equation

$$x^4 + ax^3 + bx^2 + cx + d = 0$$

with real coefficients a, b, c and d. We define new variables q and r and substitute

$$r := x^2 \quad \text{and} \quad q := x,$$

yielding the system of equations

(I) $\qquad\qquad\qquad\qquad\qquad q^2 = r \quad \text{and}$
(II) $\qquad\qquad\qquad\qquad r^2 + arq + br + cq + d = 0$

(whereby (II) could also be written as $r^2 + arq + bq^2 + cq + d = 0$). If we now interpret the variables q and r as the parameters of equations of the form $y = qx + r$ representing lines, we have just established that (I) represents the set of all tangents of the parabola with the equation $x^2 = -4y$. Equation (II) also represents some set of lines in this way (in fact, we can expect this to be the set of tangents of some conic, but this is not important for what we are doing here), and any pair of numbers $(q; r)$ solving both equations also solves any equation of the form

(2.2) $$\lambda \cdot (q^2 - r) + (r^2 + arq + br + cq + d) = 0.$$

with λ real.

Looking back to Ferarri's ideas, we note that he considered certain such expressions with λ chosen such that the solutions of the quadratic equation did not represent the coordinates of the points of a "true" conic, but rather of two (possibly identical) straight lines. As has already been mentioned a number of times, points are not primal in origami, but lines are. We must therefore consider what the analog can be in this more or less "dual" case. (At this point, it should be mentioned that several of the ideas presented here could also be presented in homogeneous coordinates. Although this would simplify some things, I have chosen not to go that route, as it would obscure the path leading to the result somewhat.)

Let us assume as given a point P_1 with coordinates (x_1, y_1). Any line passing through P_1 (and not parallel to the y-axis of our system of coordinates) is then represented by an equation of the form $y = qx + r$ with coefficients q and r such that $y_1 = qx_1 + r$ holds. We can therefore say that the equation

$$y_1 = qx_1 + r \quad \text{or} \quad x_1 \cdot q + r - y_1 = 0$$

with given real values of x_1 and y_1 and variables q and r represents the set of all lines passing through P_1 (and not parallel to the y-axis), in the sense that any pair of real numbers $(q; r)$ solving this equation yields the equation of one such line $y = qx + r$.

The same holds for a second point $P_2(x_2, y_2)$, and the set of all lines passing through P_2 and not parallel to the y-axis is given by the solutions to the equation

$$x_2 \cdot q + r - y_2 = 0.$$

The set of all lines that pass through either P_1 or P_2 (again, not parallel to the y-axis) is now the set of all lines of the form $y = qx + r$ whose parameters q and r are solutions of either

$$x_1 \cdot q + r - y_1 = 0 \quad \text{or} \quad x_2 \cdot q + r - y_2 = 0.$$

This is, however, also the set of all solutions of the equation

(2.3) $$(x_1 \cdot q + r - y_1) \cdot (x_2 \cdot q + r - y_2) = 0,$$

since a product is equal to 0 if and only if one of the factors is equal to 0. This equation can also be written as

(2.4) $$x_1 x_2 \cdot q^2 + (x_1 + x_2) \cdot qr + r^2 - (x_1 y_2 + x_2 y_1) \cdot q - (y_1 + y_2) \cdot r + y_1 y_2 = 0,$$

11 Solving quartic equations

which is a quadratic form of type

(2.5) $$Aq^2 + Bqr + Cr^2 + Dq + Er + F = 0$$

with $C = 1$.

We are now interested in finding out which such quadratic forms of type (2.5) can be expressed in form (2.3), since this will allow us to find values of λ in (2.2), such that the solutions of (2.2) yield only lines through either of a pair of determinable points.

Comparing the coefficients of (2.4) and (2.5) shows us that any choice of A and B yields x_1 and x_2 as the (possibly complex) solutions of the quadratic equation

$$x^2 - Bx + A = 0,$$

that is

$$x_1 = \frac{B}{2} + \sqrt{\frac{B^2}{4} - A} \quad \text{and} \quad x_2 = \frac{B}{2} - \sqrt{\frac{B^2}{4} - A}.$$

Similarly, any choice of E and F yields y_1 and y_2 as the (possibly complex) solutions of the quadratic equation

$$y^2 + Ey + F = 0,$$

that is

$$y_1 = -\frac{E}{2} + \sqrt{\frac{E^2}{4} - F} \quad \text{and} \quad x_2 = -\frac{E}{2} - \sqrt{\frac{E^2}{4} - F}.$$

(These choices of x_1, x_2, y_1 and y_2 mean $x_1 \geq x_2$ and $y_1 \geq y_2$ if x_1, x_2, y_1 and y_2 are all real.)

We now know that expression (2.5) is of type (2.4) if and only if

$$D = -(x_1y_2 + x_2y_1).$$

This is equivalent to

$$D = -\left[\left(\frac{B}{2} + \sqrt{\frac{B^2}{4} - A}\right)\left(-\frac{E}{2} - \sqrt{\frac{E^2}{4} - F}\right) + \left(\frac{B}{2} - \sqrt{\frac{B^2}{4} - A}\right)\left(-\frac{E}{2} + \sqrt{\frac{E^2}{4} - F}\right)\right]$$

$$= \frac{BE}{2} - 2 \cdot \sqrt{\left(\frac{B^2}{4} - A\right)\left(\frac{E^2}{4} - F\right)}$$

$$= \frac{BE}{2} - \frac{1}{2} \cdot \sqrt{(B^2 - 4A)(E^2 - 4F)}$$

$$= \frac{BE}{2} - \sqrt{\left(\frac{BE}{2}\right)^2 - (B^2F + AE^2 - 4AF)},$$

which means that D is a solution of the quadratic equation

(2.6) $$D^2 - BED + B^2F + AE^2 - 4AF = 0.$$

41

For which values of λ in equation (2.2) is this the case? We can write

$$\lambda \cdot (q^2 - r) + (r^2 + arq + br + cq + d) = 0$$
$$\Leftrightarrow \quad \lambda q^2 + aqr + r^2 + cq + (b - \lambda) \cdot r + d = 0,$$

and so, comparing this equation to (2.5), we have

$$A = \lambda, \ B = a, \ (C = 1), \ D = c, \ E = b - \lambda \quad \text{and} \quad F = d.$$

If (2.6) is to hold, λ has therefore to be a solution of

$$D^2 - BED + B^2 F + AE^2 - 4AF = 0$$
$$\Leftrightarrow \quad c^2 - abc + ac\lambda + a^2 d + b^2 \lambda - 2b\lambda^2 + \lambda^3 - 4d\lambda = 0$$
(2.7) $\quad \Leftrightarrow \quad \lambda^3 - 2b\lambda^2 + (ac + b^2 - 4d) \cdot \lambda + c^2 - abc + a^2 d = 0.$

This is a cubic equation in λ, and can therefore be solved by the method presented in section 9 on page 30.

As soon as we have a value for λ that solves this equation, it is a straightforward matter to determine the two points P_1 and P_2 associated with this value of λ, through one of which each line of the degenerate conic has to pass. The x-coordinates of these points are the solutions of the quadratic equation

$$x^2 - Bx + A = 0 \quad \text{or} \quad x^2 - ax + \lambda = 0,$$

and the y-coordinates are the solutions of the quadratic equation

$$y^2 + Ey + F = 0 \quad \text{or} \quad y^2 + (b - \lambda)y + d = 0,$$

whereby we must be careful to pair these coordinates such that the condition

$$D = -(x_1 y_2 + x_2 y_1)$$
$$\Leftrightarrow \quad c = -(x_1 y_2 + x_2 y_1)$$

holds.

Once we know the points P_1 and P_2, the solutions of (2.1) are simply the slopes of the tangents of the parabola $p : x^2 = -4y$ passing through either P_1 or P_2.

11.3 Is this always possible?

A question that arises naturally at this point is whether the steps described thus far are always possible. Obviously, P_1 and P_2 need to have real coordinates so that we can actually fold the paper in this manner. This means that the discriminants of the equations

$$x^2 - ax + \lambda = 0 \quad \text{and} \quad y^2 + (b - \lambda)y + d = 0$$

11 Solving quartic equations

both have to be non-negative real numbers. For some solution of the cubic "resolvent equation"

$$\lambda^3 - 2b\lambda^2 + (ac + b^2 - 4d) \cdot \lambda + c^2 - abc + a^2 d = 0,$$

we must have both

$$\frac{a^2}{4} - \lambda \geq 0 \quad \text{and} \quad \frac{(b - \lambda)^2}{4} - d \geq 0.$$

While the cubic equation (2.7) has to have at least one real solution, the validity of these inequalities for such a (possibly unique) real λ is not immediately obvious. As we shall see, however, there must indeed always exist a solution λ of (2.7) yielding points P_1 and P_2 with real coordinates. In order to see this, we must first investigate some properties of tangents of the parabola

$$p : x^2 = -4y.$$

As we have already seen, a tangent of this parabola represented by the equation $y = qx + r$ has the property that $q^2 = r$ holds. Each tangent is therefore represented by an equation of the form

$$t : y = qx + q^2.$$

Let us assume two tangents

$$t_1 : y = q_1 x + q_1^2 \quad \text{and} \quad t_2 : y = q_2 x + q_2^2$$

as given with $q_1 \neq q_2$, whereby the slopes q_1 and q_2 could be real or non-real complex numbers. The point of intersection $P_{1,2}$ of t_1 and t_2 is then determined by

$$q_1 x + q_1^2 = q_2 x + q_2^2$$
$$\Leftrightarrow \quad (q_1 - q_2)x = q_2^2 - q_1^2$$
$$\Leftrightarrow \quad (q_1 - q_2)x = -(q_1 - q_2)(q_1 + q_2)$$
$$\Leftrightarrow \quad x = -(q_1 + q_2)$$

and thus

$$y = -q_1(q_1 + q_2) + q_1^2$$
$$= -q_1 q_2.$$

We therefore have the point of intersection given by

$$P_{1,2}(-(q_1 + q_2), -q_1 q_2).$$

By the fundamental theorem of algebra, each fourth-degree monic polynomial in $\mathbb{C}[x]$ can be represented in the form

$$x^4 + ax^3 + bx^2 + cx + d = (x - q_1)(x - q_2)(x - q_3)(x - q_4).$$

Assuming for the moment that the values of q_i are all different, we note that each root q_i of the polynomial is associated with a tangent

$$t_i : y = q_i x + q_i^2$$

of the parabola p. The four tangents intersect pairwise in $\binom{4}{2} = 6$ points

$$P_{i,j} = t_i \cap t_j = \left(-(q_i + q_j), -q_i q_j\right),$$

as no two non-identical tangents of a parabola can be parallel (Figure 2.16).

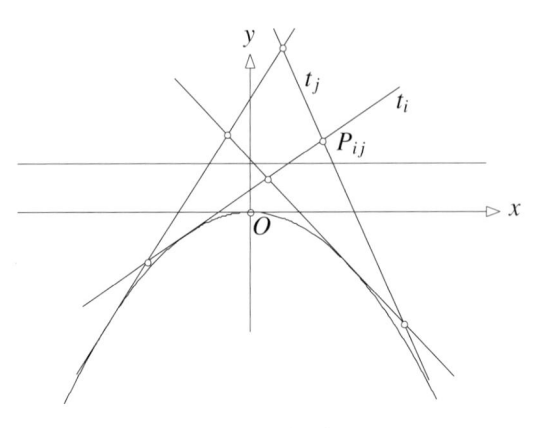

― Figure 2.16 ―

Taking a close look at polynomial (2.1), we have

$$a = -(q_1 + q_2 + q_3 + q_4),$$
$$b = q_1 q_2 + q_1 q_3 + q_1 q_4 + q_2 q_3 + q_2 q_4 + q_3 q_4,$$
$$c = -(q_1 q_2 q_3 + q_1 q_2 q_4 + q_1 q_3 q_4 + q_2 q_3 q_4) \quad \text{and}$$
$$d = q_1 q_2 q_3 q_4.$$

Since the x-coordinates of $P_{i,j}$ and $P_{k,l}$ (with $\{i, j\} \cap \{k, l\} = \emptyset$) are the solutions of

$$x^2 - ax + \lambda = 0,$$

it seems reasonable to assume

$$\lambda_1 = (q_1 + q_2)(q_3 + q_4) = q_1 q_3 + q_1 q_4 + q_2 q_3 + q_2 q_4,$$
$$\lambda_2 = (q_1 + q_3)(q_2 + q_4) = q_1 q_2 + q_1 q_4 + q_2 q_3 + q_3 q_4 \quad \text{and}$$
$$\lambda_3 = (q_1 + q_4)(q_2 + q_3) = q_1 q_2 + q_1 q_3 + q_2 q_4 + q_3 q_4,$$

which we shall now prove holds for all values of q_i (that is, even if they are not all different).

These values for λ_i are the solutions of equation (2.7) if and only if

$$(\lambda - \lambda_1)(\lambda - \lambda_2)(\lambda - \lambda_3) = \lambda^3 - 2b\lambda^2 + (ac + b^2 - 4d) \cdot \lambda + c^2 - abc + a^2 d$$

holds. This is indeed the case, because we have (the sums are all to be considered over all

11 Solving quartic equations

possible different values of the indices)

$$(\lambda - \lambda_1)(\lambda - \lambda_2)(\lambda - \lambda_3)$$
$$= \lambda^3 - (\lambda_1 + \lambda_2 + \lambda_3) \cdot \lambda^2 + (\lambda_1\lambda_2 + \lambda_2\lambda_3 + \lambda_3\lambda_1) \cdot \lambda - \lambda_1\lambda_2\lambda_3$$
$$= \lambda^3 - \left(2 \cdot \sum q_i q_j\right) \cdot \lambda^2 + \left(3 \cdot \sum q_i^2 q_j q_k + \sum q_i^2 q_j^2 + 6 \cdot q_1 q_2 q_3 q_4\right) \cdot \lambda$$
$$- \left(\sum q_i^3 q_j^2 q_k + 2 \cdot \sum q_i^3 q_j q_k q_l + 2 \cdot \sum q_i^2 q_j^2 q_k^2 + 4 \cdot \sum q_i^2 q_j^2 q_k q_l\right)$$
$$= \lambda^3 - 2b\lambda^2 + \left[\left(\sum q_i^2 q_j q_k + 4 \cdot q_1 q_2 q_3 q_4\right)\right.$$
$$+ \left(2 \cdot \sum q_i^2 q_j q_k + \sum q_i^2 q_j^2 + 6 \cdot q_1 q_2 q_3 q_4\right) - (4 \cdot q_1 q_2 q_3 q_4)\right] \cdot \lambda$$
$$+ \left[\left(\sum q_i^2 q_j^2 q_k^2 + 2 \cdot \sum q_i^2 q_j^2 q_k q_l\right) - \left(\sum q_i^3 q_j^2 q_k + 3 \cdot \sum q_i^3 q_j q_k q_l\right.\right.$$
$$\left.\left.+ 3 \cdot \sum q_i^2 q_j^2 q_k^2 + 8 \cdot \sum q_i^2 q_j^2 q_k q_l\right) + \left(\sum q_i^3 q_j q_k q_l + 2 \cdot \sum q_i^2 q_j^2 q_k q_l\right)\right]$$
$$= \lambda^3 - 2b\lambda^2 + (ac + b^2 - 4d) \cdot \lambda + c^2 - abc + a^2 d,$$

regardless of whether the q_i are all different or not.

The stated values of λ_i are therefore indeed the solutions of equation (2.7), and the points P_1 and P_2 resulting from the folding method presented in section 11.2 on page 38 can now be derived directly from these values of λ_i.

Taking

$$\lambda = \lambda_1 = (q_1 + q_2)(q_3 + q_4) = q_1 q_3 + q_1 q_4 + q_2 q_3 + q_2 q_4$$

(without loss of generality, as we can check the result in an analogous way for the other two λ_i), the coordinates of P_1 and P_2 are the solutions of the quadratic equations

$$x^2 - ax + \lambda = 0 \quad \Leftrightarrow \quad x^2 + (q_1 + q_2 + q_3 + q_4) \cdot x + (q_1 + q_2)(q_3 + q_4) = 0$$

and $y^2 + (b - \lambda) \cdot y + d = 0 \quad \Leftrightarrow \quad y^2 + (q_1 q_2 + q_3 q_4) \cdot y + q_1 q_2 q_3 q_4 = 0$

with $-(x_1 y_2 + x_2 y_1) = c = -(q_1 q_2 q_3 + q_1 q_2 q_4 + q_1 q_3 q_4 + q_2 q_3 q_4).$

This means

$$x_1 = -(q_1 + q_2), \; x_2 = -(q_3 + q_4), \; y_1 = -q_1 q_2 \;\text{ and }\; y_2 = -q_3 q_4$$

from the theorem of Vieta (or Viète) connecting the roots and coefficients of a quadratic equation, and

$$- ((-(q_1 + q_2))(-q_3 q_4) + (-(q_3 + q_4))(-q_1 q_2))$$
$$= -(q_1 q_2 q_3 + q_1 q_2 q_4 + q_1 q_3 q_4 + q_2 q_3 q_4).$$

All of these results hold for any polynomial

$$x^4 + ax^3 + bx^2 + cx + d \in \mathbb{C}[x],$$

whether the roots q_i are all different or not.

In our particular case, we have all real coefficients. If a polynomial with real coefficients has a non-real complex root, it is easy to show that its complex conjugate is also a root (see any book on elementary algebra, such as [63]).

Let us consider what cases are possible concerning the existence of real or complex roots, and how this relates to the corresponding values of λ and the corresponding points P_1 and P_2.

Case I All values of q_i are non-real.

In this case, the q_i are necessarily pairwise complex conjugate, and we can assume

$$q_2 = \overline{q_1} \quad \text{and} \quad q_4 = \overline{q_3}.$$

We therefore have

$$\lambda_1 = (q_1 + \overline{q_1})(q_3 + \overline{q_3}) = (2\operatorname{Re} q_1) \cdot (2\operatorname{Re} q_3),$$
$$\lambda_2 = (q_1 + q_3)(\overline{q_1} + \overline{q_3}) = \operatorname{Re}^2(q_1 + q_3) + \operatorname{Im}^2(q_1 + q_3)$$
and
$$\lambda_3 = (q_1 + \overline{q_3})(\overline{q_1} + q_3) = \operatorname{Re}^2(q_1 + \overline{q_3}) + \operatorname{Im}^2(q_1 + \overline{q_3}).$$

All of these values of λ_i are real, and yield the points

$\lambda_1: \quad P_1\left(-2\operatorname{Re} q_1, -(\operatorname{Re}^2 q_1 + \operatorname{Im}^2 q_1)\right) \ ; \quad P_2\left(-2\operatorname{Re} q_3, -(\operatorname{Re}^2 q_3 + \operatorname{Im}^2 q_3)\right),$

$\lambda_2: \quad P_1(-(q_1 + q_3), -q_1 q_3) \ ; \quad\quad\quad\quad\quad P_2(-(\overline{q_1} + \overline{q_3}), -\overline{q_1}\overline{q_3})$

and $\lambda_3: \quad P_1(-(q_1 + \overline{q_3}), -q_1\overline{q_3}) \ ; \quad\quad\quad\quad P_2(-(\overline{q_1} + q_3), -\overline{q_1}q_3).$

In general, only the points corresponding to λ_1 are real, and since all values of q_i are non-real, the tangents of p through P_1 and P_2 cannot be real. Points P_1 and P_2 are therefore on the "inside" of the parabola, that is, in the section of the plane described by

$$x^2 < -4y.$$

Only if $q_1 = q_3$ (or $q_1 = \overline{q_3}$) will $P_1 = P_2$ hold, and the points corresponding to λ_3 (or λ_2) be the same as these.

Case II Two values of q_i are real, and two are complex conjugate.

We assume

$$q_1, q_2 \in \mathbb{R} \quad \text{and} \quad q_4 = \overline{q_3}.$$

We then have

$$\lambda_1 = (q_1 + q_2)(q_3 + \overline{q_3}) = (q_1 + q_2) \cdot (2\operatorname{Re} q_3),$$
$$\lambda_2 = (q_1 + q_3)(q_2 + \overline{q_3})$$
and
$$\lambda_3 = (q_1 + \overline{q_3})(q_2 + q_3).$$

11 Solving quartic equations

In general, only λ_1 of these is real, and the λ_i yield the points

and
$$\begin{aligned}\lambda_1: &\quad P_1(-(q_1+q_2),-q_1q_2)\,; &\quad& P_2\left(-2\operatorname{Re} q_3,-(\operatorname{Re}^2 q_3+\operatorname{Im}^2 q_3)\right),\\ \lambda_2: &\quad P_1(-(q_1+q_3),-q_1q_3)\,; &\quad& P_2(-(q_2+\overline{q_3}),-q_2\overline{q_3})\\ \lambda_3: &\quad P_1(-(q_1+\overline{q_3}),-q_1\overline{q_3})\,; &\quad& P_2(-(q_2+q_3),-q_2q_3).\end{aligned}$$

Only the points corresponding to λ_1 are real. If $q_1 = q_2$, we have $\lambda_2 = \lambda_3$, and more importantly, the point P_1 corresponding to λ_1 is

$$P_1(-2q_1,-q_1^2).$$

Since

$$(-2q_1)^2 = -4\cdot(-q_1^2),$$

we have $x^2 = -4y$ for the coordinates of P_1, and P_1 is a point of the parabola p. We see that we must count a solution of (2.1) double in our method, if a point P_1 lies on the parabola.

Case III All four values of q_i are real.

In this case, all λ_i and corresponding P_1 and P_2 are certainly real. If all q_i are different, the arrangement of tangents and points P_1 and P_2 will be essentially as illustrated in Figure 2.15 on page 39.

As in Case II, if two values of q_i are equal, their corresponding point P lies on p. The following arrangements are possible:

IIIa $q_1 = q_2$, $q_1 \neq q_3 \neq q_4 \neq q_1$

$$\begin{aligned}\lambda_1: &\quad P_1(-2q_1,-q_1^2)\,; &\quad& P_2(-(q_3+q_4),-q_3q_4)\\ \lambda_2=\lambda_3: &\quad P_1(-(q_1+q_3),-q_1q_3)\,; &\quad& P_2(-(q_1+q_4),-q_1q_4).\end{aligned}$$

IIIb $q_1 = q_2$, $q_3 = q_4$, $q_1 \neq q_3$

$$\begin{aligned}\lambda_1: &\quad P_1(-2q_1,-q_1^2)\,; &\quad& P_2(-2q_3,-q_3^2)\\ \lambda_2=\lambda_3: &\quad P_1(-(q_1+q_3),-q_1q_3)=P_2.\end{aligned}$$

IIIc $q_1 = q_2 = q_3$, $q_1 \neq q_4$

$$\lambda_1=\lambda_2=\lambda_3:\quad P_1(-2q_1,-q_1^2)\,;\qquad P_2(-(q_1+q_4),-q_1q_4).$$

IIId $q_1 = q_2 = q_3 = q_4$

$$\lambda_1=\lambda_2=\lambda_3:\quad P_1(-2q_1,-q_1^2)=P_2.$$

In summary, we see that every quartic equation (2.1) yields at least one real solution λ of (2.7) that corresponds to real points P_1 and P_2. Complex conjugate solutions of (2.1) yield points inside the parabola, differing (and real) solutions yield points outside, and multiple solutions yield points on the parabola.

11.4 Determining actual solutions

We now turn our attention to actually folding the solutions of a quartic equation. We assume an equation (2.1) of the form

$$x^4 + ax^3 + bx^2 + cx + d = 0$$

as given. We must first determine a λ solving the resolvent equation (2.7)

$$\lambda^3 - 2b\lambda^2 + (ac + b^2 - 4d) \cdot \lambda + c^2 - abc + a^2 d = 0.$$

As shown in section 9 on page 30, the solutions of a cubic equation

$$x^3 + px^2 + qx + r = 0$$

are the slopes of the common tangents of the parabolas p_1 and p_2 given by their respective foci and directrices as

$$p_1 : \quad F_1\left(-\frac{p}{2} + \frac{r}{2}, \frac{q}{2}\right) ; \quad \ell_1 : x = -\frac{p}{2} - \frac{r}{2} \quad \text{and}$$

$$p_2 : \quad F_2\left(0, \frac{1}{2}\right) ; \quad \ell_2 : y = -\frac{1}{2}.$$

Applying this to equation (2.7) yields

$$F_1\left(b + \frac{c^2 - abc + a^2 d}{2}, \frac{ac + b^2 - 4d}{2}\right)$$

and

$$\ell_1 : \quad x = b - \frac{c^2 - abc + a^2 d}{2}.$$

Simultaneously folding F_1 onto ℓ_1 and F_2 onto ℓ_2 therefore yields the required values for λ.

Having established a possible value of λ, we must now determine the solutions of the equations

(2.8) $\qquad x^2 - ax + \lambda = 0 \quad \text{and} \quad y^2 + (b - \lambda)y + d = 0$

by the method described in section 7 on page 23. These solutions have to be paired such that

$$c = -(x_1 y_2 + x_2 y_1)$$

holds. As stated in the derivation of equation (2.6), this means that $x_1 \geq x_2$ and $y_1 \geq y_2$ if x_1, x_2, y_1 and y_2 are real-valued. We must therefore pair the larger value of x with the larger value of y, and vice versa, when these values are real. Once we have P_1 and P_2, the solutions of the quartic equation are simply the slopes of the tangents of the parabola $p : x^2 = -4y$ as discussed in section 11.2 on page 38.

11 Solving quartic equations

11.5 An example

Now we shall see how the method described in the previous section can be applied to an actual quartic equation. In order to keep things manageable, we choose coefficients that make the actual folding relatively simple, while the quartic still has an irrational real solution.

We choose $a = c = 1$ and $b = d = 0$, such that the quartic equation (2.1) is

(2.9) $$x^4 + x^3 + x = 0.$$

In this case, 0 is obviously one solution of the equation, and we could alternatively determine at least one further solution by solving the cubic equation $x^3 + x + 1 = 0$ by the method described in section 9 on page 30.

We shall see that the fact of 0 being a root makes folding the roots of (2.9) substantially easier than would otherwise be the case. Nevertheless, this equation will illustrate all important aspects of the folding process.

First of all, we must determine a real solution of the resolvent equation (2.7),

$$\lambda^3 - 2b\lambda^2 + (ac + b^2 - 4d) \cdot \lambda + c^2 - abc + a^2 d = 0,$$

which in this case reduces to

(2.10) $$\lambda^3 + \lambda + 1 = 0.$$

As stated in section 9, real solutions of this equation are obtained as the slopes of creases created by folding the point

$$F_1\left(-\frac{p}{2} + \frac{r}{2}, \frac{q}{2}\right)$$

onto line

$$\ell_1 : x = -\frac{p}{2} - \frac{r}{2}$$

and point $F_2\left(0, \frac{1}{2}\right)$ onto line $\ell_2 : y = -\frac{1}{2}$. Since we have $p = 0$ and $q = r = 1$ in the cubic equation (2.10), this means simultaneously folding

$$F_1\left(\frac{1}{2}, \frac{1}{2}\right) \quad \text{onto} \quad \ell_1 : x = -\frac{1}{2} \quad \text{and}$$

$$F_2\left(0, \frac{1}{2}\right) \quad \text{onto} \quad \ell_2 : y = -\frac{1}{2}.$$

In folding paper, we assume (as is customarily the case) that a square of paper is given. In Figure 2.17 on the following page we assume that the edge of the folding square is two units in length, and that a system of cartesian coordinates is given, such that the coordinate axes are parallel to the edges of the folding square, and the upper right-hand corner A has the coordinates $\left(\frac{1}{2}, \frac{1}{2}\right)$.

49

Chapter 2 — Origami Constructions and Algebra

— Figure 2.17 —

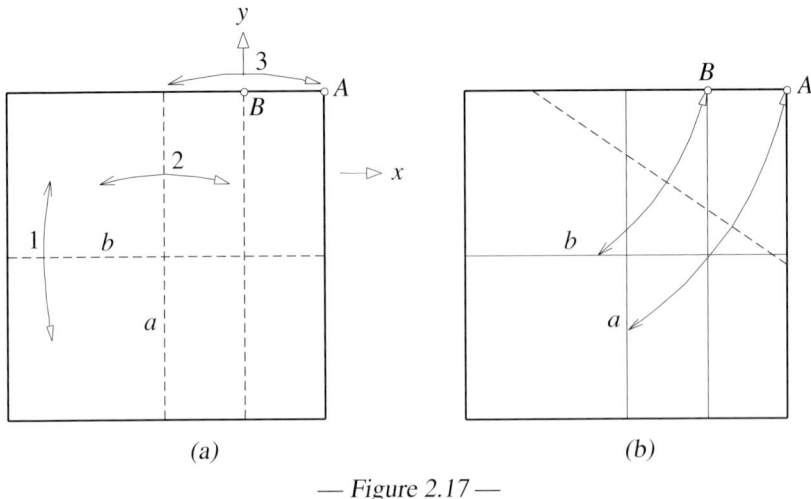

We then see that A is $F_1\left(\frac{1}{2},\frac{1}{2}\right)$ as required, and B as marked in Figure 2.17a is $F_2\left(0,\frac{1}{2}\right)$. Similarly, creases a and b are lines ℓ_1 and ℓ_2 as required. This means that folding A onto a and B onto b as shown in Figure 2.17b yields a crease whose slope is a real solution of the resolvent equation (2.10), and thus a value of λ as required. (A quick check on the calculator shows us that (2.10) has only one real solution for λ with an approximate value of -0.68233. The actual numerical value is not important here, of course.)

We must now determine the relevant points P_1 and P_2 by solving the quadratic equations (2.8) on page 48:

$$x^2 - ax + \lambda = 0 \quad \text{and} \quad y^2 + (b - \lambda)\cdot y + d = 0.$$

Since we have $a = 1$ and $b = d = 0$, this means solving

$$x^2 - x + \lambda = 0 \quad \text{and} \quad y^2 - \lambda y = 0.$$

We see that the solutions for y are 0 and λ, and since λ is negative, we have $y_1 = 0$ and $y_2 = \lambda$, since $y_1 \geq y_2$ holds.

In order to obtain the solutions for x, we must fold $F(0, 1)$ onto $\ell : y = -1$, such that the creases pass through $P_0(1, \lambda)$, as shown in section 7 on page 23. This is done in Figures 2.18a–2.18d. We assume here that the edge length of the folding square is eight units, and that the origin is in the mid-point of the folding square. The horizontal distance between the lines through E and C in Figure 2.18a is then one unit, and since the difference between the y-coordinates of E and C is therefore λ, the coordinates of G as produced in Figures 2.18a and 2.18b are therefore $(1, \lambda)$. We see that G is our required point P_0. Repeated division by a factor of 2 in Figure 2.18c means that point F has the coordinates $(0, 1)$, and is therefore our required point F, and that f has the equation $y = -1$, and is therefore our required line ℓ. Folding F onto f such that the crease passes through G in Figure 2.18d therefore yields creases with slopes x_1 and x_2 which solve the quadratic equation. Since

11 Solving quartic equations

one of these is positive and one is negative, and we require $x_1 \geq x_2$, we have x_1 as the positive slope and x_2 as the negative one.

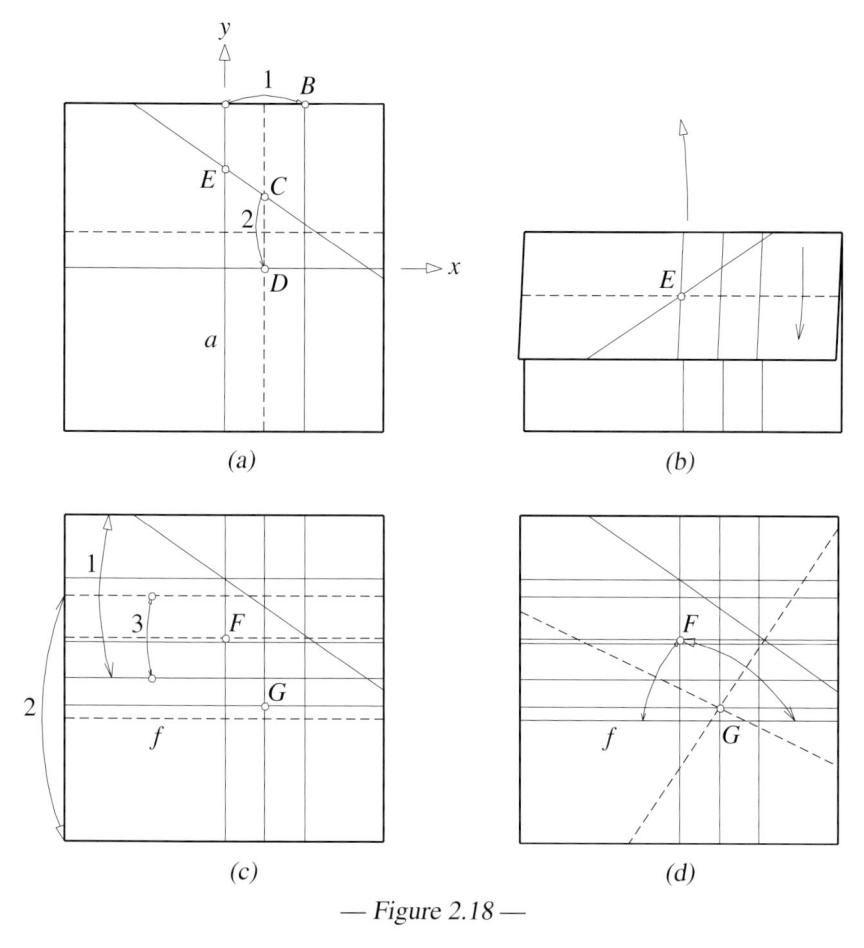

— Figure 2.18 —

As can easily be checked, equation (2.9) only has two real solutions. This means that one of the points P_1 and P_2 lies on the "inside" of the parabola $y^2 = -4x$. (This is the point P_2. In this paper, we refrain from actually illustrating a folding procedure for producing this point, as it can be accomplished by basically the same method as that required for producing P_1, and does not yield any real solutions of (2.9).)

In Figures 2.19a–2.19c on the next page, we determine P_1, whose x-coordinate is the positive slope of the crease produced in Figure 2.18d, and whose y-coordinate is 0. In order to speed up the process, we now change the orientation of the coordinate axes, and assume that the x-axis is pointing down, and the y-axis pointing right. Since points H and M are one unit apart, it follows from the fact that the slope of crease GK relative to the system of coordinates in Figure 2.19a is x_1, that the distance from M to P is also x_1. In the new system of coordinates, P therefore has the coordinates $(x_1, 0)$, and P is therefore the required point P_1.

| Chapter 2 | Origami Constructions and Algebra |

(a)   *(b)*

(c)   *(d)*

— Figure 2.19 —

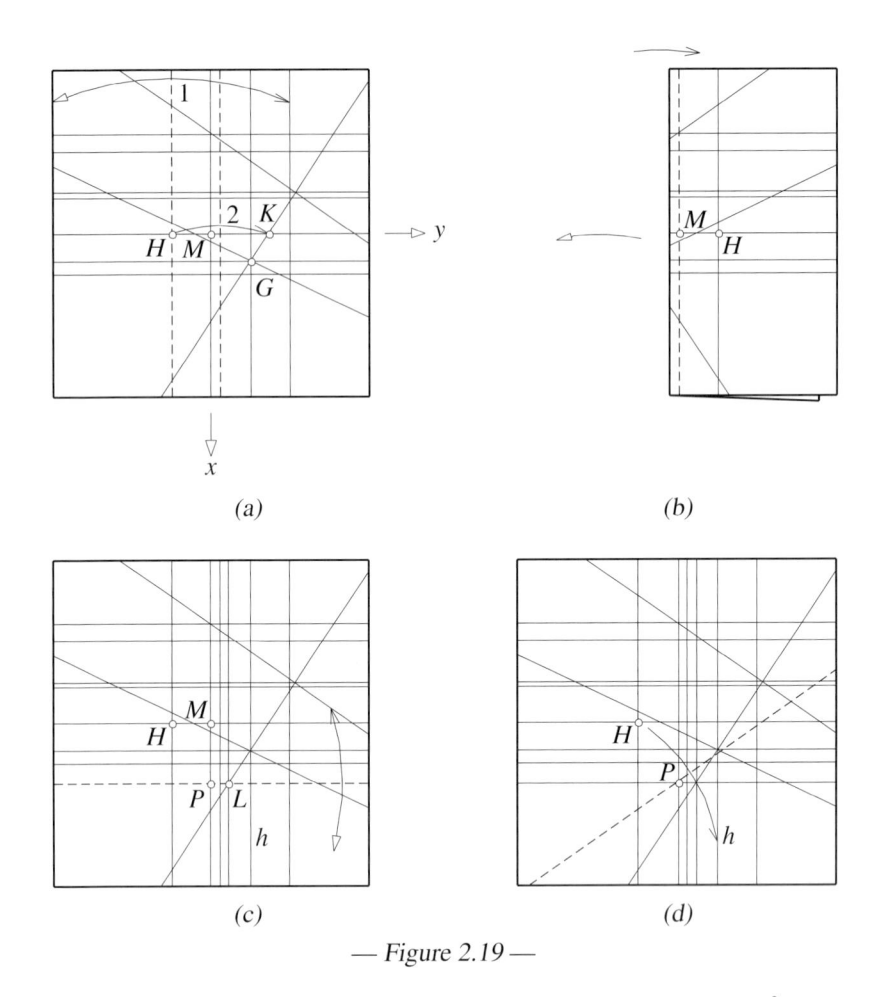

Since H has the coordinates $(0, -1)$, it is the required focus of the parabola $y^2 = -4x$, and similarly line h is its directrix $y = 1$. Folding H onto h such that the creases pass through P, as shown in Figure 2,19d, therefore yields creases whose slopes are the real solutions to our quartic equation (2.9). One of these solutions is obviously 0, and the numerical value of the other, as can easily be checked by calculator, is approximately -1.46557.

In summary, we see that the method described here always yields complete information concerning real solutions of monic quartic equations with real coefficients. All real solutions are derived as slopes of tangents of parabolas obtained by folding a point onto a line such that the resulting crease contains a specific point. If this is a point of the parabola, the solution counts at least double, and we can tell the multiplicity of the solution by the relative position of the other such point under consideration. If solutions are non-real, we see this by the fact that the relevant point is "inside" the parabola, and no tangents can be folded.

Chapter 3

Properties of Origami Constructions

12 Dividing line segments into sections of equal length

Developing folding bases for concrete origami models sometimes necessitates the precise division of the edges of the folding square into a number of pieces of equal length. Some examples for this beside Peter Messer's construction of $\sqrt[3]{2}$ as presented in section 8 on page 26 are Toshikazu Kawasaki's Coaster #1 from [36] (pp 26–27), in which a division into three equal sections is needed, or Robert J. Lang's Cube from [44] (p 57), which requires a division into five equal sections. This problem, coming from practical origami, has been discussed at length in the paper-folding literature, and this section aims to provide an overview of the various methods. (An excellent short summary of practical solutions to this problem can be found at the Origami Tanteidan web-site [79].)

From a mathematical point of view, this problem can also be seen as that of determining points on the edge of a unit square that divide the edge in a rational ratio. If we wish to divide the edge in the ratio $r : s$ (where r and s are positive integers), we must divide the edge into $r + s = n$ pieces of equal length, and count r such pieces from one end (or s from the other).

If we can determine the point P in which an edge AB of the folding square is divided in the ratio $r : s$, we can do the same for any line segment XY on the folding square by virtue of the method described in Figure 3.1 on the following page.

In Figure 3.1a, we first fold the creases AY and BY. We then fold the crease perpendicular to BY through P, and then the crease perpendicular to this crease through P. This last crease intersects AY in Q, and since BY and PQ are parallel, triangles $\triangle ABY$ and $\triangle APQ$ are similar. Therefore Q divides AY in the same ratio $r : s$ as P divides AB.

In Figure 3.1b, we then fold the crease AX, and then the crease perpendicular to AX through Q and the crease perpendicular to this crease through Q. This final crease intersects XY in a point R, and since AX and QR are parallel, triangles $\triangle YRQ$ and $\triangle YXA$ are similar and R divides XY in the same ratio as Q divides AY, which we have already seen

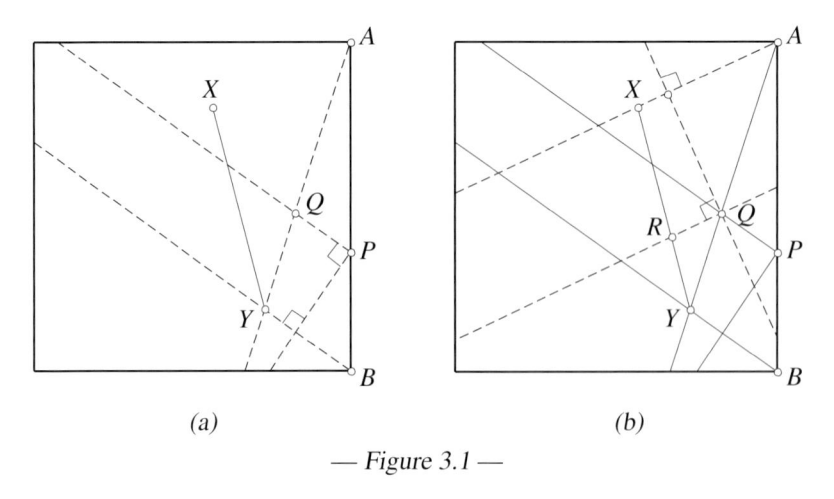

Chapter 3 — Properties of Origami Constructions

— Figure 3.1 —

to be $r : s$, as required.

This method always works, unless X, Y and A are collinear. In this case, it is sufficient to exchange the names of A and B for the method to work. This too, however, will fail if X and Y are both points on the edge AB, but in this case we can transfer P to the opposite side by folding the crease orthogonal to AB through P, and considering A, B and P on the opposite side (that is, the left side in Figure 3.1) of the folding square.

It is interesting to note here, that we are only using procedures (O1), (O4) and (O6) as defined in section 3 on page 7. This is of course due to the fact that the transfer of ratios involves only linear procedures, as we know from Euclidean constructions, where such transfer can be achieved by straight-edge constructions alone (see [48], Chapter 4 pp 69–82).

We are now ready to consider methods of determining points P on the edge AB that divide AB in a rational ratio. As before, we assume this ratio to be $r : s$ with positive integers r and s, and we define $r + s = n$.

First of all, we consider the case where n is a power of 2, that is, $n = 2^k$ with k a positive integer.

Folding A to B in Figure 3.2 yields the point P_1 on AB with

$$AP_1 = P_1B = \frac{1}{2},$$

or

$$AP_1 : P_1B = \frac{1}{2} : \frac{1}{2} = 1 : 1$$

and

$$1 + 1 = 2 = 2^1.$$

Folding A to P_1 yields P_2 on AB with

$$AP_2 = \frac{1}{2} \cdot AP_1 = \frac{1}{4},$$

12 Dividing line segments into sections of equal length

— Figure 3.2 —

or
$$AP_2 : P_2B = \frac{1}{4} : \frac{3}{4} = 1 : 3$$

and
$$1 + 3 = 4 = 2^2.$$

By continuing to fold A onto the point created by the previous step on AB, the point P_k created the the k-th step has the property that

$$AP_k = \frac{1}{2} \cdot AP_{k-1} = \frac{1}{2^k},$$

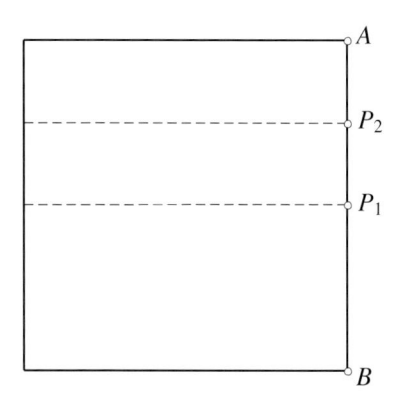

and so
$$AP_k : P_kB = \frac{1}{2^k} : \frac{2^k - 1}{2^k} = 1 : (2^k - 1)$$

and
$$1 + (2^k - 1) = 2^k.$$

This method therefore yields all points whose distance from A is $\frac{1}{2^k}$ after k steps.

More generally, we can obtain all points whose distance from A is $\frac{r}{2^k}$ with r odd and $1 \leq r < 2^k$ (if r is even, cancelling powers of 2 will yield a fraction of this type) by the following method. In the first step, we fold A to B as before, yielding the point P_1. We add this point to the set

$$S_0 = \{A, B\},$$

yielding the set

$$S_1 = \{A, P_1, B\}$$

after the first step. Then P_1 is the only point whose distance from A is $\frac{r}{2^k}$ as required with $k = 1$ (namely $\frac{1}{2^1}$, or $r = 1$).

Now folding A to P_1 yields P_2 with $|AP_2| = \frac{1}{4}$, and folding P_1 to B yields a point P'_2 with

$$|AP'_2| = |AP_1| + \frac{1}{2} \cdot |P_1B|$$

55

$$= \frac{1}{2} + \frac{1}{4}$$
$$= \frac{3}{4}.$$

These two points P_2 and P'_2 are the only points whose distance from A is $\frac{r}{2^k}$ with $k = 2$ ($r = 1$ or 3). We add these points to S_1, yielding the set

$$S_2 = \{A, P_2, P_1, P'_2, B\}.$$

We now define further sets S_k as follows. Folding every pair of adjacent points of S_{k-1} onto another yields points which are added to S_{k-1} to yield S_k. We now claim that every point whose distance from A is $\frac{r}{2^k}$ as required with r odd and $1 \le r < 2^k$ is among the points added to S_{k-1} to form S_k. This is seen by induction. It is certainly the case for S_2, as we saw above. Now, taking $1 \le r < 2^k$ and r odd, we can say that $r = 2s - 1$ with $1 \le s \le 2^{k-1}$. The point whose distance from A is $\frac{2s-1}{2^k}$ is equidistant from the points whose distances from A are $\frac{2s-2}{2^k}$ and $\frac{2s}{2^k}$ respectively. Since

$$\frac{2s-2}{2^k} = \frac{s-1}{2^{k-1}} \quad \text{and} \quad \frac{2s}{2^k} = \frac{s}{2^{k-1}},$$

these are adjacent points of S_{k-1} by the induction hypothesis, and so the point whose distance from A is

$$\frac{r}{s^k} = \frac{2s-1}{2^k}$$

is produced by folding these two onto another, as claimed.

From now on, we shall identify each point of AB with its distance from A, with $A = 0$ and $B = 1$, and we shall always assume that the numerator of the fraction is smaller than the denominator.

Having seen that it is relatively straightforward to fold any point $\frac{r}{2^k}$ (), it is worthwhile to ask how many folds are the minimum needed to determine a specific such point. The answer to this question is given by the following theorem.

Theorem 4
The smallest number of folds needed to fold the point $\frac{r}{2^k}$ with any odd value of r is k.

Proof First, we shall show that $\frac{r}{2^k}$ cannot be determined with less than k folds. In order to see this, we consider folding the points $\frac{p}{2^m}$ and $\frac{q}{2^n}$, with p and q odd and $m \ge n$, onto each other. This yields the mid-point, or the point

$$\frac{1}{2} \cdot \left(\frac{p}{2^m} + \frac{q}{2^n} \right) = \frac{p + 2^{m-n} \cdot q}{2^{m+1}}.$$

If $m = n$, we can cancel at least a factor of 2, but the power of 2 in the denominator of this fraction is not larger than $m+1$, or in other words, not more than one larger than the larger power of 2 used in determining this point. Each folding step can therefore only increase the power of 2 in the denominator by one at most, and so $\frac{r}{2^k}$ cannot be determined with less than k folds.

12 Dividing line segments into sections of equal length

Now we shall show that $\frac{r}{2^k}$ can indeed be determined with exactly k folds.

Since r is odd, r cannot be equal to 2^{k-1} for $k > 1$. If $r < 2^{k-1}$, we can obtain $\frac{r}{2^k}$ by folding 0 onto $\frac{r}{2^{k-1}}$, since this yields the mid-point

$$\frac{1}{2} \cdot \left(0 + \frac{r}{2^{k-1}}\right) = \frac{r}{2^k}.$$

If $r > 2^{k-1}$, we can obtain $\frac{r}{2^k}$ by folding $\frac{r-2^{k-1}}{2^{k-1}}$ onto 1, since this yields the mid-point

$$\frac{1}{2} \cdot \left(\frac{r-2^{k-1}}{2^{k-1}} + 1\right) = \frac{r - 2^{k-1} + 2^{k-1}}{2^{k-1}} = \frac{r}{2^k}.$$

If we therefore define $r_1 = r$ if $r < 2^{k-1}$ and $r_1 = r - 2^{k-1}$ if $r > 2^{k-1}$, we see that $\frac{r}{2^k}$ can be determined by folding $\frac{r_1}{2^{k-1}}$ onto either 0 or 1. Since r_1 is certainly odd with $1 \le r_1 < 2^{k-1}$, we can determine an r_2 by the same method, such that folding $\frac{r_2}{2^{k-2}}$ onto either 0 or 1 yields $\frac{r_1}{2^{k-1}}$, and so on. This procedure terminates after k steps, since the k-th step (counting backwards) must be to fold $\frac{r_{k-1}}{2}$ with $1 \le r_{k-1} < 2$, which means $r_{k-1} = 1$, and $\frac{1}{2}$ is the result of folding 0 to 1. This procedure therefore yields a method for folding $\frac{r}{2^k}$ in exactly k steps. ∎

Now that we know all about folding $\frac{r}{n}$ if $n = 2^k$, we turn our sites to general numbers $\frac{r}{n}$ (always with r and n positive integers, $0 < r < n$ and $\gcd(r, n) = 1$). There are many possible methods of solving this problem, and we shall consider four such methods.

Method 1 One method of solving this problem can be derived from the application of similar triangles, as shown in Figure 3.3. This method, while slightly inelegant, is easily derived from standard straight-edge methods of line segment division.

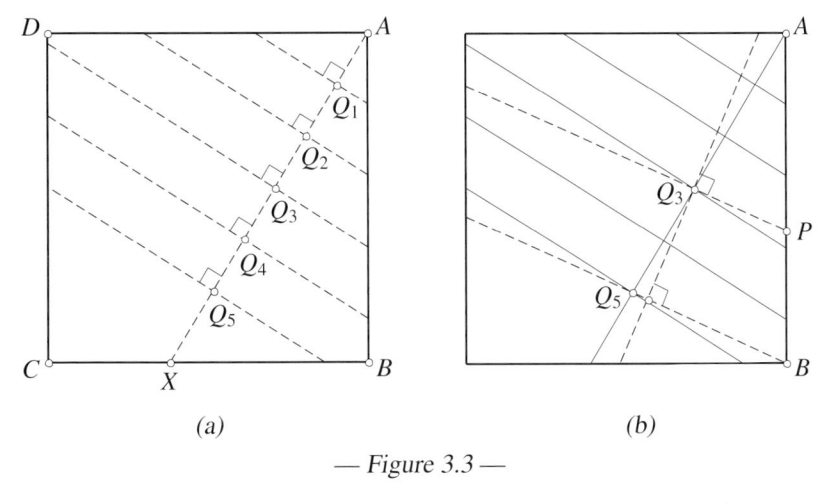

— Figure 3.3 —

This figure describes the folding of the point P whose distance from A is $\frac{3}{5}$, but the same principle holds for any integer values of r and n with $1 \le r < n$.

57

| Chapter 3 | Properties of Origami Constructions |

In Figure 3.3a, a random point X is chosen on the edge BC of the folding square (although X could also be chosen on CD or even in C), and crease AX is folded. A random point Q_1 is chosen close to A on AX, and the crease perpendicular to AX through Q_1 is folded. Then A comes to lie on a point Q_2 on AX, and the crease perpendicular to AX through Q_2 is folded. This brings Q_1 to lie on a point Q_3 on AX, and this process is repeated until we reach Q_5. Due to the way the points Q_i are determined, we have equal distances

$$|AQ_1| = |Q_1Q_2| = |Q_2Q_3| = |Q_3Q_4| = Q_4Q_5|.$$

It is therefore quite obvious that $|AQ_3|$ is $\frac{3}{5}$ of $|AQ_5|$.

In Figure 3.3b, we then fold the crease Q_5B, and then the crease perpendicular to Q_5B through Q_3 and the crease perpendicular to this crease through Q_3, which intersects AB in a point P. Since Q_5B and Q_3P are then parallel, triangles $\triangle AQ_5B$ and $\triangle AQ_3P$ are similar, and P divides AB in the same ratio as Q_3 divides AQ_5. We know that $|AQ_3|$ is $\frac{3}{5}$ of $|AQ_5|$, and so $|AP|$ is $\frac{3}{5}$ of 1.

This method is not very well suited to many practical origami applications, since it creates a large number of extraneous creases in random directions. Such creases tend to disturb the aesthetic purity of a model. They can, however, be reduced slightly in the following way.

In Figure 3.4, X was chosen in C, and rather than choosing Q_1 at random on AC, we first divide AC into $2^3 = 8$ sections of equal length by folding perpendicular bisectors. We then choose Q_1 through Q_5 as the end-points of these sections numbered from A. Then P is determined as in Figure 3.3b. Since AC and the creases perpendicular to AC determining the points Q_i are often required in the course of folding a model anyway, this can reduce the number of extraneous folds, even though the total number of creases is actually larger. For a general number $\frac{r}{n}$, it is necessary to divide AC into 2^k sections with $2^k > n$ in order to apply this method.

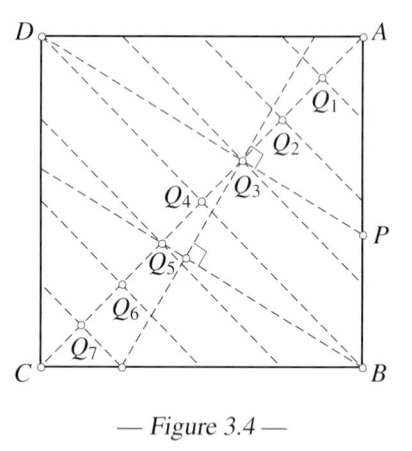

— Figure 3.4 —

Method 2 The idea of relating a regular division of the diagonal of the folding square to a different regular division of a side can be utilized in a slightly more elegant way. This idea was presented by Fumiaki Kawahata in the Origami Tanteidan newsletter, issue 29.

In Figure 3.5, we see a folding square with its diagonal AC pre-creased. Also, a crease DP has been made, which intersects AC in Q, as well as a crease orthogonal to AB through Q, which intersects AB in P'.

We name $|AP| = x$ and $|AP'| = y$. Since $\triangle AP'Q$ is a right-angled isosceles triangle, we

12 Dividing line segments into sections of equal length

have $|AQ| = y \cdot \sqrt{2}$, and we note that the length of the diagonal AC of the unit folding square is $\sqrt{2}$.

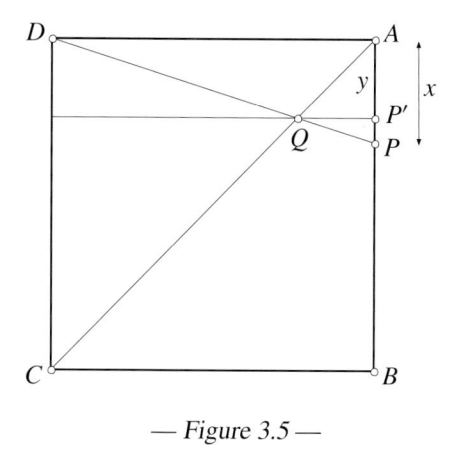

— Figure 3.5 —

Since opposite sides AB and CD of the folding square are parallel, so too are AP and CD, and so triangles $\triangle QAP$ and $\triangle QCD$ are similar, and we have

$$\frac{|AP|}{|CD|} = \frac{|AQ|}{|CQ|}$$

or, since CD is a side of the unit folding square,

$$\frac{x}{1} = \frac{y \cdot \sqrt{2}}{\sqrt{2} - y \cdot \sqrt{2}},$$

which is equivalent to

$$x = \frac{y}{1-y}$$

or

$$y = \frac{x}{1+x}.$$

If we now specifically choose $y = \frac{1}{n}$, we have

$$y = \frac{1}{n} \implies x = \frac{\frac{1}{n}}{1 - \frac{1}{n}} = \frac{1}{n-1}$$

(noting that

$$x = \frac{1}{n-1} \implies y = \frac{\frac{1}{n-1}}{1 + \frac{1}{n-1}} = \frac{1}{(n-1)+1} = \frac{1}{n}$$

also holds), and we see that AB being n times the length of AP' is equivalent to AB being $n - 1$ times the length of AP.

This means that we have an especially easy method of folding a division of the side into n pieces of equal length if n is either one more or one less than a power of 2. Fortunately,

59

| Chapter 3 | Properties of Origami Constructions |

this is the case for all odd single-digit numbers. We have (with $n = 1$ being trivial),

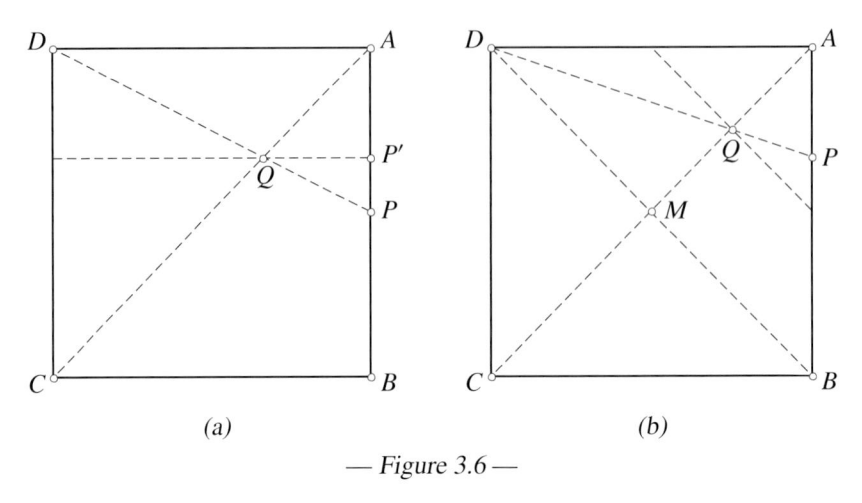

$$3 = 2^1 + 1 = 2^2 - 1, \quad 5 = 2^2 + 1, \quad 7 = 2^3 - 1 \quad \text{and} \quad 9 = 2^3 + 1.$$

— Figure 3.6 —

In Figure 3.6, we see two ways of finding one third of AB by this method. In Figure 3.6a, P is the mid-point of AB, that is, $|AP| = \frac{1}{2}$, and so $|AP'| = \frac{1}{3}$. In Figure 3.6b, Q is the mid-point of AM (with $M = AC \cap BD$), and so $|AQ| = \frac{1}{4} \cdot \sqrt{2}$, yielding $|AP| = \frac{1}{3}$.

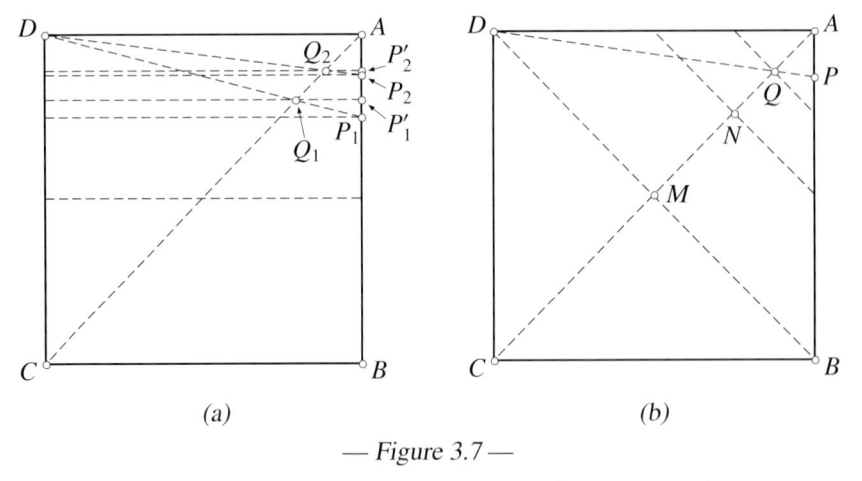

— Figure 3.7 —

In Figure 3.7a, we determine P_1 and P_2 such that $|AP_1| = \frac{1}{4}$ and $|AP_2| = \frac{1}{8}$. Then $|AP'_1| = \frac{1}{5}$ and $|AP'_2| = \frac{1}{9}$ follow. In Figure 3.7b, $M = AC \cap BD$, N is the mid-point of AM and Q the mid-point of AN. Then $|AQ| = \frac{1}{8} \cdot \sqrt{2}$, and therefore $|AP| = \frac{1}{7}$.

If we wish to use this method to divide AB into n equal sections with some other n, we can use the following property. Since $y = \frac{x}{1+x}$, choosing $x = \frac{a}{b}$ with a and b positive integers yields

$$y = \frac{\frac{a}{b}}{1 + \frac{a}{b}} = \frac{a}{a+b}.$$

12 Dividing line segments into sections of equal length

If we wish to divide AB into n equal sections, we can choose b as the largest power of 2 less than n, and $a = n - b$. We can then readily fold P such that

$$|AP| = x = \frac{a}{b},$$

and this yields

$$|AP'| = y = \frac{a}{a+b} = \frac{a}{n}$$

by Method 2. For instance, to divide AB into elevenths, choose $b = 8 = 2^3$, and $a = 11 - 8 = 3$. We then have $|AP| = \frac{3}{8}$, which is straightforward to fold, and $|AP'| = \frac{3}{11}$.

Since we choose b as a power of 2 and $1 - \frac{a}{a+b} = \frac{b}{a+b}$, we can then always determine the sections between P and B by determining mid-points.

Method 3 Rather than relating regular divisions of sides and diagonals, an alternative is to relate different regular divisions of (possibly different) sides. In Figure 3.8 we see one way of exploiting this idea.

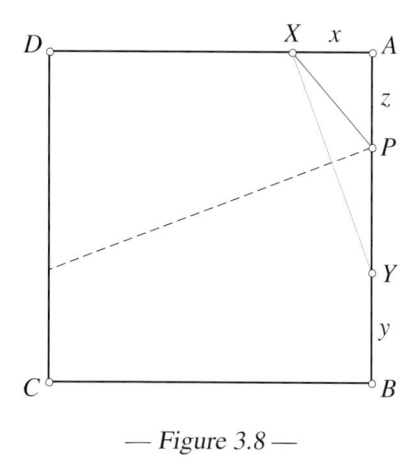

— Figure 3.8 —

On the unit folding square $ABCD$, we assume as given a point X on DA with $|AX| = x$ and a point Y on AB with $|BY| = y$. We assume that folding X to Y produces a crease which intersects AB in a point P (this is not always the case, but can always be achieved by renaming the points). We then have

$$|PX| = |PY| = |AB| - |BY| - |AP|,$$

and if we name $|AP| = z$, we have

$$|PX| = 1 - y - z.$$

Since $\triangle AXP$ is a right-angled triangle, we therefore have

$$x^2 + z^2 = (1 - y - z)^2$$

Chapter 3 — Properties of Origami Constructions

or
$$x^2 = (1-y)^2 - 2z(1-y),$$

which yields
$$z = \frac{(1-y)^2 - x^2}{2(1-y)}.$$

If we now assume the (very) special case of $x = y = \frac{1}{2m}$, that is, both points defining a regular division of their respective sides into an equal even number of sections, we have

$$z = \frac{\left(1 - \frac{1}{2m}\right)^2 - \left(\frac{1}{2m}\right)^2}{2 \cdot \left(1 - \frac{1}{2m}\right)}$$

$$= \frac{(2m-1)^2 - 1}{4m \cdot (2m-1)}$$

$$= \frac{4m^2 - 4m}{4m \cdot (2m-1)}$$

$$= \frac{m-1}{2m-1}.$$

The point P therefore determines a regular division of AB into $2m - 1$ sections, with $m - 1$ sections on one side and m on the other. Folding one side onto the other yields the difference, which is one such section. This method therefore yields a simple way to determine a division of AB into an odd number of sections, if we are given divisions of AB and DA into an equal even number of sections.

Assume, for instance, that we have $|AX| = |BY| = \frac{1}{4}$. This means $2m = 4$ or $m = 2$, and we obtain $|AP| = z = \frac{1}{3}$.

Method 4 This method is commonly referred to in the origami literature as the *Haga Theorem* (after Kazuo Haga, see [24] and [31], pp 77–80).

In origami, this mathematical result is arguably the one most talked about among non-mathematicians. Perhaps this derives from its simplicity (since it seems to involve only one fold), or perhaps from the lofty title of "Theorem" which has been bestowed upon it. It is certainly a very nice result, which exemplifies all that is aesthetically pleasing about the intrinsic geometry of origami, and in the next section, we shall see that there is a great deal more to this simple situation than first meets the eye.

We assume in Figure 3.9 that X is a point on DA with $|DX| = x$. We fold C onto a point

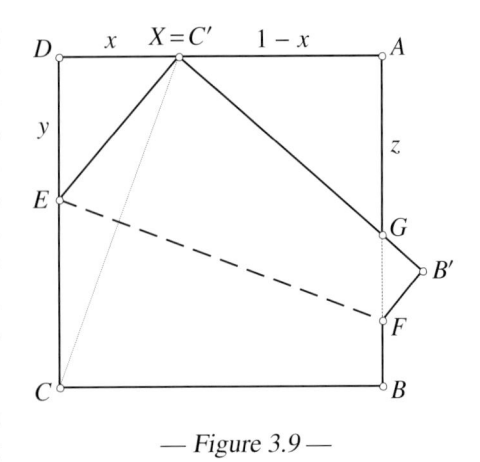

— Figure 3.9 —

12 Dividing line segments into sections of equal length

C' which is identical to X. This brings B to a point B', and creates a crease EF with E on CD and F on AB. Furthermore, we let G denote the point of intersection of AF and $C'B'$.

Naming $|ED| = y$, we have
$$|EX| = |EC'| = |EC| = 1 - y,$$
and since $\triangle EDX$ is a right-angled triangle, we have
$$x^2 + y^2 = (1-y)^2$$
or
$$x^2 = 1 - 2y,$$
which is equivalent to
$$y = \frac{1-x^2}{2}$$
$$= \frac{(1-x)(1+x)}{2}.$$

Since $\angle EXB' = \angle EC'B' = 90°$, we have
$$\angle DXE = 180° - \angle AXG - \angle EXB'$$
$$= 180° - \angle AXG - 90°$$
$$= 90° - \angle AXG,$$
and since
$$\angle AGX = 90° - \angle AXG$$
also holds in the right triangle $\triangle AGX$, we see that triangles $\triangle DXE$ and $\triangle AGX$ are similar. We name $|AG| = z$, and since $|AX| = 1 - |DX| = 1 - x$, this means that
$$\frac{|AG|}{|AX|} = \frac{|DX|}{|DE|}$$
or
$$\frac{z}{1-x} = \frac{x}{y}$$
holds. This is equivalent to
$$z = \frac{x}{y} \cdot (1-x)$$
$$= \frac{x \cdot (1-x) \cdot 2}{(1-x)(1+x)}$$
$$= \frac{2x}{1+x}.$$

If we assume $x = \frac{1}{n}$, we see that
$$z = \frac{2 \cdot \frac{1}{n}}{1 + \frac{1}{n}} = \frac{2}{n+1}$$
holds. If we choose $|DX| = x = \frac{1}{2}$, for instance, we have $|AG| = z = \frac{2}{3}$ (and therefore $|BG| = 1 - \frac{2}{3} = \frac{1}{3}$. If $x = \frac{1}{4}$, we have $z = \frac{2}{5}$, and so on.

63

Chapter 3   Properties of Origami Constructions

13 Six problems from one fold

In this section we consider six intimately related problems, which all result from folding a square of paper once. These problems demonstrate the power of the Haga Theorem in all it's nuances.

I suggest that readers of this section attempt to solve the problems themselves before they read the solutions so that they gain greater familiarity with the situation. In order to make this easier, I will state the problems first, and save the solutions for the end of the section.

The situation we are given in all of the problems is the following (Figure 3.10).

Let $ABCD$ be a square of paper placed on a plane surface. Holding corners A and B on the surface (and identifying the points immediately below C and D in the surface with C and D themselves), C is folded onto the point C' on AB. Simultaneously, D is folded onto a point D'. Folding C onto C' in this way creates a crease EF in the paper with E on BC and F on DA. Furthermore, we let G designate the point of intersection of DA and $C'D'$.

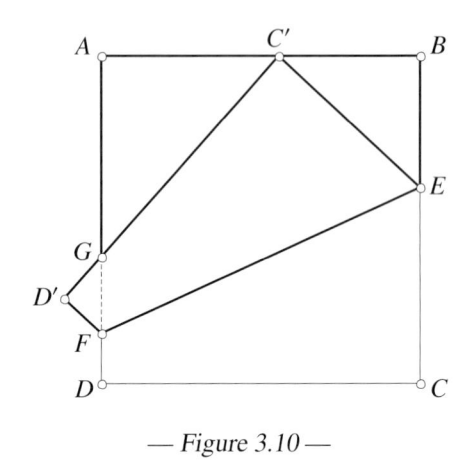

— Figure 3.10 —

Problem[a] 1
Prove that $C'D'$ is a tangent of the circle with center in C, passing through B and D.

Problem[b] 2
Prove that the perimeter of triangle GAC' is equal to half the perimeter of $ABCD$.

Problem 3
Prove the identity $AG = C'B + GD'$.

Problem[c] 4
Prove that the sum of the perimeters of triangles $C'BE$ and $GD'F$ is equal to the perimeter of triangle GAC'.

Problem 5
Prove that the perimeter of triangle $GD'F$ is equal to the length of line segment AC'.

Problem[d] 6
Prove that the inradius of GAC' is equal to the length of line segment GD'.

---

[a] Posed on p 11 of [29].
[b] Problem Number 2 in the VIII Nordic Mathematical Contest, 1994.
[c] Problem Number 4, Grade Two, Final Round in the 37th Slovenian Mathematical Olympiad, 1993.
[d] Example 3.1 on page 37 of [10].

13 Six problems from one fold

Problem 6 is a traditional sangaku, a geometry problem found on tablets mounted in many Edo-period Shinto temples in Japan.

13.1 Solution to Problem 1

Since EF is the crease resulting from folding C onto C' and D onto D', C is symmetric to C' with respect to EF, as is D to D'.

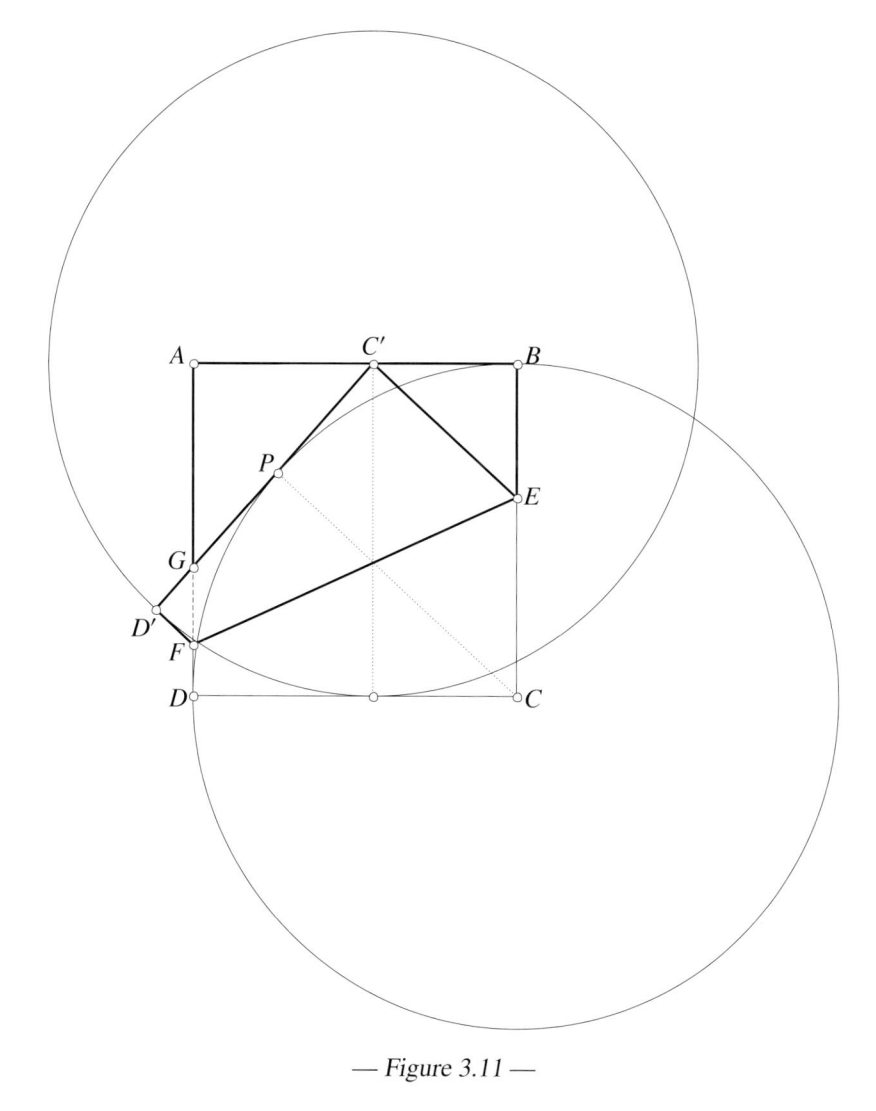

— Figure 3.11 —

The circle c' with center in C' and radius equal to the length of the sides of $ABCD$ is tangent to CD, as the distance from C' to CD is equal to the length of the sides of the square. Since reflection of the circle c' in EF yields the circle with center C passing through B and D, and reflection of CD in EF yields $C'D'$, the result is shown.

13.2 Solution to Problem 2

We know from Problem 1 that $C'D'$ is tangent to the circle with center C passing through B and D. Also B is the point of tangency of this circle with AB, and D is its point of tangency with AD. We let P designate the point of tangency of this circle with $C'D'$. Since $C'P$ and $C'B$ are both tangents of this circle, their lengths are equal, and similarly so are the lengths of GP and GD.

The perimeter of GAC' is equal to the sum of the lengths of the three sides, and we have

$$AC' + C'G + GA = AC' + C'P + GP + GA$$
$$= AC' + C'B + GD + GA$$
$$= AB + DA.$$

The perimeter of GAC' is therefore equal to the sum of the lengths of two sides of $ABCD$, which is half its perimeter.

13.3 Solution to Problem 3

We know from Problem 2 that the perimeter of GAC' is equal to half the perimeter of $ABCD$. We therefore have

$$AC' + C'G + AG = AB + CD$$
$$= AB + C'D'$$
$$= AC' + C'B + C'G + GD',$$

and therefore
$$AG = C'B + GD'.$$

Another way to see this is as follows. Since AD and $C'D'$ are both the length of sides of $ABCD$, and therefore equal, we have

$$AG = AD - GD$$
$$= C'D' - GP$$
$$= C'P + GD'$$
$$= C'B + GD'.$$

13.4 Solution to Problem 4

We note that $\angle C'BE$, $\angle GD'F$ and $\angle GAC'$ are all right angles.

Furthermore, we have
$$\angle D'GF = \angle C'GA$$

13 Six problems from one fold

since these are opposing angles, and

$$\angle BC'E = 180° - \angle EC'D - \angle D'C'A$$
$$= 180° - 90° - \angle GC'A$$
$$= 90° - \angle GC'A$$
$$= \angle C'GA.$$

The triangles GAC', $C'BE$ and $GD'F$ are therefore all similar with

$$AG : C'B : GD' = AC' : BE : D'F = C'G : EC' : FG.$$

From Problem 3, we know that $AG = C'B + GD'$ holds, and therefore we have $AC' = BE + D'F$ and $C'G = EC' + FG$, from which

$$AG + AC' + C'G = (C'B + BE + EC') + (GD' + D'F + FG)$$

follows.

This result can also be proven by analytic methods. Without loss of generality, we assume that the length of the sides of $ABCD$ is 1. Naming $C'B = x$ and $BE = y$, we see that $C'E = CE = 1 - y$ (Figure 3.12), and since $C'BE$ is a right triangle, we have

$$x^2 + y^2 = (1-y)^2 \quad \Leftrightarrow \quad x^2 = 1 - 2y$$
$$\Leftrightarrow \quad y = \frac{1-x^2}{2}.$$

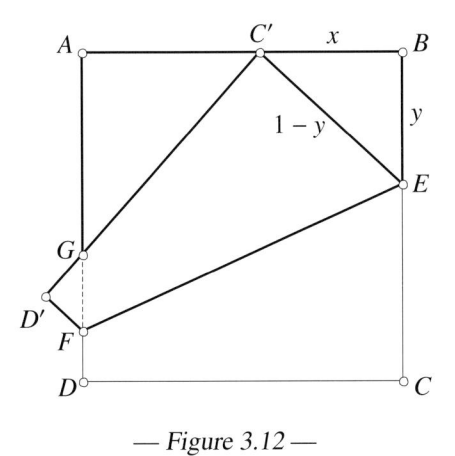

— Figure 3.12 —

Since triangles GAC', $C'BE$ and $GD'F$ are similar, and $AC' = 1 - x$, we have

$$GC' : AC' = C'E : BE$$
$$= 1 - y : y,$$

67

and therefore
$$GC' = \frac{(1-y)(1-x)}{y}$$
$$= \frac{\frac{1+x^2}{2}(1-x)}{\frac{1-x^2}{2}}$$
$$= \frac{1+x^2}{1+x},$$
and
$$GD' = 1 - GC'$$
$$= 1 - \frac{1+x^2}{1+x}$$
$$= \frac{x-x^2}{1+x}.$$

We know from Problem 2 that the perimeter p_1 of GAC' is 2, and the perimeter p_2 of $C'BE$ is
$$p_2 = C'B + BE + C'E$$
$$= x + y + 1 - y$$
$$= 1 + x.$$

The perimeter p_3 of $GD'F$ now results from the fact that $GD'F$ and $C'BE$ are similar, and we have
$$p_3 : p_2 = GD' : C'B$$
$$= \frac{x-x^2}{1+x} : x$$
and therefore
$$p_3 = p_2 \cdot \frac{x-x^2}{1+x} \cdot \frac{1}{x}$$
$$= (1+x) \cdot \frac{x(1-x)}{1+x} \cdot \frac{1}{x}$$
$$= 1 - x,$$
and
$$p_2 + p_3 = (1+x) + (1-x) = 2 = p_1$$
follows.

13.5 Solution to Problem 5

In the second proof of problem 4, we define the length of line segment $C'B$ as x, and assume without loss of generality that the length of the sides of $ABCD$ is 1. We immediately

13 Six problems from one fold

see that $AC' = 1 - x$, and as was proven in Problem 4, the perimeter of $GD'F$ is also $1 - x$, yielding the result.

Another way to see this is as follows. The sides of $ABCD$ are all the same length, and so we have

$$AB = CD = C'D'$$
$$= C'P + PD'$$
$$= C'B + PD',$$

since $C'P$ and $C'B$ are both tangents of the circle with center in C passing through B and D, as noted in Problem 1. It therefore follows that

$$AC' + C'B = AB$$
$$= C'B + PD',$$

and therefore

$$AC' = PD'$$
$$= GP + GD'$$
$$= GD + GD',$$

as GP and GD are also both tangents of this circle. We therefore have

$$AC' = GF + FD + GD'$$
$$= GF + FD' + GD',$$

as claimed.

13.6 Solution to Problem 6

Let I designate the point of tangency of the incircle with AC', II the point of tangency with AG, and III the point of tangency with GC' (Figure 3.13 on the next page).

The incenter M of GAC' is the fourth corner of a square with corners A, I and II, since the two tangents AI and AII of the incircle are of equal length, and $\angle IAII = 90° = \angle MIA = \angle MIIA$. For the inradius r of GAC', we therefore have $r = AI = AII$. Furthermore, since tangents of the incircle through a common point are of equal length, we also have $C'I = C'III = x$ and $GII = GIII = y$.

From Problem 2, we know that the perimeter of GAC' is equal to half the perimeter of $ABCD$, or twice the length of a side of this square. We therefore have

$$2 \cdot C'D' = AC' + AG + GC'$$
$$= (r + x) + (r + y) + (x + y)$$
$$= 2 \cdot (x + y + r),$$

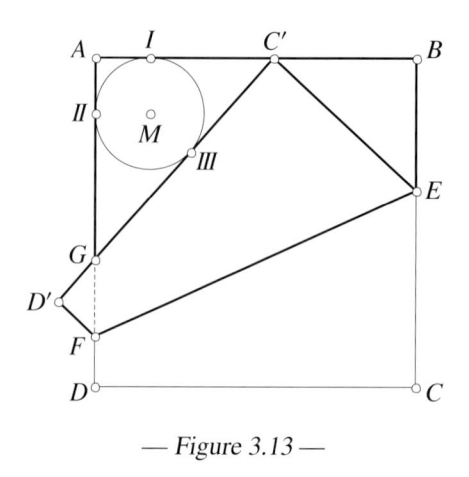

Figure 3.13

and since
$$C'D' = C'III + GIII + GD'$$
$$= x + y + GD',$$

it follows that
$$2 \cdot (x + y + GD') = 2 \cdot (x + y + r),$$

and we therefore have
$$x + y + GD' = x + y + r,$$

and so $GD' = r$ follows, as required.

14 Determining common folding methods for given creases

By virtue of (O7), we can fold a given point P onto any point ($\neq P$) on a given line ℓ. As discussed in section 3 (page 7), this yields as creases all lines perpendicular to ℓ not containing P if $P \in \ell$, and all tangents of the parabola with focus P and directrix ℓ if $P \notin \ell$.

A question that arises naturally is the following: If we are given a crease (or a number of creases), how can we choose a point P and a line ℓ, such that folding P onto ℓ produces the given crease (or creases)? In this section, we shall determine necessary and sufficient conditions for this to be possible, and give methods for determining such points P and lines ℓ when they exist.

14.1 One crease given

For a single given crease c_1, the situation is quite simple. First of all, we note that we cannot choose P on c_1, since folding a point P onto any point $Q \neq P$ yields the perpendicular bisector of the line segment PQ by virtue of (O5), which cannot pass through P or Q.

On the other hand, we can choose any point not on c_1 as P. If P' is the unique point symmetric to P with respect to c_1 (Figure 3.14), we can choose any line passing through P' as ℓ, and it is then certainly possible to produce c_1 by folding P onto a point of ℓ, namely P'.

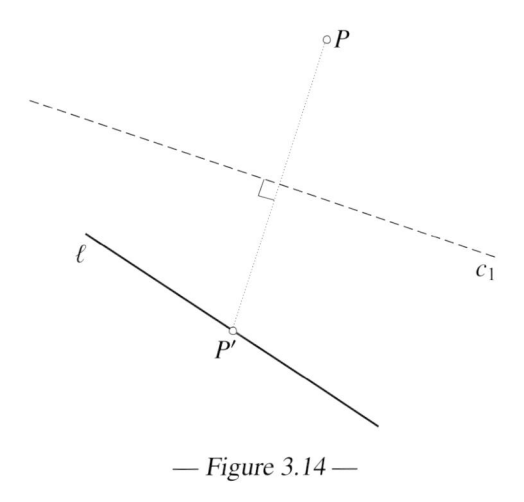

— Figure 3.14 —

Conversely, if we wish to choose ℓ first, we note again that the point P' of ℓ onto which we are to fold P in order to produce the crease c_1 may not be located on c_1. We may therefore not choose ℓ in such a way that it consists solely of points on c_1. In other words, we may not choose c_1 itself as ℓ.

We may, however, choose any other line as ℓ (Figure 3.15). We can then choose any point on the line ℓ' symmetric to ℓ with respect to c_1 as P (as long as we choose $P \notin \ell$, which is then certainly possible). Then P' is a point on ℓ and not on c_1, as required.

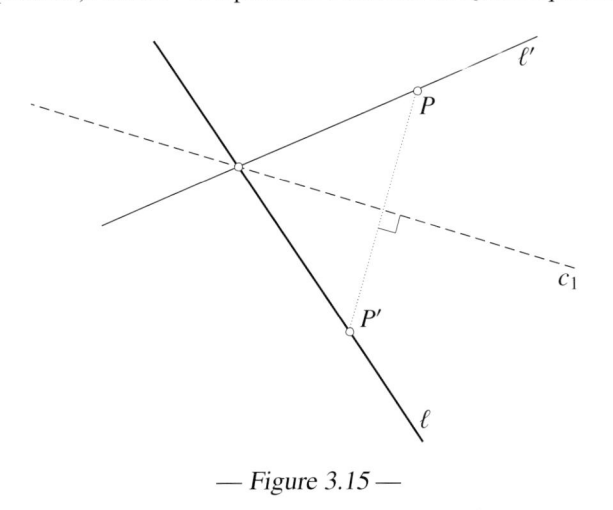

— Figure 3.15 —

14.2 Two creases given

How can we choose P and ℓ if two creases $c_1 \neq c_2$ are given? As for one crease, we can choose any point of the folding plane as P, as long as P is not a point of either c_1 or c_2 (Figure 3.16). If we use P' to refer to the point symmetric to P with respect to c_1 and P'' to refer to the point symmetric to P with respect to c_2, we must then choose ℓ through both P' and P''. The two points P' and P'' are certainly not equal, since this would mean that c_1 (as the perpendicular bisector of the line segment PP') and c_2 (as the perpendicular bisector of the line segment PP'') would be equal, in contradiction to the assumption that they are not. Any choice of P therefore uniquely determines the associated line ℓ as the line joining P' and P''.

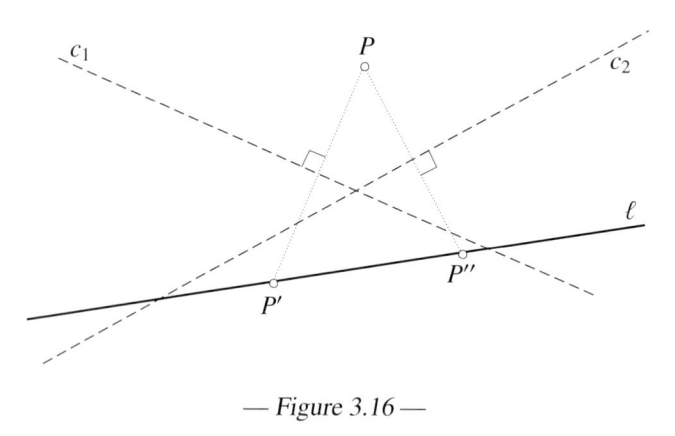

— Figure 3.16 —

If c_1 and c_2 are parallel (Figure 3.17), we note that both PP' and PP'' are perpendicular to both c_1 and c_2. We therefore have $PP' = PP'' = \ell$, and ℓ therefore passes through P in this case.

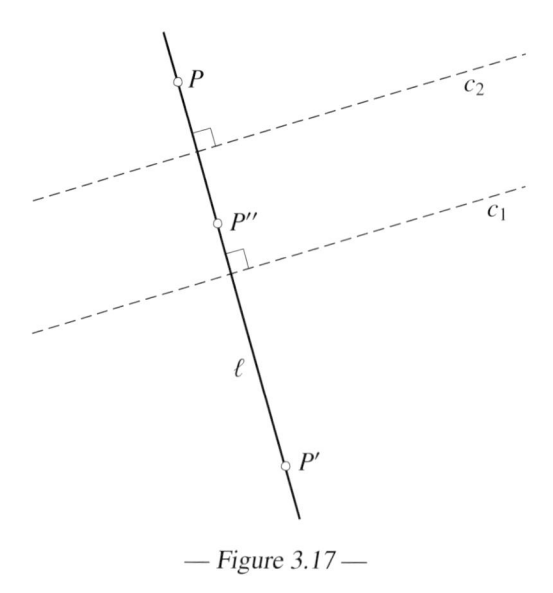

— Figure 3.17 —

14 Determining common folding methods for given creases

If c_1 and c_2 are given, which lines can we choose as ℓ? This is a slightly more difficult question to answer completely. From section 14.1, we know that ℓ can not be chosen equal to either c_1 or c_2. If we choose a line ℓ, the corresponding point P needs to lie on both the line ℓ' symmetric to ℓ with respect to c_1 and the line ℓ'' symmetric to ℓ with respect to c_2 (Figure 3.18). Such a point certainly exists, unless we have $\ell' \neq \ell''$ and $\ell' \parallel \ell''$. Also, P has to be chosen such that it does not lie on either c_1 or c_2.

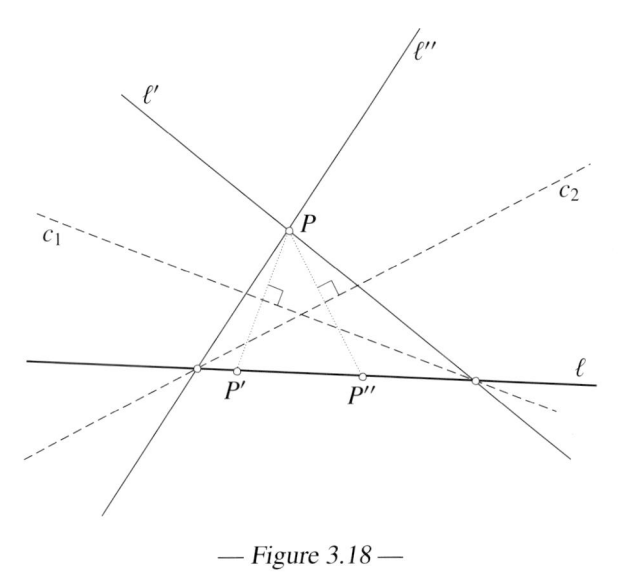

— Figure 3.18 —

Which lines, then, can we not choose as ℓ because they would not allow the choice of a corresponding point P? In order to answer this question, we consider three possible cases for the relative positions of c_1 and c_2.

Case I $c_1 \parallel c_2$ (Figure 3.19)

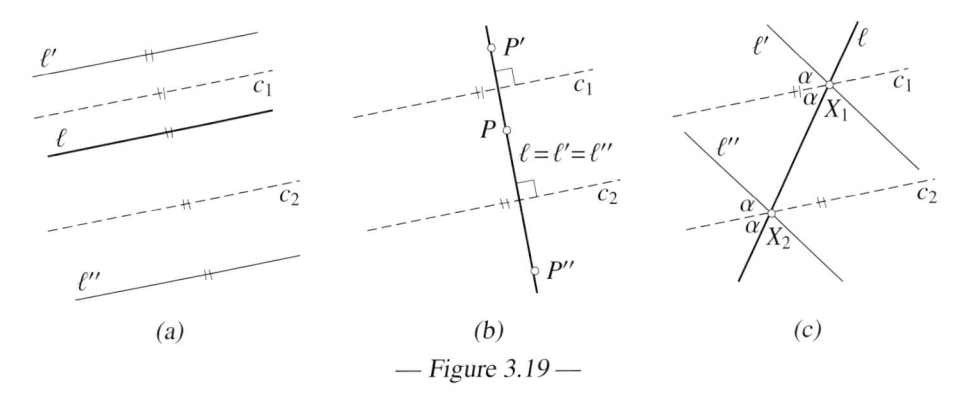

(a)   (b)   (c)

— Figure 3.19 —

If c_1 and c_2 are parallel and ℓ is parallel to both (Figure 3.19a), both ℓ' and ℓ'' are also parallel to both, and therefore to each other. In this case, there is no possible choice for P, and we cannot therefore choose ℓ parallel to c_1 and c_2.

73

If ℓ is perpendicular to c_1 and c_2 (Figure 3.19b), both ℓ' and ℓ'' are identical to ℓ. Therefore P can be chosen anywhere on ℓ (except in the points of intersection with c_1 or c_2).

If ℓ intersects c_1 in X_1 and c_2 in X_2, and $\angle \ell c_1 = \angle \ell c_2 = \alpha$ with $0° < \alpha < 90°$ (Figure 3.19c), we see that $\angle \ell \ell' = \angle \ell \ell'' = 2\alpha$ with $0° < 2\alpha < 180°$. In this case, ℓ' and ℓ'' are two lines passing through different points (X_1 and X_2) of ℓ, and intersecting ℓ at equal (oriented) angles not equal to $0°$ or $180°$, and ℓ' and ℓ'' are therefore parallel and not equal. Again there is no possible choice for P.

We see that we must choose ℓ perpendicular to c_1 and c_2 if c_1 and c_2 are parallel.

Case II $c_1 \perp c_2$ (Figure 3.20)

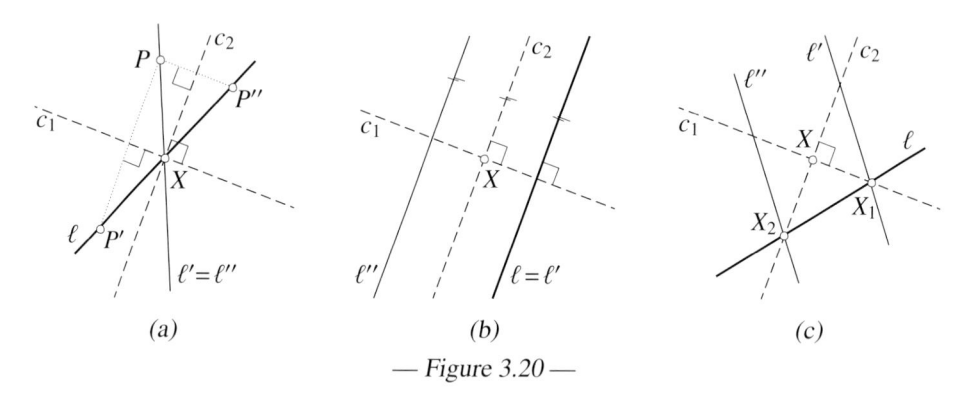

— Figure 3.20 —

If $c_1 \perp c_2$ and ℓ contains the common point X of c_1 and c_2 (with $\ell \neq c_1$ and $\ell \neq c_2$) (Figure 3.20a), ℓ' and ℓ'' are equal. This can be seen in the following manner. If we name $\angle \ell c_1 = \alpha$ (taking oriented angles), we certainly have $0° < \alpha < 90°$. Since $c_1 \perp c_2$, we have $\angle \ell c_2 = 90° - \alpha$. It therefore follows that $\angle \ell \ell' = 2 \cdot \angle \ell c_1 = 2\alpha$ and $\angle \ell \ell'' = 2 \cdot \angle \ell c_2 = 2 \cdot (90° - \alpha)$. It therefore follows that $\angle \ell \ell' + \angle \ell \ell'' = 180°$, and since ℓ, and therefore ℓ' and ℓ'' pass through the common point X of c_1 and c_2, we have $\ell' = \ell''$. Therefore P can be chosen anywhere on $\ell' = \ell''$, except in X.

If ℓ does not contain X, but is orthogonal to c_1 (the analogous argument holds for $\ell \perp c_2$), we have $\ell' = \ell$, and since ℓ and c_2 are both orthogonal to c_1, we have $c_2 \parallel \ell$, and therefore $\ell'' \parallel \ell = \ell'$ (Figure 3.20b). Since $\ell \neq c_2$, we have $\ell' \neq \ell''$, and there is again no possible choice for P.

Finally, if ℓ does not contain X, and is not perpendicular to either c_1 or c_2, we find that ℓ' and ℓ'' are parallel and not equal (Figure 3.20c). We see this in the following manner. If we name $X_1 = \ell \cap c_1$ and $X_2 = \ell \cap c_2$, we certainly have $X_1 \neq X_2$. Also, if we name $\angle \ell c_1 = \alpha$, we have $\angle \ell c_2 = 90° - \alpha$. It therefore follows that $\angle \ell \ell' = 2 \cdot \angle \ell c_1 = 2\alpha$ and $\angle \ell \ell'' = 2 \cdot \angle \ell c_2 = 2 \cdot (90° - \alpha)$, and since the sum of these two angles is $180°$, we see that ℓ' and ℓ'' intersect ℓ at equal (oriented) angles, but in different points. They are therefore parallel and not equal, and there is once more no possible choice for P.

14 Determining common folding methods for given creases

Case III c_1 not parallel or perpendicular to c_2 (Figure 3.21)

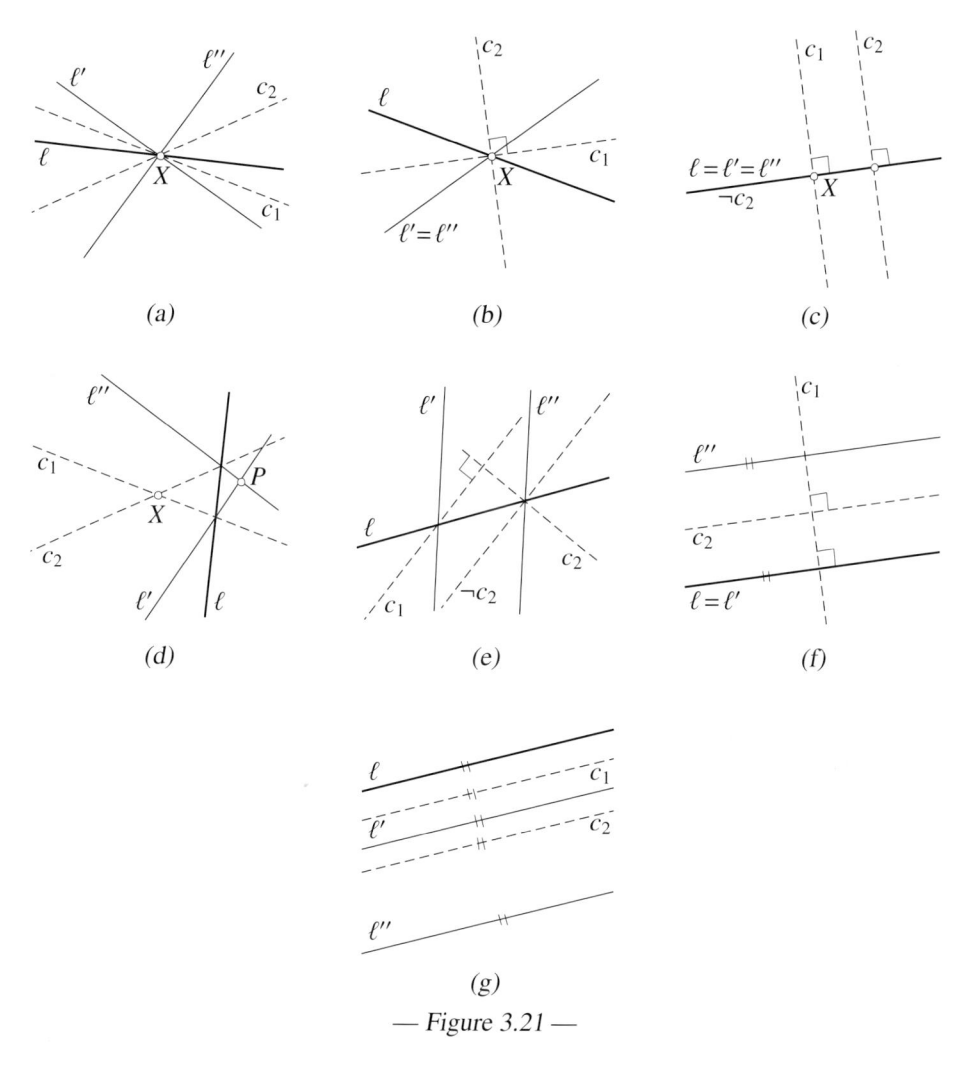

(a)

(b)

(c)

(d)

(e)

(f)

(g)

— Figure 3.21 —

If c_1 and c_2 intersect in a point X and ℓ passes through X, ℓ' and ℓ'' will also pass through X. If c_1 and c_2 are not perpendicular, this means that we cannot choose ℓ through X, since ℓ' and ℓ'' cannot be equal in this case (Figure 3.21a). Why is this? If ℓ' and ℓ'' were equal and ℓ not perpendicular to c_1, c_1 and c_2 would both be lines of symmetry of ℓ and $\ell' = \ell''$, and therefore either equal or perpendicular (Figure 3.21b). On the other hand, if $\ell' = \ell''$ and $\ell \perp c_1$ (or analogously for $\ell \perp c_2$), we would have $\ell = \ell' = \ell''$, and therefore $c_2 \perp \ell''$ (since $c_2 = \ell$ is not possible) (Figure 3.21c). Creases c_1 and c_2 would therefore be parallel, in contradiction to the assumption that they intersect in X. We see that ℓ cannot be chosen through X.

If, however, c_1 and c_2 intersect in X and are not perpendicular, we can choose ℓ anywhere with $X \notin \ell$, and an appropriate P certainly exists in the unique point of intersection of ℓ'

and ℓ'' (Figure 3.21d). We can see this in the following manner.

Let us assume that c_1 and c_2 intersect in X with c_1 not perpendicular to c_2, $X \notin \ell$ and $\ell' \parallel \ell''$ (or $\ell' = \ell''$). If ℓ is not parallel to c_1 and ℓ not perpendicular to c_1 (Figure 3.21e), we name $\angle \ell c_1 = \angle c_1 \ell' = \alpha$. Since $\ell' \parallel \ell''$, we have $\angle \ell \ell' = \angle \ell \ell''$, and since c_2 has to be a line of symmetry of ℓ and ℓ'', we have either $\angle \ell c_2 = \angle c_2 \ell'' = \alpha$ (in which case $c_1 \parallel c_2$ in contradiction to $c_1 \cap c_2 = X$), or $\angle \ell c_2 = \angle c_2 \ell'' = 90° - \alpha$, in which case $\angle c_1 c_2$ is the third angle in a triangle with sides ℓ, c_1 and c_2, and since $\angle \ell c_1 = \alpha$ and $\angle \ell c_2 = 90° - \alpha$, we have $\angle c_1 c_2 = 90°$, in contradiction to the assumption that c_1 is not perpendicular to c_2.

If $\ell \perp c_1$ (Figure 3.21f) and $\ell' \parallel \ell''$, we have $\ell = \ell'$ and therefore c_2 is the mid-parallel of ℓ and ℓ'', which means $c_1 \perp c_2$ in contradiction to the assumption that c_1 is not perpendicular to c_2. (The configuration $\ell = \ell' = \ell''$ is also not possible, since this would mean $c_2 \perp \ell$, and therefore $c_1 \parallel c_2$, contradicting $c_1 \cap c_2 = X$.)

Finally, if $\ell \parallel c_1$ (or analogously $\ell \parallel c_2$) and $\ell' \parallel \ell''$ (Figure 3.21g), we have $\ell' \parallel \ell \parallel \ell''$, and since c_2 is the mid-parallel of ℓ and ℓ'', we have $c_1 \parallel c_2$, again contradicting $c_1 \cap c_2 = X$. (The only other possibility is $\ell'' = \ell$ and $c_2 \perp \ell$, which means $c_1 \perp c_2$ in contradiction to the assumption that c_1 is not perpendicular to c_2.)

In summary, depending on the relative positions of c_1 and c_2, we can choose ℓ (and then P) in the following manner:

$c_1 \parallel c_2$: $\quad \ell \perp c_1$ and $\ell \perp c_2$; $\qquad\qquad P \in \ell' = \ell'' = \ell$ with $P \notin c_1, P \notin c_2$).

$c_1 \perp c_2$: $\quad \ell \neq c_1$ and $\ell \neq c_2$ with $c_1 \cap c_2 \in \ell$; $\qquad P \in \ell' = \ell''$ with $P \neq c_1 \cap c_2$).

c_1 not parallel or perpendicular to c_2:

$\qquad \ell$ anywhere with $c_1 \cap c_2 \notin \ell$; $\qquad\qquad P = \ell' \cap \ell''$ uniquely.

14.3 Three creases given

Things get even more interesting when we wish to find out which points P and which lines ℓ can solve our problem if three creases are given. Put another way, given three lines c_1, c_2 and c_3 in the plane, which points P not on any of the lines c_i have the quality that the points P', P'' and P''' symmetric to P with respect to c_1, c_2 and c_3 respectively, are collinear (Figure 3.22)?

Or, given c_1, c_2 and c_3, which lines ℓ have the quality that the lines ℓ', ℓ'' and ℓ''' symmetric to ℓ with respect to c_1, c_2 and c_3 respectively, pass through a common point, not on any of the lines c_i?

If the three lines c_1, c_2 and c_3 are parallel, all points P not on one of the lines c_i have this quality (Figure 3.23a). As was shown in section 14.2, ℓ is then the line through P and orthogonal to all three lines c_i. (Since this holds for any two, it holds for all three.)

As for two creases, we can conversely choose ℓ anywhere at right angles to the parallel lines c_i, and P anywhere on ℓ except in the points of intersection with one of the lines c_i.

14 Determining common folding methods for given creases

— Figure 3.22 —

(a) (b)

— Figure 3.23 —

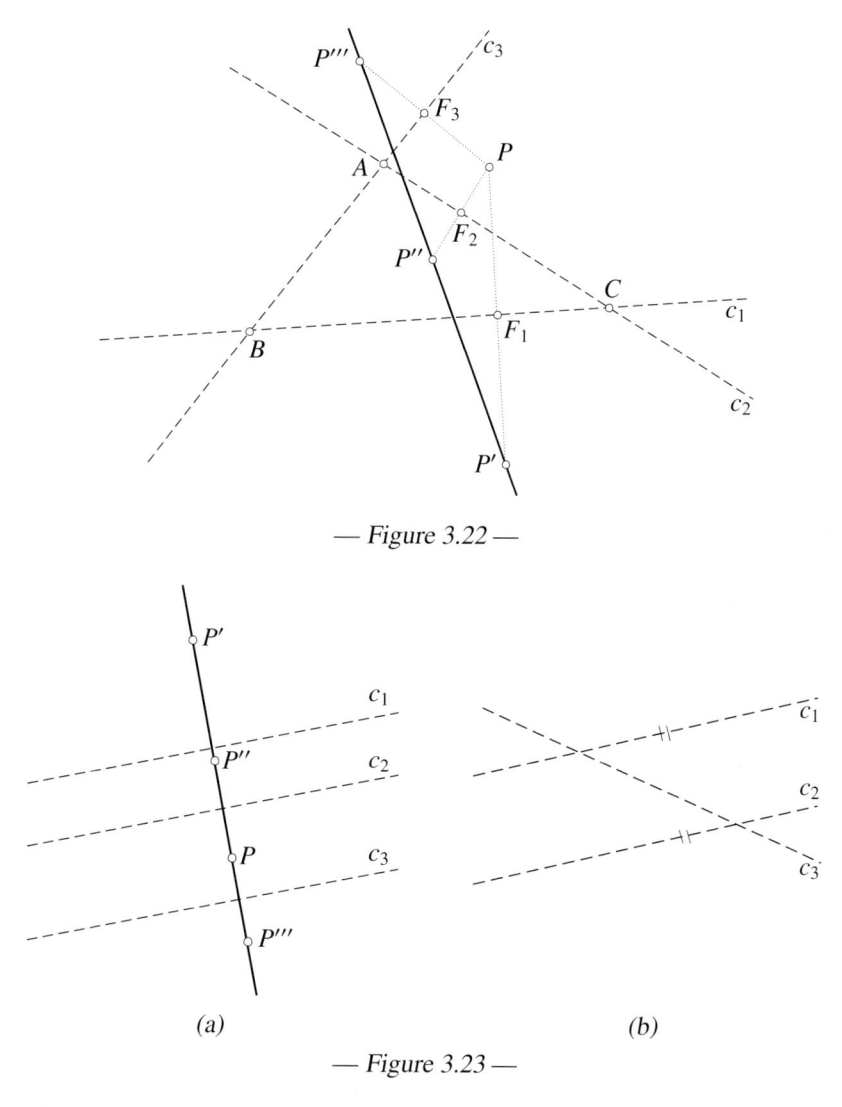

What if two creases, say c_1 and c_2 are parallel, and c_3 is not parallel to c_1 and c_2 (Figure 3.23b)?

Since $c_1 \parallel c_2$, we know from section 14.2 that ℓ has to be chosen orthogonal to c_1 and c_2, and P on ℓ, but not on any of the c_i. Folding P onto any point on ℓ then yields a crease orthogonal to ℓ however, and since c_3 is not parallel to c_1 and c_2, we cannot therefore obtain c_3 by folding any such P onto ℓ. We see that there is no possible choice of P or ℓ in this case.

Similarly, there can be no such P or ℓ if the three creases c_i pass through a common point Q (Figure 3.24 on the following page).

If we assume that such a point P exists, we note that the feet F_1, F_2 and F_3 of P on creases

Chapter 3   Properties of Origami Constructions

— *Figure 3.24* —

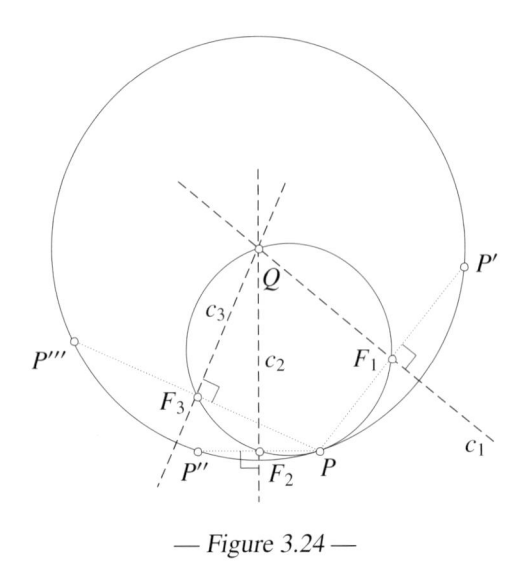

c_1, c_2 and c_3 respectively all lie on the circle with diameter PQ, since $\angle PF_1Q$, $\angle PF_2Q$ and $\angle PF_3Q$ are all right angles. Since the homothety with center P and homothetic ratio 2 maps F_1 onto P', F_2 onto P'' and F_3 onto P''', we see that P', P'' and P''' lie on the circle passing through P with center in Q. No three concyclic points can be collinear, however, and we see that there can be no point P in this case, since there can never be a corresponding ℓ.

The impossibility of the last two cases can also be seen in the following manner. We know from (O7) on page 11 that folding a point onto the points of a line ℓ yields either the lines orthogonal to ℓ and not passing through P if $P \in \ell$, or the tangents of the parabola with focus P and directrix ℓ if $P \notin \ell$. If we can fold two parallel creases c_1 and c_2 and a third crease c_3 not parallel to c_1 and c_2 (or alternately c_1, c_2 and c_3 passing through a common point Q) by folding some point P onto some line ℓ, we must have $P \notin \ell$, since not all creases are parallel. All three creases are therefore tangents of a common parabola. Parabolas, however, can neither have two parallel tangents nor three tangents passing through a common point. In neither of these cases does a P or an ℓ therefore exist. (These are very elementary properties of the parabola, proofs of which can be found in many books on conics. An excellent and readily available example of such a text is [55], Section IX: The Projective Generation of Conics and Quadrics, pp 321–400.)

Let us now assume that c_1, c_2 and c_3 intersect in three different points $A = c_2 \cap c_3$, $B = c_3 \cap c_1$ and $C = c_1 \cap c_2$ (Figure 3.22). These three points cannot be collinear, since the three creases would then be identical, with $c_1 = BC = CA = c_2 = AB = c_3$. We are therefore now searching for points P such that the points symmetric to P with respect to the sides of a triangle $\triangle ABC$ are collinear. If we again use F_1, F_2 and F_3 to denote the feet of P on c_1, c_2 and c_3 respectively, we see that this is equivalent to finding P such that the points F_1, F_2 and F_3 are collinear, since F_1, F_2 and F_3 are the mid-points of PP', PP'' and PP''' respectively, and therefore result from P', P'' and P''' by means of the homothety with center P and homothetic ratio $\frac{1}{2}$.

This is a well known problem of Euclidean geometry, and the answer is that P can be any point of the circumcircle of $\triangle ABC$. The line $F_1F_2F_3$ is then called the "Simson line" (or "Wallis line") of P with respect to $\triangle ABC$. Proving the fact that the points F_i are collinear if P is a point of the circumcircle is a fairly easy exercise in angles subtended over arcs, and is left to the interested reader. Proving the converse, that is, that collinearity of the F_i implies that P is a point of the circumcircle is slightly more difficult, as it involves proving the impossibility of a number of different relative positions of P and $\triangle ABC$. More on this subject can be found in [33], pp 131–144, or [26], pp 76–79.)

The set of all possible points P, for which a line ℓ exists such that we can fold P onto points of ℓ in order to produce the given creases c_1, c_2 and c_3 is therefore precisely the set of all points of the circumcircle of $\triangle ABC$, not including the points A, B and C, since P can not be located on one of the creases c_i.

On the other hand, which lines can be chosen as ℓ, such that there exists a corresponding point P? We shall prove the following theorem:

Theorem 5
Given a triangle $\triangle ABC$, the set of all lines ℓ with the property that there exists a point P such that each side of the triangle can be produced as a crease by folding P onto ℓ is the set of all lines through the orthocenter O of $\triangle ABC$, not including the three altitudes of $\triangle ABC$.

Proof If a line ℓ is given, such that a corresponding point P exists and these conditions are fulfilled, P is certainly a point of the circumcircle of $\triangle ABC$. As a first step, we shall prove that ℓ therefore contains O.

If $\triangle ABC$ is acute-angled, we have the following nice synthetic proof due to Andrej Storozhev (Figure 3.25 on the next page).

We assume that P is a point on the arc BC of the circumcircle of $\triangle ABC$. (For P on the arcs AB or CA, we can simply rename the points to achieve this configuration.) Since ℓ is the line joining P'' and P''', it is sufficient to prove that P'', P''' and O are collinear for any such a point P. Since

$$\angle P'''OO''' = \angle PO'''O \quad \text{and} \quad \angle P''OO'' = \angle PO''O,$$

it follows that

$$\angle P''OO'' + \angle P'''OO''' = \angle PO''O + \angle PO'''O$$
$$= \angle PO''B + \angle PO'''C$$
$$= \angle PAB + \angle PAC$$
$$= \angle BAC$$
$$= \angle BO'''C$$
$$= \angle BO'''O$$
$$= \angle BOO'''.$$

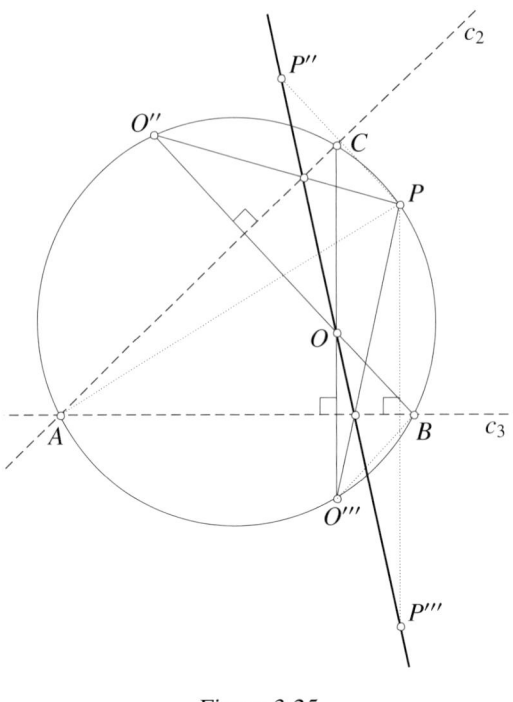

— Figure 3.25 —

It therefore follows that

$$\angle BOP''' = \angle BOO''' - \angle P'''OO'''$$
$$= \angle P''OO'',$$

and since B, O and O'' all lie on an altitude of $\triangle ABC$ and are therefore collinear, so too are P'', P''' and O, as required. ∎

This proof can readily be adapted to right- and obtuse-angled triangles $\triangle ABC$, but this requires considering a myriad of cases with respect to the relative positions of P, B, C, O'' and O'''.

We can also prove this result analytically. This method has the advantage of including all possible cases, even though the calculations are a bit long. In order to do this, we make the following assumptions. First of all, we assume a system of cartesian coordinates to be given with it's origin in the circumcenter O of $\triangle ABC$ (Figure 3.26). We assume that the x-axis is parallel to c_1, and since the circumcenter of $\triangle ABC$ is equidistant from A, B and C, we can assume that the coordinates of A are $(-a; b)$ and the coordinates of B are $(a; b)$.

Furthermore, we assume that the slope of c_2 is the finite number k. (If c_2 is perpendicular to c_1, we can certainly rename A, B and C such that k is finite, since a triangle cannot have two interior right angles.)

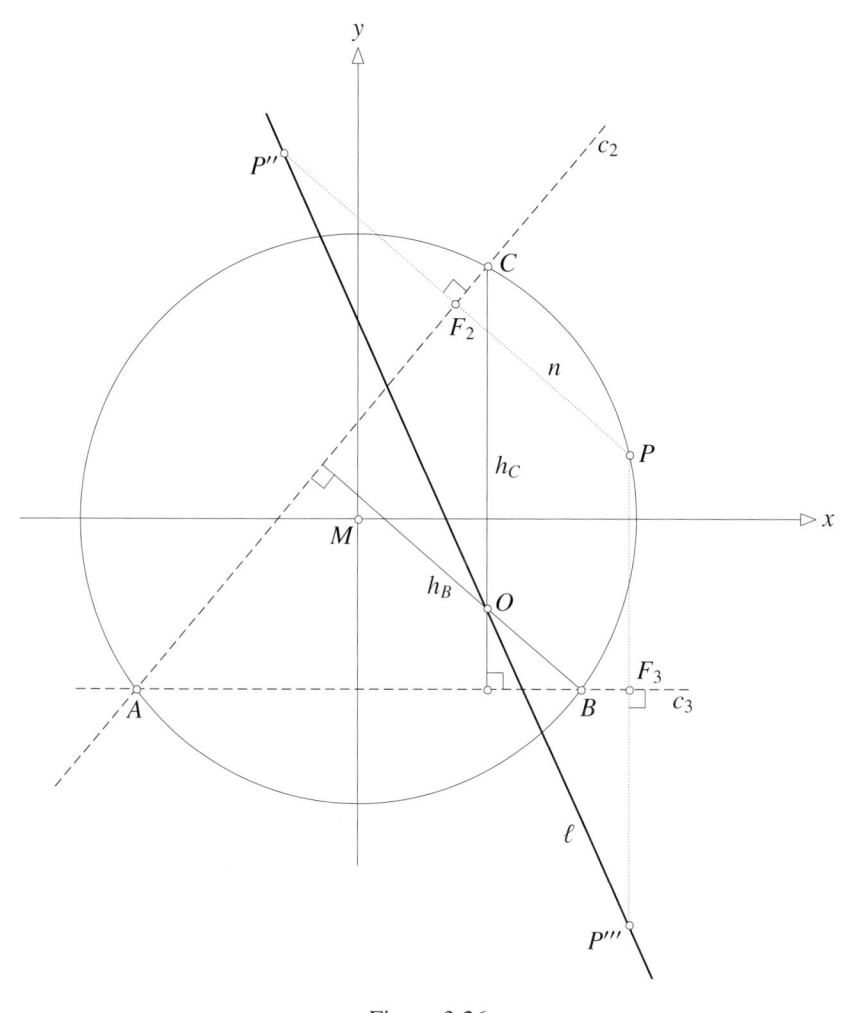

14 Determining common folding methods for given creases

— Figure 3.26 —

Having made these assumptions, $c_3 = AB$ is represented by the equation

$$c_3 : y = b,$$

and $c_2 = AC$ is represented by the equation

$$c_2 : y = k(x + a) + b.$$

If we assume that P is a point on the circumcircle of $\triangle ABC$ with coordinates $(x_0; y_0)$, the point P''' symmetric to P with respect to c_3 has the coordinates

$$P'''(x_0; 2b - y_0).$$

In order to determine the coordinates of the point P'' symmetric to P with respect to c_2,

Chapter 3   Properties of Origami Constructions

we first note that the equation of the line through P and perpendicular to c_2 is

$$y = -\frac{1}{k} \cdot (x - x_0) + y_0.$$

The point F_2 is then the point of intersection of this line and c_2, and we have

$$F_2 \left(\frac{x_0 + ky_0 - ak^2 - bk}{k^2 + 1} ; \frac{kx_0 + k^2 y_0 + ak + b}{k^2 + 1} \right).$$

The vector $\overrightarrow{PF_2}$ is therefore represented by

$$\overrightarrow{PF_2} = \frac{1}{k^2 + 1} \cdot \left(\begin{array}{c} -k^2 x_0 + ky_0 - ak^2 - bk \\ kx_0 - y_0 + ak + b \end{array} \right),$$

and since $\overrightarrow{PP''} = 2 \cdot \overrightarrow{PF_2}$, we see that P'' has the coordinates

$$P'' \left(\frac{-k^2 x_0 + x_0 + 2ky_0 - 2ak^2 - 2bk}{k^2 + 1} ; \frac{2kx_0 + k^2 y_0 - y_0 + 2ak + 2b}{k^2 + 1} \right).$$

We can now calculate that the vector $\overrightarrow{P'''P''}$ is of the form

$$\overrightarrow{P'''P''} = \frac{2k}{k^2 + 1} \cdot \left(\begin{array}{c} -kx_0 + y_0 - ak - b \\ x_0 + ky_0 + a - bk \end{array} \right),$$

and the line ℓ, which joins P''' and P'' (and also contains P') is therefore represented by the equation

$$\ell : (x_0 + ky_0 + a - bk) \cdot x + (kx_0 - y_0 + ak + b) \cdot y$$
$$= ax_0 + bkx_0 - 3by_0 - aky_0 + 2abk + a^2 + 3b^2.$$

In order to show that O is always a point of ℓ, we must now determine the coordinates of O, and then show that inserting them into this equation always yields a true statement.

Since $c_3 = AB$ is parallel to the x-axis, the altitude through C is orthogonal to the x-axis. This means that the x-coordinate of O is the same as the x-coordinate x_C of C. We calculate x_C by noting that C is the point of intersection of c_2 with the circumcircle of $\triangle ABC$ which is not equal to A. The circumcircle of $\triangle ABC$ is represented by the equation

$$x^2 + y^2 = r^2 = a^2 + b^2,$$

since A and B are points on the circumcircle. Intersecting this circle with the line $c_2 : y = k(x + a) + b$ yields the quadratic equation

$$x^2 + (kx + ka + b)^2 = a^2 + b^2,$$

which is equivalent to

$$x^2 + \frac{2ak^2 + 2bk}{k^2 + 1} \cdot x + \frac{2abk + a^2 + a^2 k^2}{k^2 + 1} = 0.$$

Since the sum of the roots of a quadratic equation is the negative value of the linear coefficient, and we want to determine the root not equal to $-a$, we have

$$x_C = \frac{-2ak^2 - 2bk}{k^2 + 1} + a = \frac{a - ak^2 - 2bk}{k^2 + 1} = x_O.$$

Now, in order to determine the y-coordinate of the orthocenter, we note that the altitude through B is represented by the equation

$$y = -\frac{1}{k}(x - a) + b.$$

Substituting x_C for x in this equation yields the value of the y-coordinate of O as

$$y_O = -\frac{1}{k}(x_O - a) + b$$

$$= \frac{2ak + 3b + bk^2}{k^2 + 1}.$$

We have therefore determined the coordinates of the orthocenter as

$$O\left(\frac{a - ak^2 - 2bk}{k^2 + 1}; \frac{2ak + 3b + bk^2}{k^2 + 1}\right).$$

We wish to show that O is a point of ℓ independent of the choice of P on the circumcircle, and so must show that substituting the coordinates of O in the equation representing ℓ yields a true statement, no matter which values are substituted for $(x_0; y_0)$ on the circumcircle.

Indeed, it is easy to verify that

$$(x_0 + ky_0 + a - bk) \cdot \frac{a - ak^2 - 2bk}{k^2 + 1} + (kx_0 - y_0 + ak + b) \cdot \frac{2ak + 3b + bk^2}{k^2 + 1}$$

$$= ax_0 + bkx_0 - 3by_0 - aky_0 + 2abk + a^2 + 3b^2$$

always holds by simply multiplying by $k^2 + 1$ and factoring out.

We see that ℓ always passes through O, no matter how P is chosen on the circumcircle of $\triangle ABC$. If P is chosen in a corner of the triangle, say $P = C$, we have $P'' = P' = P = C$, and since P''' is the point symmetric to P with respect to $c_3 = AB$, ℓ is then the altitude of $\triangle ABC$ through C. Obviously, P cannot be chosen in this way if we wish to solve the problem of folding P onto ℓ such that the c_i are produced as creases, however.

It remains to be shown that all lines through O can be chosen as ℓ, yielding an appropriate P, as long as ℓ is not such an altitude of the triangle.

In order to show this, we require the following result.

Lemma
Let $\triangle ABC$ be a triangle with sides $c_1 = BC$, $c_2 = CA$ and $c_3 = AB$ and orthocenter O. Furthermore, let O', O'' and O''' be the points symmetric to O with respect to c_1, c_2 and c_3 respectively. Then O', O'' and O''' are all points on the circumcircle of $\triangle ABC$.

Proof If $\triangle ABC$ is a right triangle (without loss of generality, we assume $\angle c_1 c_2 = 90°$, Figure 3.27), this is quite obvious.

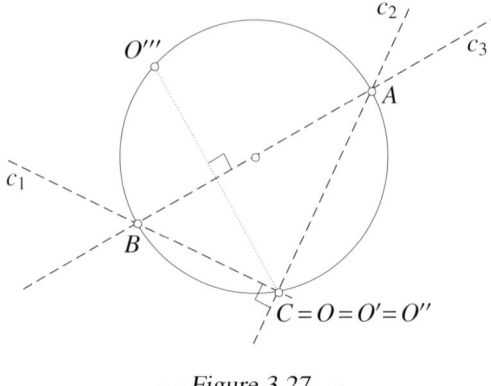

— Figure 3.27 —

The point $C = O = O' = O''$ is certainly a point of the circumcircle, and O''' is symmetric to this point C with respect to c_3, which is a diameter of the circumcircle. Therefore O''' is also on the circumcircle.

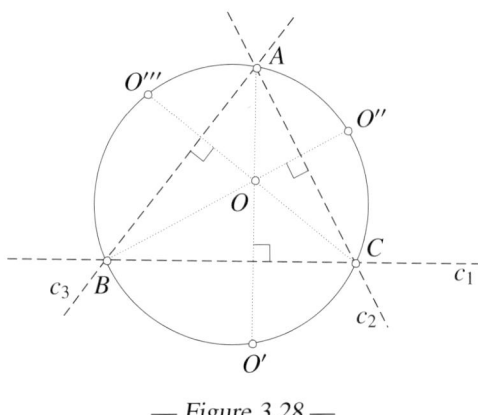

— Figure 3.28 —

If $\triangle ABC$ is acute angled (Figure 3.28), we have

$$\angle BO'C = \angle BOC$$
$$= 180° - \angle OBC - \angle OCB$$
$$= 180° - (90° - \angle ACB) - (90° - \angle ABC)$$
$$= \angle ACB + \angle ABC$$
$$= 180° - \angle BAC,$$

and O', A, B and C are concyclic. The result follows analogously for O'' and O'''.

If $\triangle ABC$ is obtuse angled (Figure 3.29), there are three possible relative positions of the points symmetric to O with respect to O and the corners of the triangle.

14 Determining common folding methods for given creases

— Figure 3.29 —

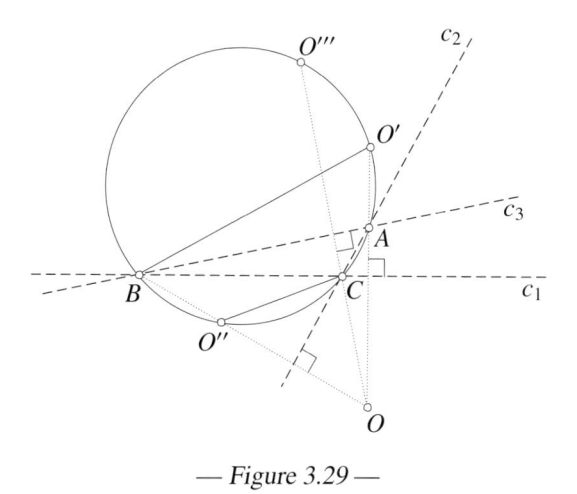

For O' we have

$$\angle AO'B = \angle AOB$$
$$= 180° - \angle OAB - \angle OBA$$
$$= 180° - (90° - \angle ABC) - (90° - \angle CAB)$$
$$= \angle ABC + \angle CAB$$
$$= 180° - \angle ACB,$$

and O', A, B and C are concyclic. For O'' we have

$$\angle BO''C = 180° - \angle CO''O$$
$$= 180° - \angle COB$$
$$= 180° - (90° - \angle ABO)$$
$$= 180° - \angle BAC,$$

and O'', A, B and C are also concyclic. Finally, for O''' we have

$$\angle BO'''A = \angle BOA$$
$$= 180° - \angle OBA - \angle OAB$$
$$= 180° - (90° - \angle BAC) - (90° - \angle ABC)$$
$$= \angle BAC + \angle ABC$$
$$= 180° - \angle BCA,$$

and O''', A, B and C are also concyclic. ∎

Next, we must prove the following results.

Theorem 6

Let $\triangle ABC$ be a triangle with orthocenter O and circumcenter M. Let $c_1 = BC$, $c_2 = CA$ and $c_3 = AB$ be the lines on which the sides of $\triangle ABC$ lie, and let O', O'' and O''' be the points symmetric to O with respect to c_1, c_2 and c_3 respectively, and M' the point symmetric to M with respect to c_1. Furthermore, let $(O')''$ and $(O')'''$ be the points symmetric to O' with respect to c_2 and c_3 respectively. Then the following statements hold:

(a) The lines $O(O')''$ and $O(O')'''$ are equal and orthogonal to $M'O$.

(b) The unique parabola with tangents c_1, c_2 and c_3, whose focus is O' (the existence of which was shown earlier), has the line symmetric to the tangent of the circumcircle of $\triangle ABC$ in O' with respect to c_1 as it's directrix ℓ.

Proof The proof of part (a) that follows is due to Gottfried Perz.

(a) As the previous lemma on page 83 shows, O' is certainly a point of the circumcircle of $\triangle ABC$. The feet of O' on the sides of $\triangle ABC$ are therefore certainly collinear, as they all lie on the Simson line of O' with respect to $\triangle ABC$. Since the homothety with center O' and homothetic ratio 2 maps the feet of O' on the sides of $\triangle ABC$ onto the points O, $(O')''$ and $(O')'''$ respectively, these points are also collinear.

In order to prove the validity of (a), it is therefore sufficient to show that $M'O$ is perpendicular to the line $(O')''(O')'''$ joining these three points.

We now note the following facts. Firstly, AO is an altitude of $\triangle ABC$ and therefore perpendicular to $c_1 = BC$. Furthermore, $c_1 = BC$ is the axis of symmetry of the line segment OO'. It therefore follows that A, O and O' are collinear. Due to the defining symmetries involved, it also follows that A, O'' and $(O')''$ are collinear, as are A, O''' and $(O')'''$. Also, we have $AO' = A(O')'' = A(O')'''$ and $AO = AO'' = AO'''$. Both triangles $\triangle A(O')''(O')'''$ and $AO''O'''$ are therefore isosceles, and it therefore follows that $(O')''(O')'''$ and $O''O'''$ are parallel.

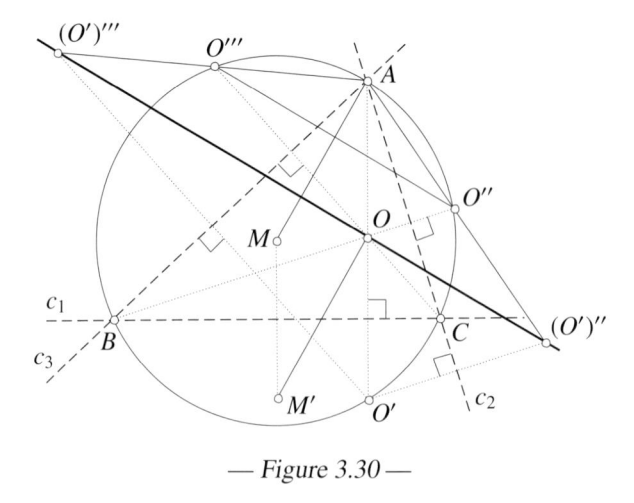

— Figure 3.30 —

Furthermore, the vectors $\overrightarrow{M'O}$ and $\overrightarrow{MA}$ are equal. This is due to the fact that MO' and $M'O$

14 Determining common folding methods for given creases

are symmetric with respect to $c_1 = BC$, and MO' and MA are symmetric with respect to the axis of symmetry of AO', which passes through M (as A and O' are both points of the circumcircle) and is parallel to c_1 (as AO' is perpendicular to c_1). The two axes of symmetry are therefore parallel, and the vectors $\overrightarrow{M'O}$ and $\overrightarrow{MA}$ are equal.

Specifically, $M'O$ and MA are parallel, and it is now sufficient to show that MA and $O''O'''$ are perpendicular in order to prove that $M'O$ and $O(O')''$ (or $M'O$ and $O(O')'''$) are.

This however follows immediately from the fact that $AO'' = AO'''$ holds on the one hand, and $MO'' = MO'''$ holds on the other, since both O'' and O''' lie on the circumcircle.

We therefore have $MA \perp O''O'''$, and therefore both $M'O \perp O(O')''$ and $M'O \perp O(O')'''$ hold as claimed.

We note that this proof is equally valid, no matter whether the triangle $\triangle ABC$ is acute-, right- or obtuse-angled (Figures 3.30, 3.31a, and 3.31b).

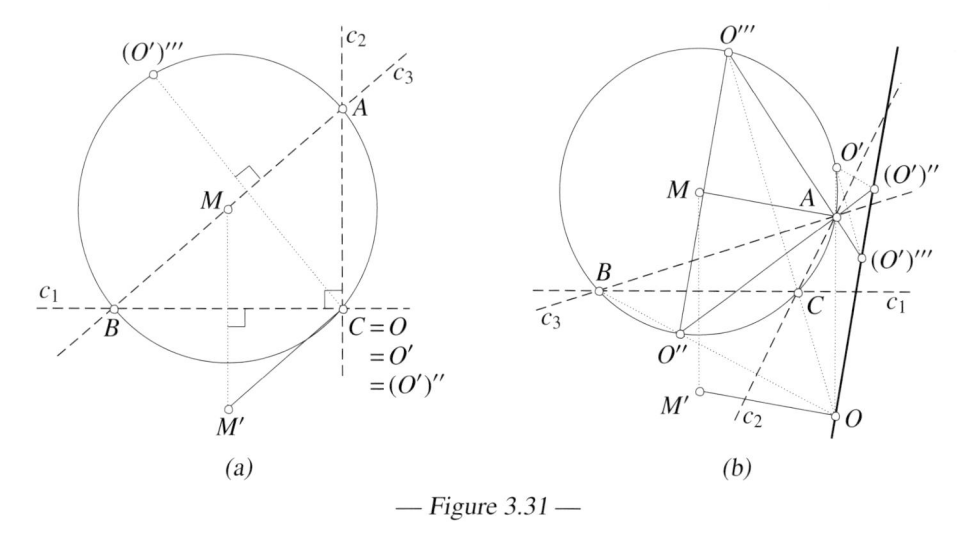

(a)   (b)

— Figure 3.31 —

(b) This is an immediate consequence of (a).

The directrix of the unique parabola with tangents c_1, c_2 and c_3 and focus O' is the line ℓ on which the points symmetric to O' with respect to c_1, c_2 and c_3 lie. These are O, $(O')''$ and $(O')'''$ respectively, and as shown in (a), ℓ is perpendicular to $M'O$.

This means that MO' is perpendicular to the line ℓ' symmetric to ℓ with respect to c_1, and since MO' is a radius of the circumcircle of $\triangle ABC$, we see that ℓ' is the tangent of the circumcircle in O'. ∎

We are now ready to prove the following result.

Theorem 7

Let $\triangle ABC$ be a triangle with orthocenter O. Let $c_1 = BC$, $c_2 = CA$ and $c_3 = AB$ be the lines on which the sides of $\triangle ABC$ lie, and let O', O'' and O''' be the points symmetric to O with respect to c_1, c_2 and c_3 respectively.

(a) *Every line passing through O has the property that the lines ℓ', ℓ'' and ℓ''' symmetric to ℓ with respect to c_1, c_2 and c_3 respectively, pass through a common point on the circumcircle of $\triangle ABC$. If ℓ is an altitude of $\triangle ABC$, this point is the corner of $\triangle ABC$ on ℓ opposite the side to which ℓ is orthogonal. If ℓ is symmetric to the tangent of the circumcircle of $\triangle ABC$ in O' with respect to c_1 (or to the tangent in O'' with respect to c_2 or the tangent in O''' with respect to c_3), this point is O' (or O'' or O''' respectively).*

(b) *Every line ℓ passing through O which does not also pass through a corner of $\triangle ABC$ is the directrix of a unique parabola with c_1, c_2 and c_3 as tangents. The focus of this parabola is the unique common point of the lines ℓ', ℓ'' and ℓ''' symmetric to ℓ with respect to c_1, c_2 and c_3 respectively. If ℓ is symmetric to the tangent of the circumcircle of $\triangle ABC$ in O' with respect to c_1, the focus of the parabola is O' (and analogously O'' or O''' if ℓ is symmetric to the appropriate tangents with respect to the appropriate sides of $\triangle ABC$).*

(c) *The locus of the directrices of all parabolas with tangents c_1, c_2 and c_3 is the set of all lines passing through O, not including the altitudes of $\triangle ABC$.*

Proof Let us first assume that $\triangle ABC$ is a right triangle, and without loss of generality, let us assume that the right angle is in C (Figure 3.32).

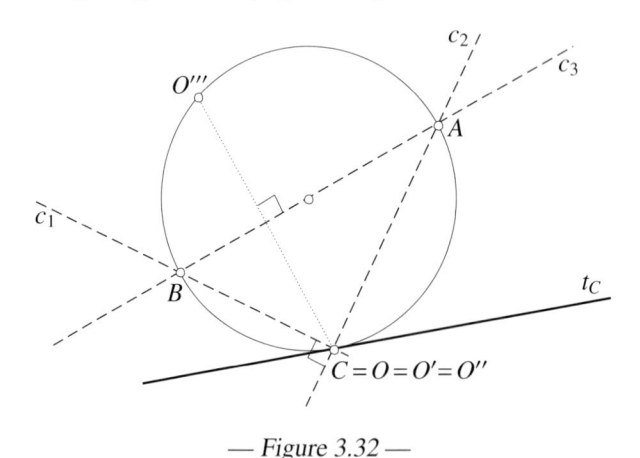

— Figure 3.32 —

If ℓ is a side (and therefore also an altitude) of $\triangle ABC$, say $\ell = c_1 = BC$, we have $\ell = \ell' = \ell''$ and $\ell''' = BO'''$, and the result is shown. If ℓ is the altitude in C, we have $\ell = \ell''' = CO'''$ and $\ell' = \ell''$ since c_1 and c_2 are the orthogonal angle bisectors of ℓ' and ℓ''. Therefore ℓ', ℓ'' and ℓ''' intersect in C and the result is again shown. This line is also the line symmetric to the tangent t_C of the circumcircle in C with respect to c_1 (and therefore also with respect to c_2), since we have $\angle \ell c_1 = \angle \ell' t_C = \angle c_2 c_3$ for this line ℓ.

Again, by the previous result we see that $C = O' = O''$ is the common point of ℓ', ℓ'' and ℓ'''. If ℓ is the tangent of the circumcircle in C, it is symmetric to the tangent of the circumcircle in O''' with respect to c_3, and by the previous result, ℓ', ℓ'' and ℓ''' intersect in O''' (whereby $\ell' = \ell''$ again holds).

If ℓ is any other line through C (Figure 3.33), the line ℓ' symmetric to ℓ with respect to c_1 cannot be a tangent of the circumcircle, and since it has the point C in common with the circumcircle, it will also intersect the circumcircle in a further point P, which cannot be a corner of $\triangle ABC$.

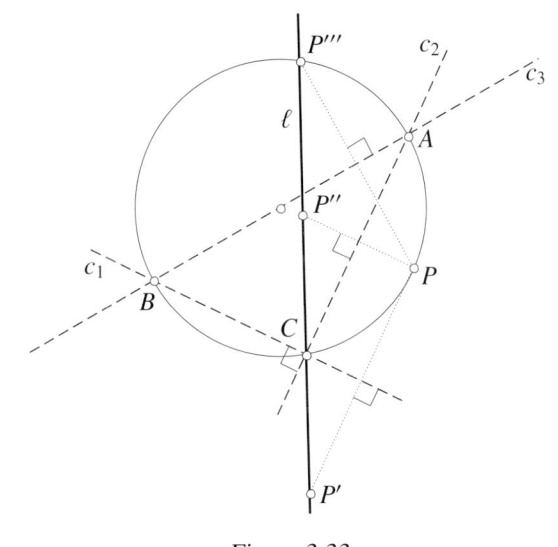

— Figure 3.33 —

Since P is a point of the circumcircle of $\triangle ABC$, the feet of P on c_1, c_2 and c_3 are collinear, since they all lie on the Simson line of P with respect to $\triangle ABC$. The points P', P'' and P''' are therefore also collinear, since the homothety with center P and homothetic ratio 2 maps the feet of P on c_1, c_2 and c_3 onto these points respectively. As shown in theorem 5 on page 79, this line passes through the orthocenter $O = C$ of $\triangle ABC$, and since it is the line joining O and P' and we have $P \in \ell'$ and therefore $P' \in \ell$, this line is ℓ itself. We see that P is a common point of $\ell' = \ell'' = \ell'''$ as claimed.

We now assume that $\triangle ABC$ is not right-angled (Figure 3.34 on the following page).

If ℓ is an altitude of $\triangle ABC$, we assume without loss of generality that ℓ passes through A. Then we have $\ell = \ell'$, and since both ℓ'' and ℓ''' intersect ℓ in A (because A is a point of both c_2 and c_3), we have shown that A is the common point of ℓ', ℓ'' and ℓ''' as claimed.

If ℓ is symmetric to a tangent of the circumcircle in either O', O'' or O''' with respect to c_1, c_2 or c_3 respectively, the previous result shows that ℓ', ℓ'' and ℓ''' intersect in the appropriate point O', O'' or O'''.

If we now assume that ℓ does not pass through a corner of $\triangle ABC$ and is not symmetric to a tangent of the circumcircle in this way, the line ℓ' symmetric to ℓ with respect to c_1 will

Chapter 3   Properties of Origami Constructions

(a)   (b)

— Figure 3.34 —

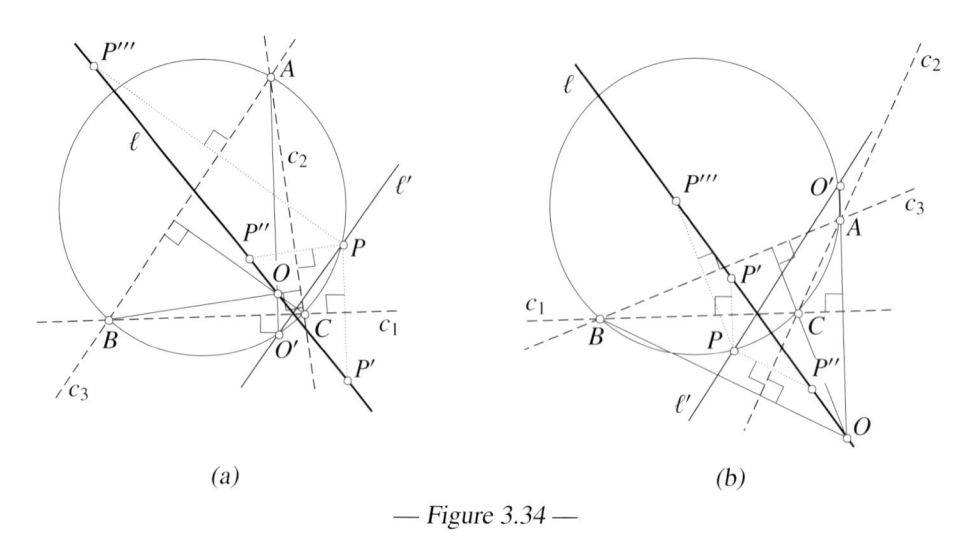

intersect the circumcircle in a second point P beside O'. As for the right triangle, P', P'' and P''' are collinear and the line joining these passes through O. Since $P \in \ell'$, we also have $P' \in \ell$, and since $P \neq O'$, we also have $P' \neq O$, and ℓ is the line joining P' and O. Therefore P is the unique common point of ℓ', ℓ'' and ℓ''' as claimed.

Statements (b) and (c) are now immediate consequences of (a). ∎

An interesting fact that immediately follows is the following.

Corollary
If a parabola has two orthogonal tangents, the directrix of the parabola passes through the point of intersection of these tangents.

Proof Since no three tangents of a parabola can pass through a common point and no two can be parallel, we can choose any other tangent of the parabola, and this tangent will determine a right triangle along with the two given orthogonal tangents. The directrix of every parabola with these three tangents passes through the orthocenter of this triangle, and the orthocenter is the corner of the triangle in which the given orthogonal tangents intersect. ∎

This fact can also be deduced by considering much more elementary facts about parabolas, of course, but it is interesting to note that it follows in a very natural way from the foregoing considerations.

14.4   Four creases given

Solving the problem of determining points P and lines ℓ such that each of four given creases c_1, c_2, c_3 and c_4 can be produced by folding P onto ℓ now does not involve much more than a group of simple corollaries of the preceding results.

14 Determining common folding methods for given creases

First of all, if any two of the given creases are parallel, they will all be parallel if there is to be a solution to the problem, as was determined in the previous section. Then, P and ℓ can again be chosen in a random way under the conditions that ℓ is orthogonal to the creases c_i and P lies on ℓ but not on any of the creases c_i. In fact, this is possible for any number of parallel folds for the same reasons as detailed in section 14.3 for three parallel folds.

Also, we have already established that no three of the creases c_i may have a point in common if there is to be a solution to the problem. Apart from the case where all c_i are parallel, there can only be a solution if the c_i are given such that any three of them are the sides of a triangle.

Let us assume that creases c_1, c_2, c_3 and c_4 are given satisfying this condition (Figure 3.35).

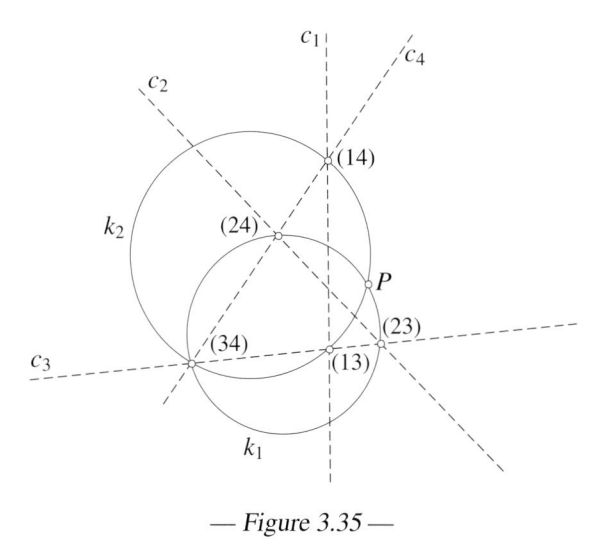

— *Figure 3.35* —

Points P solving the problem are then subject to the following constraints. On one hand, such points P need to lie on the circumcircle k_1 of the triangle with sides c_2, c_3 and c_4. On the other hand, they also need to lie on the circumcircle k_2 of the triangle with sides c_1, c_3 and c_4. (Of course, we can also choose one or both of the analogously defined circles k_3 or k_4.)

For ease of notation in this section, we shall use (ij) to denote the point of intersection of creases c_i and c_j.

Since k_1 is the circumcircle of $\triangle(23)(34)(24)$ and k_2 is the circumcircle of $\triangle(13)(34)(14)$, we see that k_1 and k_2 certainly have one point in common, namely (34). But k_1 and k_2 cannot be identical, because this would mean that the collinear points (13), (23) and (34) are also concyclic, which is impossible. Also, k_1 and k_2 cannot be tangent in (34), because there would then exist a homothety with center in (34) (Figure 3.36), mapping k_1 onto k_2, (24) onto (14) and (23) onto (13).

— Figure 3.36 —

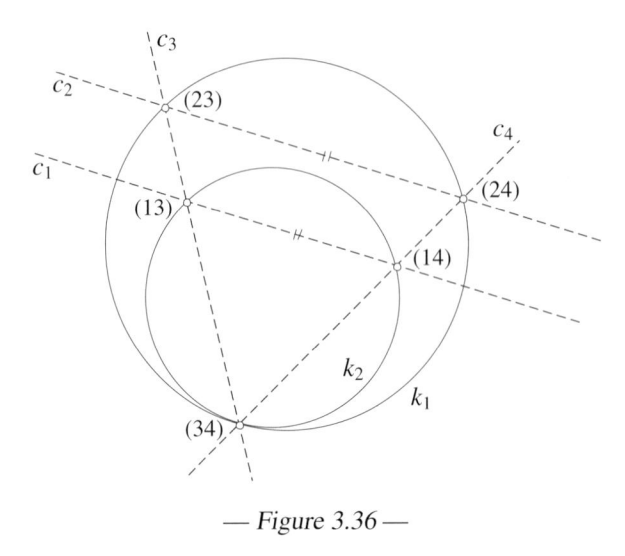

This homothety would map $c_2 = (23)(24)$ onto $c_1 = (13)(14)$, and we would have $c_1 \parallel c_2$ in contradiction to the assumption that no two creases are parallel.

The circles k_1 and k_2 therefore have a point P in common, which does not lie on any of the creases c_i. If we denote the points symmetric to P with respect to the creases as before, we note that P'', P''' and P'''' are collinear because P is a point of the circumcircle of the triangle with sides c_2, c_3 and c_4. Also, P', P''' and P'''' are collinear, because P is a point of the circumcircle of the triangle with sides c_1, c_3 and c_4. Since P''' and P'''' lie on both lines, the lines are equal, and we see that P', P'', P''' and P'''' lie on a common line ℓ. The point P and the line ℓ are certainly unique.

Furthermore, since any line ℓ associated with P with respect to $\triangle(23)(34)(24)$ passes through the orthocenter O_{234} of $\triangle(23)(34)(24)$, and similarly any line ℓ associated with P with respect to $\triangle(13)(34)(14)$ passes through the orthocenter O_{134} of $\triangle(13)(34)(14)$, ℓ has to be the line joining O_{234} and O_{134}.

Of course, the choice of triangles was random, and the same results hold for the triangles $\triangle(12)(24)(14)$ and $\triangle(12)(23)(13)$. In summary, we have the following results.

Theorem 8
Let c_1, c_2, c_3 and c_4 be four lines, no two of which are parallel and no three of which pass through a common point. Then the following results hold:

(a) The four circumcircles of the triangles formed by any three of the given lines pass through a unique common point P, which does not lie on any of the four given lines.

(b) The four orthocenters of these triangles are collinear.

(c) There exists a unique parabola tangent to all four given lines. The focus of this parabola is the point P common to the circumcircles of the triangles formed by the lines, and the directrix of the parabola is the line ℓ joining the orthocenters of these triangles.

14 Determining common folding methods for given creases

The fact that such a unique parabola exists is simply a special case of the theorem stating that there always exists a unique conic if we are given five tangents in the projective plane, no three of which have a point in common. (For more information on the generation of line conics, see [55].) A parabola is simply a conic with the line at infinity as one tangent, and the restriction that no two lines c_i may be parallel results from the fact that parallel lines have a common point at infinity in the projective plane, which they also have in common with the line at infinity.

14.5 Folding procedures solving the four crease problem

In this section, we shall consider some concrete methods for determining P and ℓ by folding when four creases c_1, c_2, c_3 and c_4 are given such that any three of them form the sides of a triangle. As before, we use the notation (ij) to denote the point of intersection of c_i and c_j.

First of all, an interesting special case results if two pairs of perpendicular creases $c_1 \perp c_2$ and $c_3 \perp c_4$ are given (Figure 3.37). In this case, as we have just seen, ℓ is already known as the line joining the two points (12) and (34).

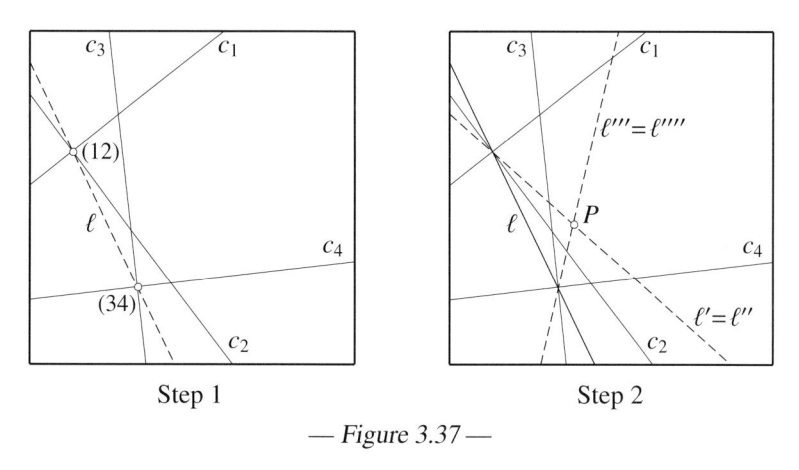

— Figure 3.37 —

This is shown in Step 1. Since $c_1 \perp c_2$, the same line is symmetric to ℓ with respect to both c_1 and c_2, as we have seen in section 14.2, and this line $\ell' = \ell''$ is determined by virtue of (O5) by folding either the crease c_1 or c_2 in Step 2. Similarly, since $c_3 \perp c_4$, the same line $\ell''' = \ell''''$ is symmetric to ℓ with respect to both c_3 and c_4, and this line is determined in Step 2 by folding either the crease c_3 or c_4. Then P is the common point of $\ell' = \ell''$ and $\ell''' = \ell''''$.

For the general case, we have a number of options at our disposal. One method of first determining P (and then ℓ) is illustrated in Figure 3.38 on the next page.

We know from section 14.3 that P has to lie on the circumcircle of any triangle whose sides are among the lines c_1, c_2, c_3 and c_4. It is therefore possible to determine P as a point of intersection of two such circumcircles, and since any two triangles formed by the four

— *Figure 3.38* —

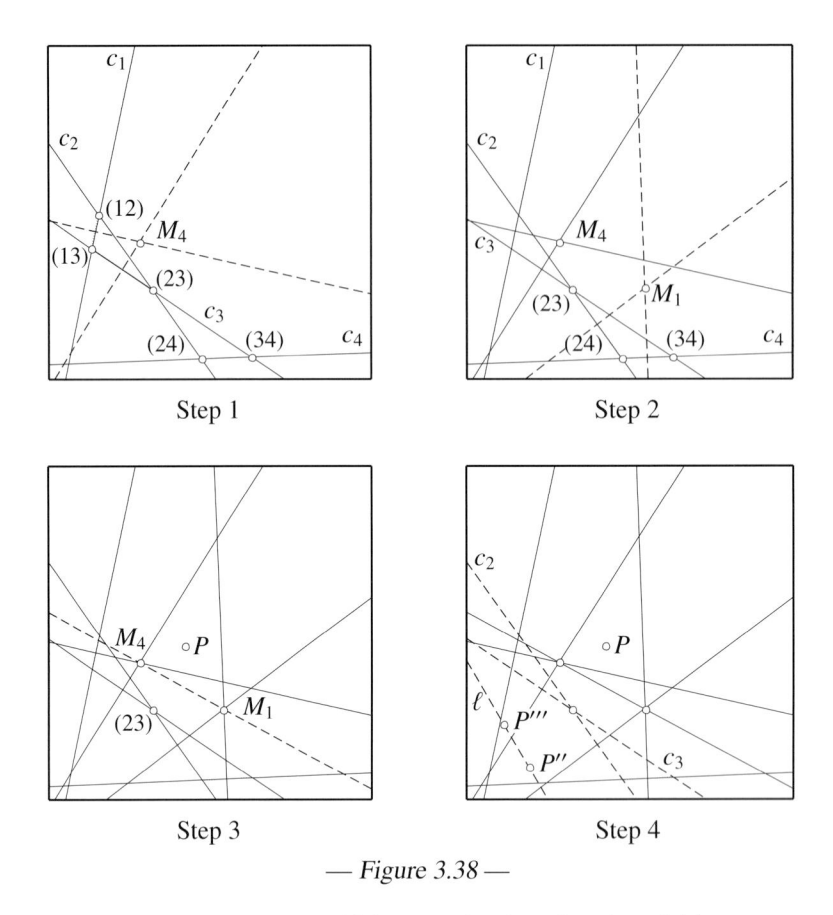

given lines have a common vertex (which cannot be the point P), and this common vertex is one of the two common points of the circumcircles, P will always be the other.

In Step 1, we determine the mid-point M_4 of the circumcircle of $\triangle(12)(23)(13)$ by folding (13) onto (23), yielding the perpendicular bisector of one side of the triangle, and then folding (12) onto (13), yielding the bisector of another side. These bisectors intersect in M_4. In Step 2, we do the same for triangle $\triangle(23)(34)(24)$, yielding the point M_1 as the mid-point of the circumcircle.

Obviously, one common point of the two circumcircles is the common vertex (23) of the two triangles, and since the other common point of the circles, namely the point P we wish to determine, is symmetric to this point with respect to the line joining the mid-points, in Step 3 we determine P by folding the crease joining M_4 and M_1, which yields P by virtue of (O4). In Step 4 we fold the creases c_2 and c_3, yielding the points P'' and P''' respectively, as the points symmetric to P. Finally, ℓ is obtained by folding the crease joining P'' and P'''.

Another possible method, which utilizes Theorem 5, is presented in Figure 3.39.

Since the orthocenter of any triangle whose sides are among the lines c_1, c_2, c_3 and c_4

94

14 Determining common folding methods for given creases

— Figure 3.39 —

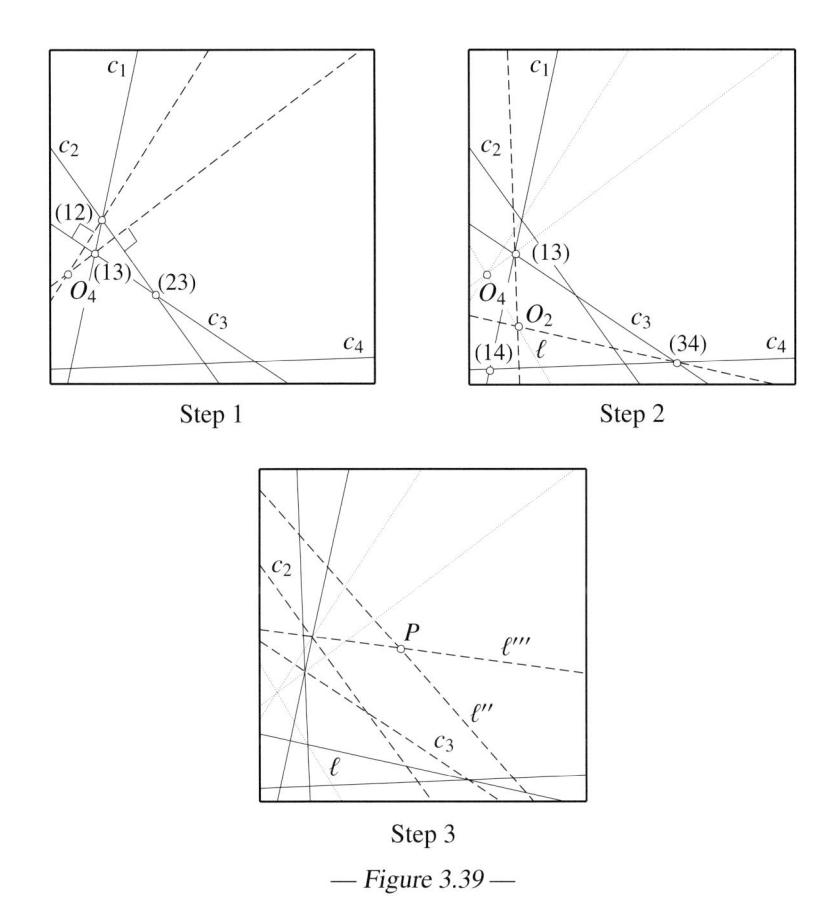

lies on the line ℓ, we can simply determine two such orthocenters, yielding ℓ as the line joining them.

In Step 1, we determine the orthocenter of $\triangle(12)(23)(13)$ by folding c_3 onto itself such that the crease passes through (12) and then folding c_2 onto itself such that the crease passes through (13). This yields two altitudes of the triangle, and these intersect in the orthocenter O_4. In Step 2, the same thing is done for $\triangle(13)(34)(14)$, yielding the altitudes through (34) and (13), which intersect in the orthocenter O_2. This yields the line ℓ joining O_4 and O_2 as required. Finally, in Step 3 we fold the creases c_2 and c_3, yielding the lines ℓ'' and ℓ''' respectively, as the lines symmetric to ℓ. The required point P is then simply the point of intersection of these two lines.

A further method for solving the four crease problem can be derived from polarity properties of conics in general, and parabolas in particular. It is known (see for instance [43], pp 336–343) that the diagonal point triangle of any quadrangle of points of a conic is a self-polar triangle with regard to the conic. The dual of this holds as well, that is, the diagonal line triangle of any quadrangle of tangents of a conic is also a self-polar triangle with regard to the conic. This fact, along with the fact that the pole of the line at infinity of any parabola is the point at infinity of its axis, as well as some further investigation, yields another solution of the four crease problem. Since the results in projective geometry required to present this solution go well beyond the scope of this book, and the result is a good deal more complicated than the solutions presented, this method is not presented in its entirety here. Deriving this method may however be an interesting exercise for any readers familiar with the projective generation of conics.

15 Origami constructions on a parabola

Since they are so elementary to origami constructions, it is quite natural to ask questions pertaining to the manipulation of parabolas with the aid of origami constructions. Assuming that a parabola $par(F; d)$ is given by its focus F and its directrix d (Figure 3.40), (O7) states that we can determine all tangents of the parabola by folding F onto the points F' of d.

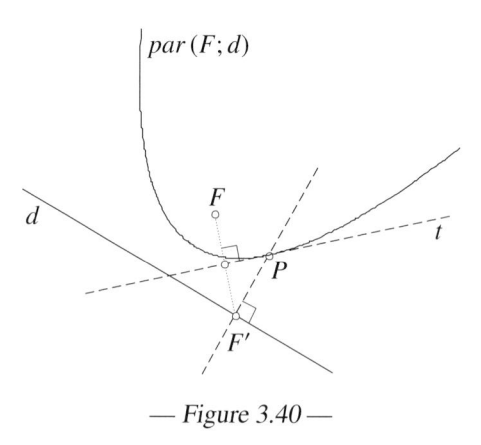

— Figure 3.40 —

Once we have folded F onto one specific such point F', creating the crease t, we can fold d onto itself such that the crease passes through F' by virtue of (O6). The resulting crease intersects t in a point P. Since PF' is perpendicular to d and all points of t are equidistant from F and F', P is the point on t equidistant from F and d. This is, of course, the defining property of the points of the parabola, and we see that any point of the parabola can be determined by folding two specific creases. (Note that since points are only determined by knowledge of two creases by (O1), this is a number that cannot possibly be reduced by some other method.)

Since we know how to determine random tangents and random points of $par(F; d)$, we can turn our attention to determining tangents and points with specific defining characteristics.

15.1 Tangents through a given point

If we are given $par(F; d)$ and a point X, it is possible to fold F onto d such that the crease(s) pass through X (if such creases exist) by virtue of (O7) (Figure 3.41). The resulting creases are therefore the tangents t_1 and t_2 of $par(F;d)$ passing through X as required.

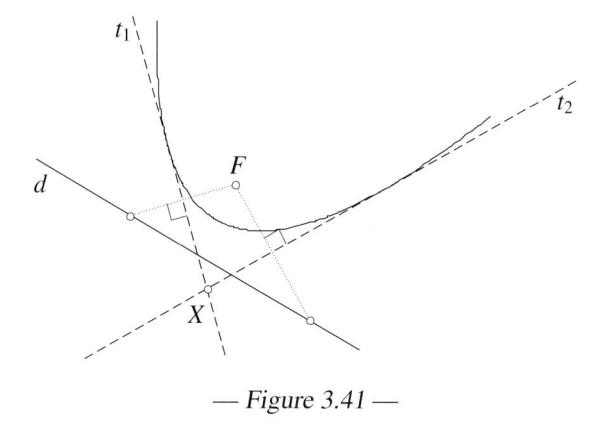

— Figure 3.41 —

15.2 Tangents perpendicular to a given line

If we are given $par(F;d)$ and a line ℓ, it is possible to fold F onto d and ℓ onto itself simultaneously by virtue of (O7*), since folding ℓ onto itself can be interpreted as folding a random point of ℓ (not on the resulting crease) onto ℓ (Figure 3.42). The resulting crease is the (unique) tangent of $par(F;d)$ orthogonal to ℓ.

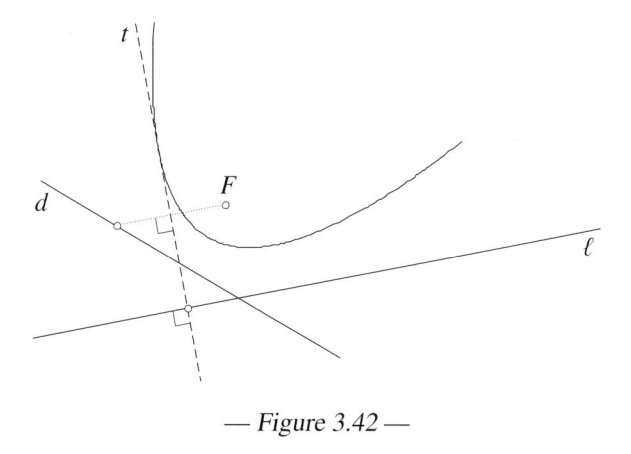

— Figure 3.42 —

15.3 Tangents parallel to a given line

If we are given $par(F;d)$ and a line ℓ not perpendicular to d (Figure 3.43 on the following page), we first fold ℓ onto itself such that the crease passes through F (O6). The resulting crease is perpendicular to ℓ and intersects d in a point F'. Folding F onto F' (O5) then yields a tangent of the parabola perpendicular to FF', and therefore parallel to ℓ as required.

97

— Figure 3.43 —

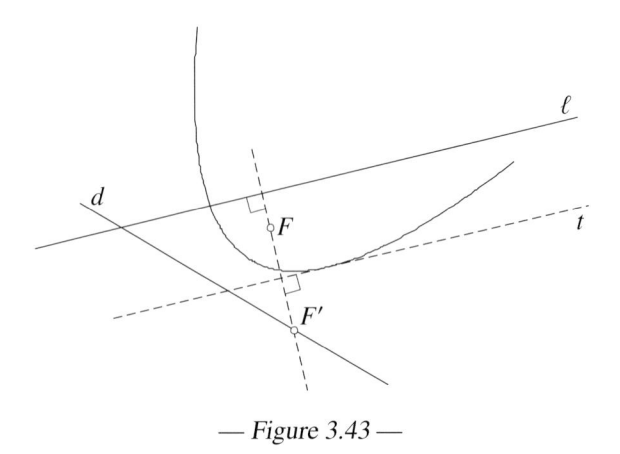

15.4 Points on a given line

This construction is not quite as straightforward as the previous three. In order to solve this problem, we consider $par\,(F;d)$ as given embedded in a system of coordinates such that F has the coordinates $\left(0, \frac{p}{2}\right)$, and d is represented by the equation $y = -\frac{p}{2}$ (Figure 3.44).

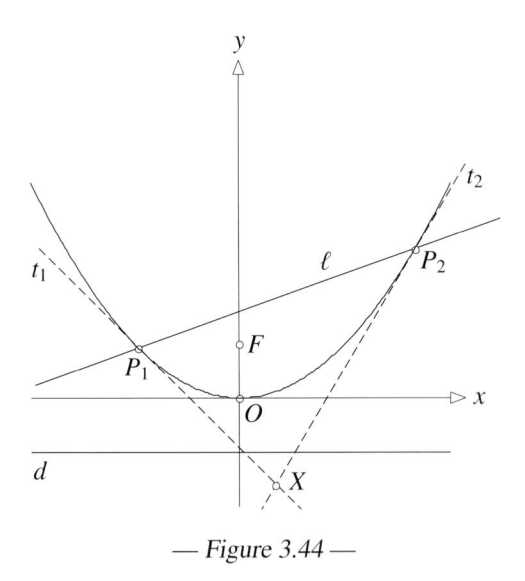

— Figure 3.44 —

The points of the parabola are then precisely those points whose coordinates are solutions of the equation
$$par : x^2 = 2py.$$

We assume that we are also given a straight line ℓ whose points have coordinates solving the equation
$$l : y = ax + b.$$

15 Origami constructions on a parabola

(For the moment, we assume that ℓ intersects $par(F; d)$ in two distinct points P_1 and P_2. In this case, ℓ is not parallel to the axis and such an equation certainly exists.) Letting t_1 and t_2 denote the tangents of the parabola in P_1 and P_2 respectively, t_1 and t_2 certainly intersect in a point X with coordinates $X(q, r)$.

This point X is the pole of ℓ with respect to the parabola (and ℓ the polar line of X), and if a point has coordinates (q, r), its polar line with respect to the parabola with the equation $x^2 = 2py$ is the line with the equation

$$qx = py + pr,$$

which can also be written as

$$y = \frac{q}{p} \cdot x - r.$$

(This is an important elementary property of parabolas, that can be verified by calculating the coordinates of the points of intersection of this line with the parabola, and then checking that (q, r) is indeed the point of intersection of the tangents in these points.)

Since the equation of ℓ can therefore be written either as

$$\ell : y = ax + b$$

or

$$\ell : y = \frac{q}{p} \cdot x - r,$$

it follows that both

$$a = \frac{q}{p} \quad \text{and} \quad b = -r$$

hold. We therefore have

$$q = ap \quad \text{and} \quad r = -b,$$

and X has the coordinates $(ap, -b)$, where p is the parameter of the parabola (that is, the distance from focus to directrix), a the slope of ℓ, and b the y-intercept of ℓ.

We can now easily deduce a method of folding the points of intersection of ℓ and the parabola. Choosing p as the unit length, we must determine the point X with coordinates $(a, -b)$, and then fold F onto d such that the crease passes through X. This yields the tangents t_1 and t_2, which intersect ℓ in P_1 and P_2 as required. This is demonstrated in Figure 3.45 on the next page.

In Step 1 we first fold d onto itself such that the crease passes through F, yielding the axis s of the parabola as a crease, which we simultaneously consider to be the y-axis. Folding F onto $I = s \cap d$ creates the x-axis as a crease and brings $II = \ell \cap s$ to lie on the point III, whose coordinates are therefore $(0, -b)$.

In Step 2 we then fold s onto itself such that the crease passes through this point III. The resulting crease is then represented by the equation $y = -b$, and X has to lie on this crease. Next, we fold ℓ onto itself such that the crease passes through F. The resulting

Chapter 3 — Properties of Origami Constructions

Step 1

Step 2

Step 3

— *Figure 3.45* —

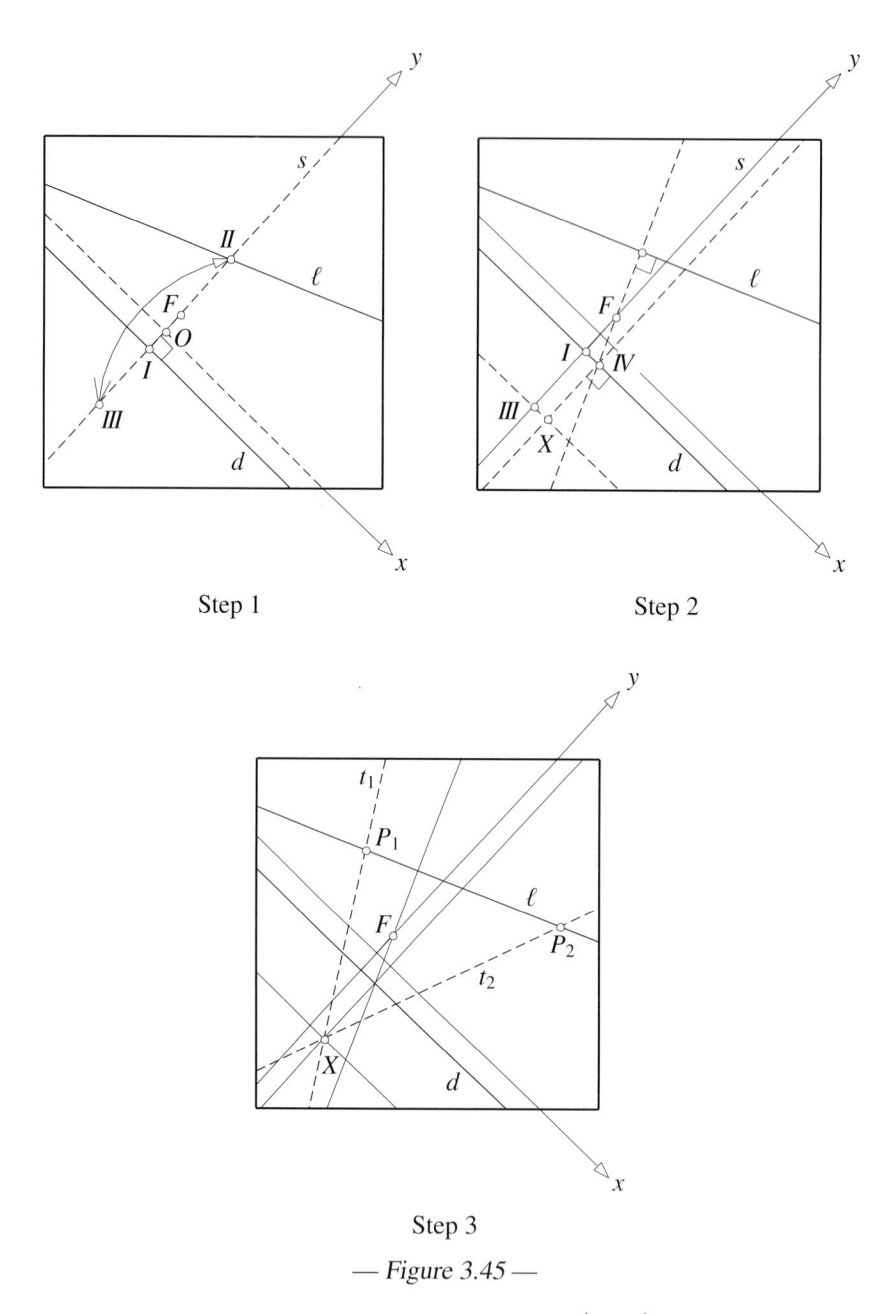

crease intersects d in a point IV, whose coordinates are $\left(a, -\frac{1}{2}\right)$, since the slope of FIV will be $\frac{1}{a}$ due to the fact that it is perpendicular to ℓ, and the right triangle $\triangle FIIV$ has one side (FI) whose (oriented) length is the (negative) unit length. Folding d onto itself, such that the crease passes through IV therefore yields the crease represented by the equation $x = a$, and this crease intersects the crease $y = -b$ in $X(a, -b)$. (Note that this step is not necessary if $\ell \parallel d$, since this means $a = 0$, and therefore $III = X$.)

15 Origami constructions on a parabola

Folding F onto d such that the creases pass through X in Step 3 therefore yields t_1 and t_2 as creases, and these intersect ℓ in P_1 and P_2 respectively, as required.

Note that we have so far assumed that ℓ intersects the parabola in two points. If ℓ intersects the parabola in exactly one point, it can either be a tangent of the parabola or perpendicular to d. In the first case, the same assumptions for ℓ hold as before, and X shall turn out to be a point of the parabola, allowing only one fold in Step 3.

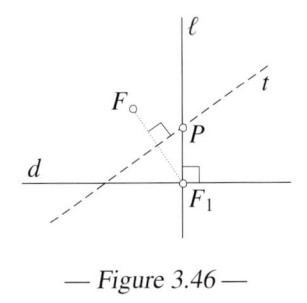

— Figure 3.46 —

If $\ell \perp d$ (Figure 3.46), we can simply fold F onto $F_1 \cap d$, yielding the tangent t of the parabola, intersecting ℓ in its unique common point P with the parabola.

Chapter 4

The Maximum Polygon Problem

When an origamist creates a model, he or she often has more or less practical reasons for starting their model from a regular polygon. For instance, many animal models might be developed from a regular hexagon, with four of the corners of the hexagon gradually becoming the legs of the animal in question, one further corner becoming the head, and another the tail. For tail-less animals, a regular pentagon may be preferable. For many insect models, six legs, a head and an abdomen may make a regular octagon an optimal shape to begin with.

For this reason, it has long been of interest to origamists to determine methods of folding regular polygons, either in a mathematically precise way or as good approximations. In this book, we restrict ourselves to the former, although some citations will be given for interesting approximations in the literature.

Standard origami paper is almost always cut into squares, and since it is preferable to have as little waste as possible in folding regular polygons, a question that arises naturally is that of determining the largest possible regular polygon with a given number of sides that can fit into a given square. (In order to simplify notation, we shall use the term "n-gon" to denote a regular polygon with n sides. A 3-gon is therefore an equilateral triangle, a 4-gon is a square, a 5-gon is a regular pentagon, and so on. The term "maximum n-gon" will be used to denote an n-gon of largest possible area that can be inscribed in the square, that is, any inscribed n-gon with the property that the area of any other inscribed n-gon has an area less than or equal to the area of that n-gon.) A method of solving this problem using analytic methods was described by David Dureisseix in [6]. In this section, a method is presented using synthetic methods. This method is a bit longer, but should give some added insight into the inscription of n-gons in squares.

A first result is the following.

Theorem 9
The maximum $(4k)$-gon (with $k \in \mathbb{N}$) has two vertices on each side of the square. The maximum $(4k)$-gon is therefore unique.

Proof If $n = 4k$, there certainly exists an n-gon with two vertices on each side of the square. The principle is illustrated in Figure 4.1 for the 12-gon.

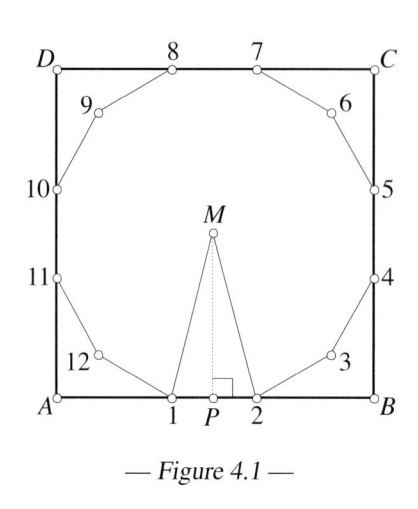

Naming the corners of the square A, B, C and D, let M be the mid-point of the square and P the mid-point of the side AB. We determine points 1 and 2 on AB such that

$$\angle PM1 = \angle PM2 = \frac{360°}{8k}.$$

(For the 12-gon, this means $\angle PM1 = \angle PM2 = \frac{360°}{24} = 15°$.) Since 1 and 2 are an equal distance from M, 1 and 2 are vertices of a $(4k)$-gon with mid-point M, and we name the other vertices of this $(4k)$-gon (counter-clockwise) 3, 4, ..., $4k$. Since the points $1+k$ and $2+k$ (4 and 5 in the case of the 12-gon) result by counter-clockwise rotation around M by 90°, and BC similarly results from AB by counter-clockwise rotation around M by 90°, the points $1 + k$ and $2 + k$ lie on BC. By analogous reasoning (rotation by 180° and 270°, respectively), we see that the points $1 + 2k$ and $2 + 2k$ lie on CD and $1 + 3k$ and $2 + 3k$ lie on DA. (For the 12-gon, 4 and 5 lie on BC, 7 and 8 on CD and 10 and 11 on DA.)

— Figure 4.1 —

It now only remains to be shown that this $(4k)$-gon is indeed the largest possible inscribed in the square. This can be seen by considering the incircle of the square. The incircle is the largest possible circle that can be inscribed in the square. Due to the way the $(4k)$-gon was defined, MP is a radius of the incircle of the $(4k)$-gon, and therefore the incircle of the square is also the incircle of the $(4k)$-gon. If we assume the existence of a larger $(4k)$-gon that can also be inscribed in the square, it would have a larger incircle, which could then also be inscribed in the square, contradicting the fact that the incircle of the square is the largest such circle. The $(4k)$-gon as constructed is therefore indeed maximum. Since the common incircle cannot be translated within the square, and the $(4k)$-gon cannot be continuously rotated within the square, the $(4k)$-gon is indeed unique. ∎

In order to determine how maximum n-gons are placed in the square if $n \neq 4k$, we first require the following result.

Lemma 1
Every maximum n-gon has a vertex on each side of the square.

Proof We shall prove this lemma in steps, by considering the various possible cases in which there exist sides of the square on which no vertices of a n-gon lie, and showing in each case that there exists a larger such n-gon, which can still be inscribed in the square.

Case I There are no vertices of the n-gon on either BC or CD.

In this case, we can assume without loss of generality that one vertex of the n-gon lies on AB, and one lies on DA. If this were not the case (Figure 4.2), naming the vertices of the n-gon $1, 2, \ldots, n$ and their orthogonal projections onto AB $1', 2', \ldots n'$, respectively, all vectors $\overrightarrow{11'}$, $\overrightarrow{22'}, \ldots, \overrightarrow{nn'}$ are oriented in the same direction, and at least one has a minimal length. Let this be $\overrightarrow{11'}$. Translating the n-gon by this vector yields a congruent n-gon with $1'$ (on AB) as a vertex, and all vertices within $ABCD$, as the vector $\overrightarrow{11'}$ was chosen of minimal length. Similarly, we can name the orthogonal projections of $1', 2', \ldots,$ and n' as $1'', 2'', \ldots$ and n'', respectively. All vectors $\overrightarrow{1'1''}, \overrightarrow{2'2''}, \ldots$ and $\overrightarrow{n'n''}$ are again oriented in the same direction, and at least one has a minimal length. Let this be $\overrightarrow{k'k''}$. Translating the (second) n-gon by this vector yields an n-gon congruent to the original one with k'' (on DA) and $1''$ (on AB) as vertices.

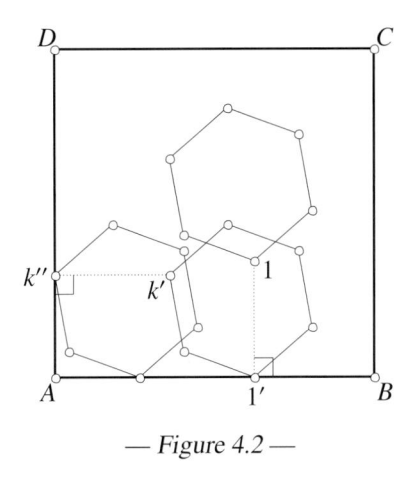

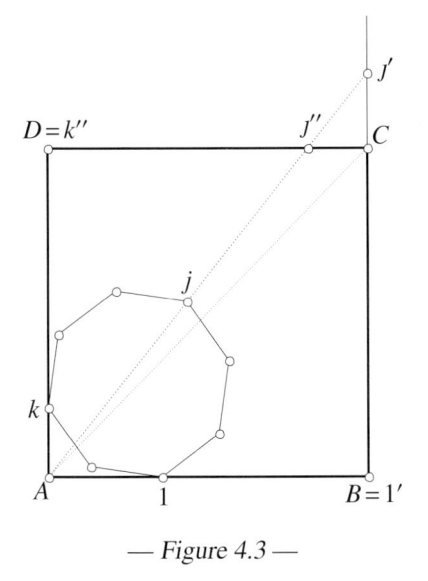

— Figure 4.2 —

We can therefore assume, as stated, that we are given an n-gon with vertex 1 on AB, vertex k on DA, and no vertex on either BC or CD (Figure 4.3). Note that for $n = 3$, it is possible that this means $1 = k = A$.

For each vertex $j \neq 1, k$ of the n-gon, there exists a homothety whose center is A that transforms j to a point j' on the line BC. We name the homothetic ratio of this mapping r'_j, and we note that $r'_j > 1$ since $j \notin BC$ holds. Similarly, for each $j \neq 1, k$, there exists such a homothety that transforms j to a point j'' on the line CD. We name the homothetic ratio of this mapping r''_j, and we note that $r''_j > 1$ since $j \notin CD$ holds. If j is inside the triangle $\triangle ACD$, we have j'' on the line segment CD, j' outside the line segment BC, and $r''_j < r'_j$. Similarly, if j is inside $\triangle ABC$, we have j' on the line segment BC, j'' outside the line segment CD, and $r'_j < r''_j$. If j is on AC, we have

— Figure 4.3 —

$j' = j'' = C$ and $r'_j = r''_j$. Of all these homotheties, at least one has a minimal homothetic ratio $r_{\min} > 1$, and the homothety with this ratio has the property of transforming at least one point j onto either a point j' on the line segment BC or a point j'' on the line segment CD. We say it maps each vertex j onto a point $\bar{j}$. This homothety maps vertex 1 onto a point $\overline{1}$ on AB, k onto a point $\overline{k}$ on DA (except in the case $n = 3$ and $1 = k = A$, in which case we have $\overline{1} = \overline{k} = A$), and all vertices $1, 2, \ldots, n$ onto points $\overline{1}, \overline{2}, \ldots, \overline{n}$ not outside the square $ABCD$. Since $r_{\min} > 1$, the area of the transformed n-gon $\overline{1}\,\overline{2}\ldots\overline{n}$ is certainly larger than that of $1\,2\ldots n$, and the new n- gon has all the properties we set out to prove.

Case II There are no vertices of the n-gon on CD.

We can now assume without loss of generality that there is a vertex of the n-gon on each of the sides AB, BC and DA. If there is no vertex on BC, we know from Case I that there exists a larger n-gon inscribed in the square, and the same holds if there is no vertex on DA, since we can simply rename the corners of the square $BADC$ instead of $ABCD$, and obtain the same situation as before. If there are vertices on both BC and DA, but not on either AB or CD (Figure 4.4), we assume much as in Case I that the vertices of the n-gon are named $1, 2, \ldots$ and n (with i on BC and k on DA) and that their orthogonal projections onto AB are named $1', 2', \ldots$ and n', respectively, (and therefore $i' = B$ and $k' = A$). As before, all vectors $\overrightarrow{11'}, \overrightarrow{22'}, \ldots, \overrightarrow{nn'}$ are oriented in the same direction, and at least one has minimal length. Let this again be $\overrightarrow{11'}$. Translating the n-gon by this vector yields a congruent n-gon with $1'$ on AB as a vertex, vertices on BC and DA resulting from i and k, respectively, and no vertices outside the square.

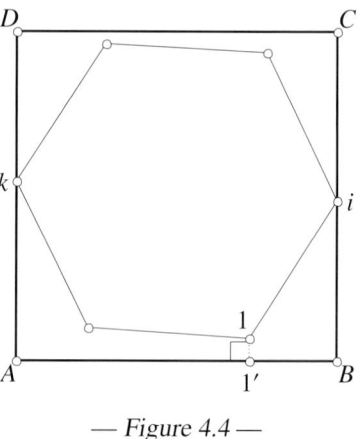

— Figure 4.4 —

We can therefore assume that vertices 1, i and k are on the sides AB, BC and DA of the square, respectively (Figure 4.5). (Note that we could use i to simply denote the vertex on BC nearest B in case there were two vertices of the n-gon on BC. This case is not actually possible however, as lengthy but ultimately unnecessary computation of the altitudes and the diagonals of regular n-gons can show.)

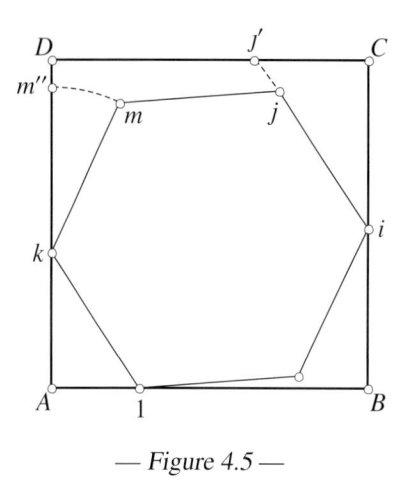

— Figure 4.5 —

Without loss of generality, we also assume $|Ak| \leq |Bi|$, that is, i is not nearer to B than k to A. (If this were not true, we could consider the symmetric case.) For each vertex $j \neq k$ of the n-gon, there exists a rotation with center k (counter-clockwise, if we choose the orientation as in Figure 4.5) that maps j either onto a point j' on CD, a point j'' on DA or a point j''' on BC, and we name the angle of this rotation α_j. (If more than one such rotation exists, we let α_j denote the smallest positive angle of such a rotation. For points i on BC, we therefore still have $\alpha_i > 0$.) All of these angles α_j are positive, and the rotation with center k and the smallest such angle α_{min} therefore maps all vertices 1, 2, ..., n onto points inside $ABCD$ or on one of the edges. The rotation with center k and angle $\frac{1}{2} \cdot \alpha_{min}$ therefore maps all vertices of $1\,2\ldots n$ except k onto points in the interior of the square, while leaving k on AD. We know from Case I, however, that there exists an n-gon with a larger area than this one, that can still be inscribed in the square, which was what we had set out to prove.

Any regular polygon that does not have a vertex on each side of the square $ABCD$ can therefore never be maximum, and the validity of the lemma is shown. ∎

Having proven this, we can now advance to the next result.

Lemma 2
Any maximum n-gon has a diagonal of ABCD as an axis of symmetry.

Proof We already know this to be true for $n = 4k$, since the n-gon and the square then have a common incircle, and rotations around the common mid-point by 90°, 180° and 270° map both the n-gon and the square onto themselves. All axes of symmetry of the square are therefore also axes of symmetry of the n-gon, and so in particular are the diagonals of $ABCD$.

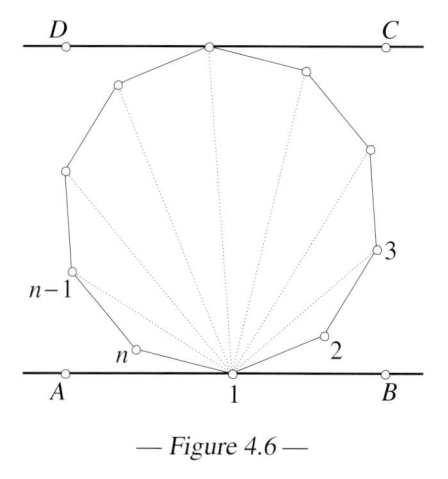

— Figure 4.6 —

We now assume that we are given a maximum n-gon with $n \neq 4k$ inscribed in the square. From the previous lemma, we know that one vertex of the n-gon lies on each side of the square. We assume without loss of generality that 1 lies on AB (Figure 4.6).

Since

$$\angle 21B < \angle 31B < \ldots$$

and

$$|2\,1| < |3\,1| < \ldots,$$

Chapter 4   The Maximum Polygon Problem

it follows that
$$|2\overline{AB}| < |3\overline{AB}| < \ldots .$$

Similarly, on the other side we have
$$\angle n1A < \angle (n-1)1A < \ldots$$
and
$$|n1| < |(n-1)1| < \ldots ,$$

and it therefore follows that
$$|n\overline{AB}| < |(n-1)\overline{AB}| < \ldots .$$

Since the vertex of the n-gon that lies on CD is the one that is the greatest distance from AB, for even n this is the vertex $\frac{n}{2} + 1$, and for odd n it is either $\frac{n-1}{2} + 1$ or $\frac{n+1}{2} + 1$, since both the distance from 1 and the angle to AB are maximal in this case.

We now have two distinct cases to consider.

Case A n is even, but $n \neq 4k$ (that is, $n \equiv 2 \pmod{4}$).

The diagonal joining points 1 and $\frac{n}{2} + 1$ on AB and CD, respectively, is a diameter of the circumcircle of the n-gon, and passes through the mid-point M of the n-gon. If we assume that vertex j is point on BC, then vertex $\frac{n}{2} + j$ is a point on DA by the same argument as before. Since both diagonals $1\left(\frac{n}{2} + 1\right)$ and $j\left(\frac{n}{2} + j\right)$ are of the same length, and the opposite sides of the square are equal distances apart, these diagonals of the n-gon and the respective sides intersect at equal angles. There are two ways in which this is possible (Figure 4.7).

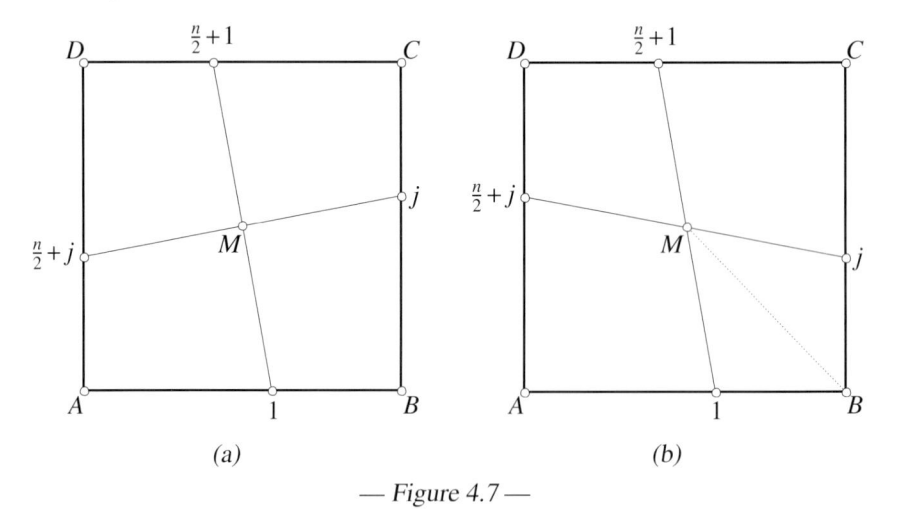

(a)   (b)

— Figure 4.7 —

We can either have $\angle A1M = \angle BjM$ as in Figure 4.7a, or $\angle A1M = \angle CjM$ as in Figure 4.7b.

If the diagonals are arranged as in Figure 4.7a, we have
$$\angle M1B = 180° - \angle M1A = 180° - \angle BjM.$$

Since $\angle 1Bj = 90°$, this means

$$\angle 1Mj = 360° - \angle M1B - \angle BjM - \angle 1Bj$$
$$= 360° - (180° - \angle BjM) - \angle BjM - 90°$$
$$= 90°.$$

Since any two main diagonals of an n-gon with even n intersect at an angle of $k \cdot \frac{360°}{n}$, this means

$$k \cdot \frac{360°}{n} = 90°,$$

or $n = 4k$. The configuration of Figure 4.7a is therefore not possible in this case.

In configuration Figure 4.7b, we assume without loss of generality that $\angle M1A \leq 90°$, and therefore $\angle M1B = \angle MjB \geq 90°$. Joining M and B, we then see that $M1 = Mj$, and since MB is a common side of triangles $\triangle M1B$ and $\triangle MjB$, they are congruent. Since $\angle 1Bj = 90°$, we have $\angle 1BM = 45°$, and M is therefore a point on the diagonal BD of the square. Also, we have $B1 = Bj$, and therefore 1 and j are symmetric with respect to BD, as is therefore the whole n-gon, since the perpendicular bisector of any diagonal of a regular n-gon is an axis of symmetry of the n-gon. We have therefore shown what we set out to prove in this case.

Case B n is odd.

As before, the line segments joining the vertices of the n-gon on opposite sides of the square $ABCD$ are both diagonals of the n-gon of maximum length. Since both pairs of opposing sides of the square are the same distance apart, these diagonals intersect the respective sides of the square at equal angles. As in Case A, there are two configurations in which this is possible (Figure 4.8).

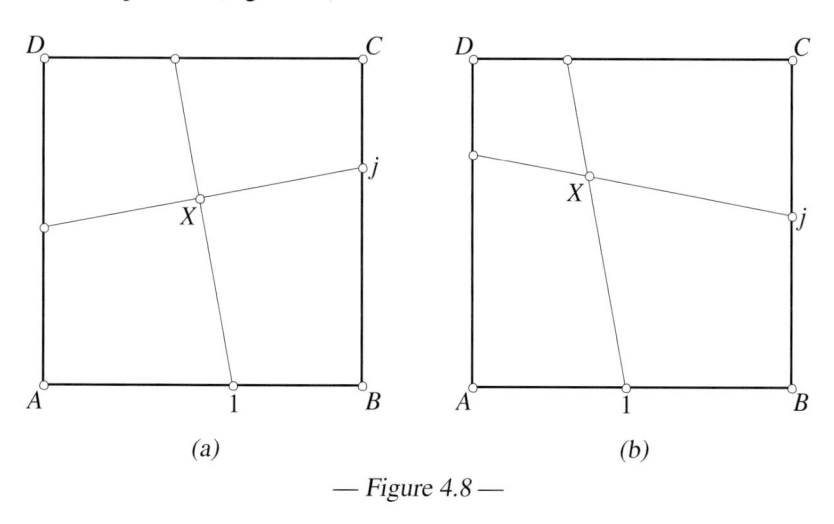

— Figure 4.8 —

Naming the point in which the diagonals intersect X, and assuming as before that vertex 1 lies on AB and vertex j on BC, we can either have $\angle A1X = \angle BjX$ as illustrated in Figure 4.8a or $\angle A1X = \angle CjX$ as illustrated in Figure 4.8b.

As in Case A, if the diagonals are arranged as in Figure 4.8a, we have

$$\angle X1B = 180° - \angle X1A = 180° - \angle BjX.$$

Since $\angle 1Bj = 90°$, this means

$$\angle 1Xj = 360° - \angle X1B - \angle BjX - \angle 1Bj$$
$$= 360° - (180° - \angle BjX) - \angle BjX - 90°$$
$$= 90°.$$

This is not possible for odd values of n, however (Figure 4.9).

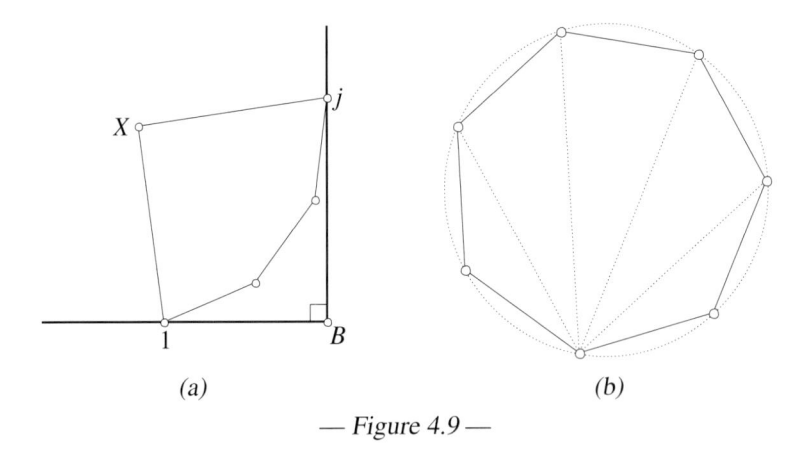

— Figure 4.9 —

If we assume that two main diagonals of the n-gon are orthogonal, there exists a (not regular) $(j+1)$-gon as shown in Figure 4.9a with a right angle in X and angles of $\frac{n-2}{n} \cdot 180°$ in each of the vertices $2, 3, \ldots, (j-1)$. Since each main diagonal divides the angle in the vertex into angles of $\frac{n-1}{2n} \cdot 180°$ and $\frac{n-3}{2n} \cdot 180°$ (as we see in Figure 4.9b, the diagonals through the vertex 1 divide the n-gon into $n-2$ triangles, and the angles in 1 are all equal in these triangles, as they are all angles subtended over chords of equal length, that is, the sides of the n-gon, in the circumcircle of the n-gon), considering the sum of angles in the $(j+1)$-gon yields

$$(j-1) \cdot 180° = \angle 1Xj + \angle X12 + \angle Xj(j-1) + (j-2) \cdot \frac{n-2}{n} \cdot 180°.$$

If $\angle 1Xj = 90°$, this is equivalent to

$$(j-1) \cdot 180° = 90° + \frac{1}{2n} \cdot 180° \cdot (a+b) + (j-2) \cdot \frac{n-2}{n} \cdot 180°$$
$$\Leftrightarrow \quad 2n(j-1) = n + (a+b) + 2(j-2)(n-2)$$
$$\Leftrightarrow \quad -2n = n + (a+b) - 4j - 4n + 8$$
$$\Leftrightarrow \quad n = (a+b) - 4(j-2).$$

Since a and b are either both equal to $n-1$ or $n-3$, or one equal to $n-1$ and the other to $n-3$, we have either

$$a+b = 2(n-1)$$
or
$$a+b = 2(n-3)$$
or
$$a+b = (n-1)+(n-3)$$
$$= 2(n-2).$$

In either case, n is equal to an expression of the form

$$n = 2 \cdot c - 4(j-2),$$

with integer c. Therefore n is even, contradicting the basic assumption of Case B.

We see that the situation illustrated in Figure 4.8a is once again not possible, and so we have the situation of Figure 4.8b (reproduced in Figure 4.10).

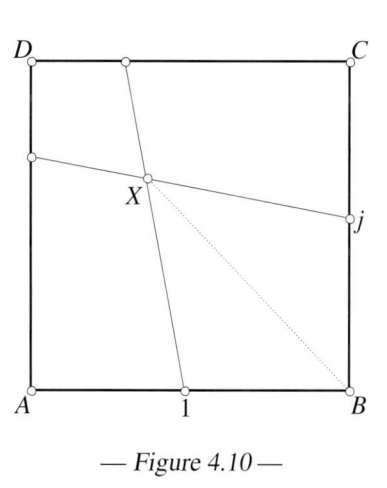

If the vertex of the n-gon on AB is named 1 and the vertex on BC is named j, the vertex on CD is either $\left(1 + \frac{n-3}{2}\right)$ or $\left(1 + \frac{n-1}{2}\right)$, that is, either $1 + m$ or $1 + (m+1)$. Similarly, the vertex on DA is either $j+m$ or $j+(m+1)$, and without loss of generality we can assume that these vertices are $1+m$ and $j+(m+1)$ (the reasoning is analogous if they are $1+(m+1)$ and $j+m$), since this can certainly be achieved by rotating the configuration by 90° and renaming the points if it is not the case.

— Figure 4.10 —

This means that the perpendicular bisector of the line segment $1j$ is also the bisector of $(1+m)(j+(m+1))$, since the diagonals $1j$ and $(1+m)(j+(m+1))$ are parallel (Figure 4.11), and all parallel diagonals of a (regular) n-gon with odd n have a bisector in common with the parallel side.

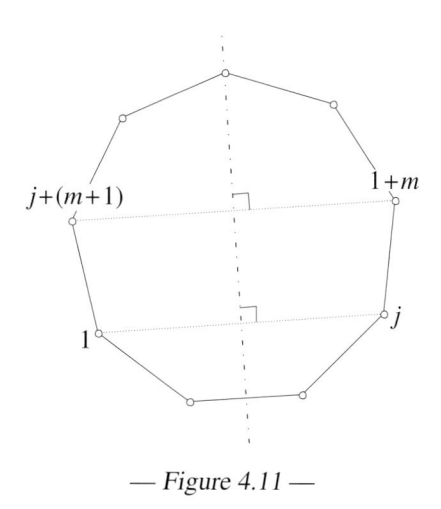

It therefore follows that this common bisector is also an angle bisector of the diagonals $1(1+m)$ and $j(j+(m+1))$, and X is therefore a point on this bisector. Furthermore, the line segments $X1$ and Xj are of equal length.

As in Case A, it therefore follows that triangles $\triangle M1B$ and $\triangle MjB$ are congruent (since the angles in B are acute, the side-side-angle theorem yields a unique triangle), and we see that

— Figure 4.11 —

$\angle 1BX = \angle jBX = 45°$ and $B1 = Bj$. Therefore X is a point of BD, and BD is the common bisector of $1j$ and $(1+m)(j+(m+1))$. We see that BD is once again an axis of symmetry of the n-gon, and the lemma is proven. ∎

The following result summarises all the results of this chapter (Figure 4.12).

Theorem 10
For any integer $n \geq 3$, the regular n-gon with largest possible area that can be inscribed in a given square has at least one vertex on each side of the square and at least one diagonal of the square as an axis of symmetry.

For $n = 3$, one vertex lies in a corner of the square, and is therefore common to two of its sides.

For $n = 4k$ ($k \in \mathbb{N}$), two vertices of the n-gon lie on each side of the square.

For $n = 2k$, both diagonals of the square are axes of symmetry of the n-gon.

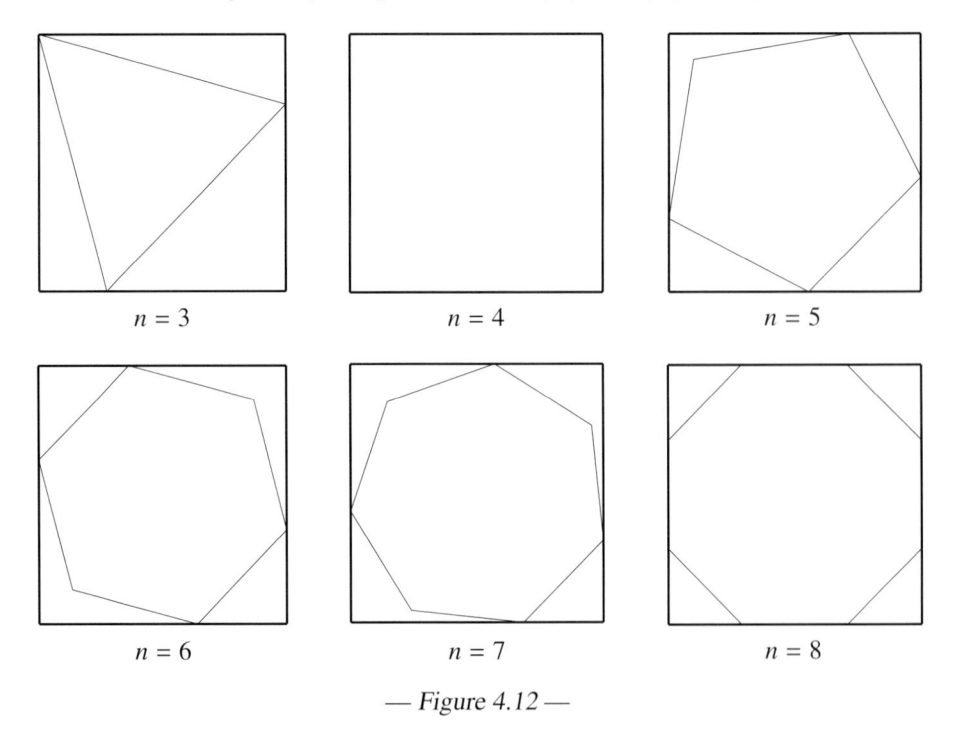

$n = 3$

$n = 4$

$n = 5$

$n = 6$

$n = 7$

$n = 8$

— Figure 4.12 —

Part II

Some Practice

Chapter 5

Triangles, Squares and More

16 Triangles

16.1 Some thoughts on folding general triangles

We know from chapter 1 that any construction problem that can be solved with straight-edge and compass can also be solved by origami methods. Methods of drawing triangles given either by the lengths of all three sides (SSS), the lengths of two sides and their enclosed angle (SAS), the length of one side and the two adjoining angles (or equivalently, any two angles, since the three angles sum to 180°) (ASA) or the lengths of two sides and an angle not enclosed by them (SSA) are quite standard, and can be found in many school books. We can therefore fold such triangles as well, assuming that they exist.

As a short reference, we can now pose a few elementary, but important questions. When do such triangles exist, and when are they unique, in the sense that all triangles with the given angles and sides are congruent? Which folding steps (as defined in section 3, page 7) do we require to fold the triangle(s) in each case?

(SSS) If we are given three line segments, whose lengths are a, b and c, a unique triangle with sides of these lengths exists if and only if the triangle inequalities hold, that is, we must have

$$a + b > c,$$
$$b + c > a$$
$$c + a > b.$$

and

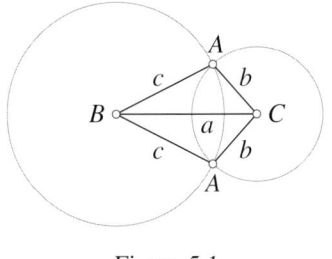

— *Figure 5.1* —

As explained on page 10 in section 3, we can transfer the line segment of length a to any position by means of (O3) and (O5). If we name the end-points of the resulting line segment B and C (Figure 5.1), the third corner of the triangle is either of the points in which the circle with mid-point B and radius c and the circle with mid-point C and radius b intersect.

These points may be determined by applying the folding techniques shown in section 4.5, page 15. (Note that the two solutions in Figure 5.1 are congruent, and therefore represent the same triangle in the sense we are considering here.)

(SAS) If we are given two line segments whose lengths are a and b and an angle γ, a unique triangle exists for any values of a and b and

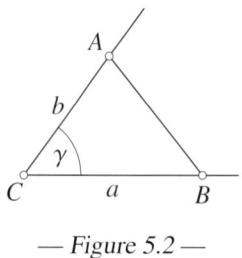

$$0° < \gamma < 180°.$$

Again, as explained in section 3, we can transfer γ to any position by means of (O3) and (O5). Letting C denote the vertex of γ (Figure 5.2), we can then transfer a to one arm of γ such that one end-point is in C, again by means of (O3) and (O5).

— Figure 5.2 —

We name the other end-point of the resulting segment B, and similar transfer of b onto the other arm yields A, giving us the triangle.

(ASA) If we are given a line segment whose length is a and two angles β and γ, a unique triangle exists for any value of a and any positive values of β and γ such that

$$0° < \beta + \gamma < 180°.$$

As before, we can transfer a to any position (Figure 5.3). Naming its end-points B and C respectively, we can then transfer β such that its vertex comes to lie in B and a lies on one arm of β. Similarly, we can transfer γ such that its vertex comes to lie in C, a lies on one arm of γ, and the arms of both angles not containing a are on the same side of the line BC.

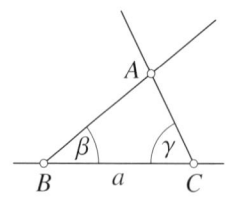

— Figure 5.3 —

These arms intersect in A, yielding the triangle.

(SSA) If we are given two line segments whose lengths are a and b and an angle α (that is, the angle α is opposite side a in the triangle we wish to fold), there can exist 0, 1 or 2 triangles, depending on the relative values of a, b and α.

If $a \geq b$, there certainly exists a unique triangle for any value of α with

$$0° < \alpha < 180°.$$

Once again, we can transfer b to any position (Figure 5.4a), naming its end-points A and C.

We can then transfer α such that its vertex comes to lie in A and b lies on one arm of α. Transferring a such that one end-point coincides with C by (O5), we can then transfer

16 Triangles

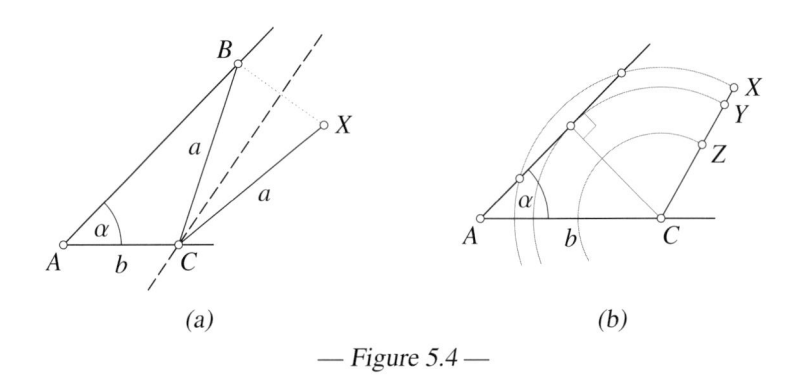

— Figure 5.4 —

the other resulting end-point X of a onto the arm of α not containing b in such a way (by (O7)) that the crease contains C. This would yield two points B on the line of the arm of α, but since $a \geq b$, only one of these results in a viable triangle $\triangle ABC$.

If $a < b$ (Figure 5.4b), the folding method is the same as described for $a \geq b$, but there can be 2, 1 or 0 solutions for B (with intermediate points X, Y and Z), depending on whether we have $a > b \cdot \sin \alpha$, $a = b \cdot \sin \alpha$ or $a < b \cdot \sin \alpha$ respectively. (This is true for acute angles α. If $\alpha \geq 90°$, there is certainly no triangle with $a < b$, since the largest angle in a triangle has to be opposite the longest side.)

A question that arises in this context is that of which whole numbered angles can be folded in theory. It is known (see [4]) that Euclidean methods can produce any angle whose measure in degrees is a multiple of three, but no other whole numbered angles. Origami methods, being more extensive, allow any whole numbered angle to be folded.

As we shall see in the next section, folding an equilateral triangle, and therefore 60°, is quite easy. In chapter 6, we shall see that folding a regular pentagon is also possible. Any two adjacent sides of a regular pentagon meet at an angle of 108°. Since adding, subtracting and bisecting angles are all simple applications of (O3) and (O5), and trisecting angles is possible (as was shown in section 10, page 33), we can apply these methods to these angles. Noting, for instance, that

$$108 = 2 \cdot 2 \cdot 3 \cdot 3 \cdot 3$$

or
$$60 + 60 - 108 = 12 = 2 \cdot 2 \cdot 3$$

hold, we can therefore fold an angle of 1°, and hence any whole numbered angle.

117

Chapter 5 — Triangles, Squares and More

16.2 The maximum equilateral triangle

In order to fold equilateral triangles, we must fold angles of 60°. In order to do this, we note that any altitude divides an equilateral triangle into two right triangles (Figure 5.5) with angles of 30°, 60° and 90°.

— *Figure 5.5* —

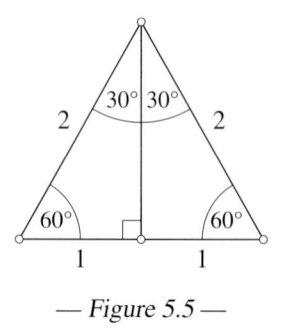

The hypotenuse of each such triangle is twice the length of its shortest side. We use this fact to our advantage in Model I.

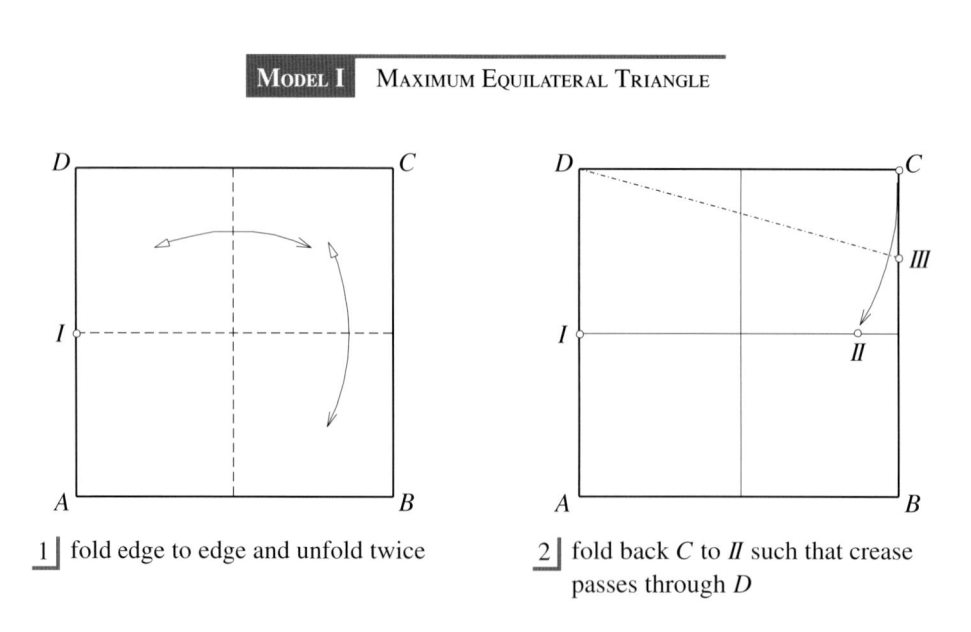

MODEL I MAXIMUM EQUILATERAL TRIANGLE

1| fold edge to edge and unfold twice

2| fold back *C* to *II* such that crease passes through *D*

16 Triangles

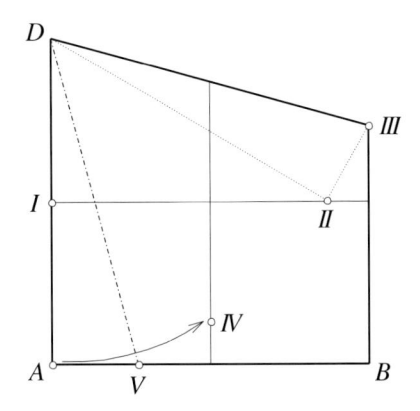

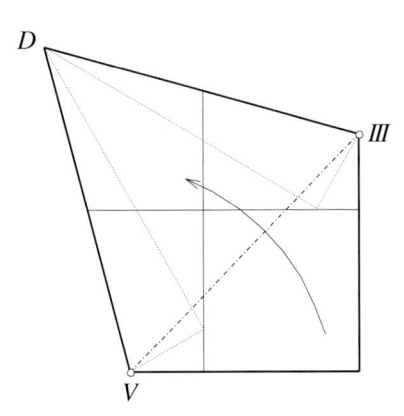

3 fold back A to IV such that crease passes through D

4 fold back line joining III and V

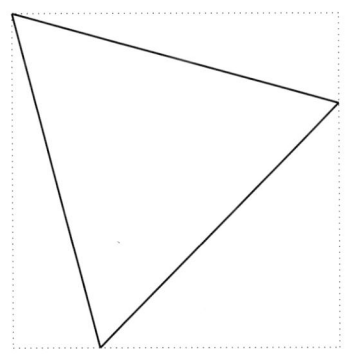

5 the maximum equilateral triangle

Considering the triangle $\triangle DI II$ (best seen in step 3), we see that $\angle DIII$ is obviously a right angle, and since DI is half of the edge DA and $DII = DC$, the hypotenuse DII is twice the length of the side DI. It therefore follows that $\angle IDII = 60°$, and therefore $\angle IIDC = 90° - 60° = 30°$. Since $DIII$ is the angle bisector of $\angle IIDC$, we have

$$\angle IIDIII = \angle IIIDC = 15°,$$

and since the same argument holds for A, IV and V as for C, II and III, we also have $\angle VDA = 15°$. It therefore follows that

$$\angle IIIDV = \angle CDA - \angle CDIII - \angle VDA$$
$$= 90° - 15° - 15°$$
$$= 60°,$$

and since $DIII$ and DV are obviously of the same length for reasons of symmetry, it follows that $\triangle IIIDV$ is isosceles with an angle of 60°, and therefore equilateral. Since one vertex is in a corner of the folding square, and the other two are on sides of the square, it is also maximal, as was shown in chapter 4.

16.3 A regular triangular grid

Certain geometric origami models, such as regular tetrahedra or octahedra, may require pre-creasing a square in a regular triangular grid with one side of each grid triangle parallel to a side of the folding square. One method of achieving this is shown in Model II.

By folding B onto the perpendicular bisector of AB in step 1, the resulting point I is the third vertex of an equilateral triangle $\triangle ABI$. Step 2 is simply the completion of this triangle. By folding the lines parallel to the sides of $\triangle ABI$ that divide the sides into equal halves in step 3, we obtain part of a quasi-regular division of the square with six equilateral triangles and half of four others. Completing this simple first grid in step 4 yields parts of five other such triangles at the top of the folding square.

In step 6, the grid is further refined by folding mid-parallels to all neighboring pairs of parallel grid lines from step 5. This yields the second grid of step 7. Of course, this can be repeated to yield even finer grids if desired.

MODEL II   REGULAR TRIANGULAR GRID

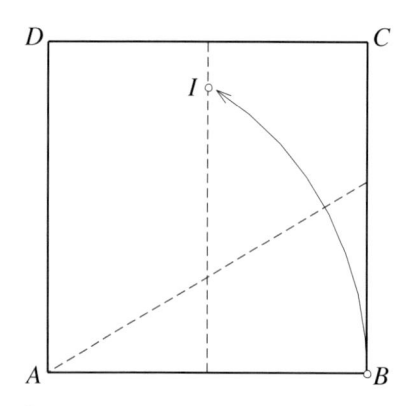

1. fold edge to edge and unfold; then fold B to I on crease

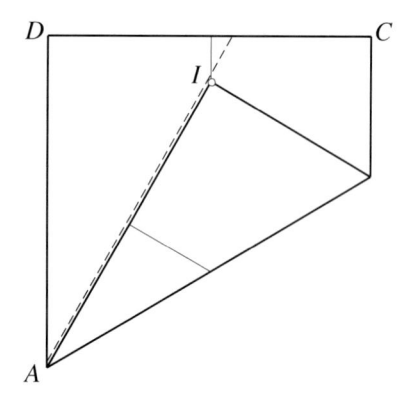

2. fold line joining A and I; unfold everything and repeat on other side, interchanging the roles of A and B

16 Triangles

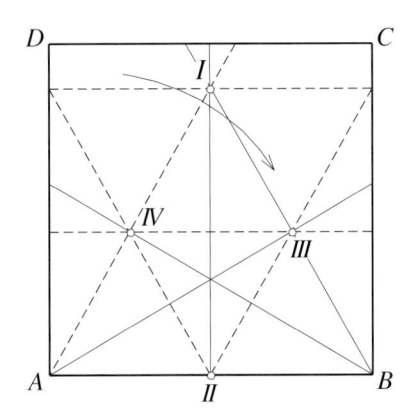

3| fold creases joining *II*, *III* and *IV* as well as line perpendicular to *III* through *I* and unfold; fold along *AI*

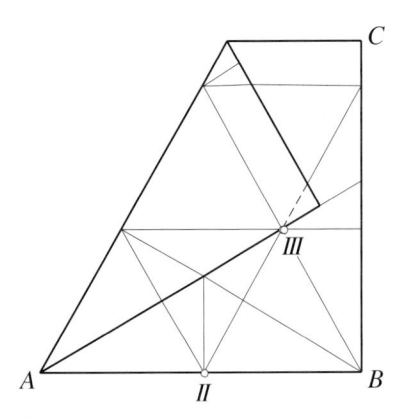

4| fold corner using *II III* as guideline and repeat on other side

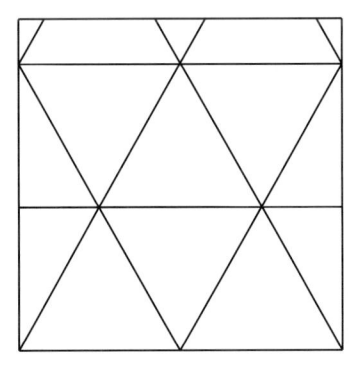

5| first grid

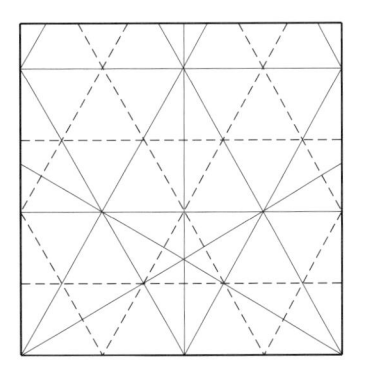

6| folding each line of the grid to the nearest parallel lines and folding in the lower corners to join crease end-points yields a finer grid

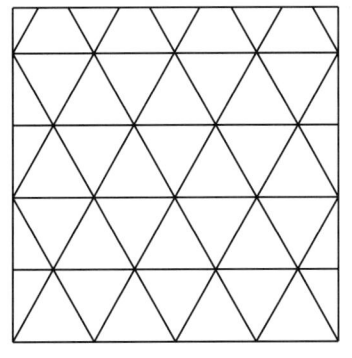

7| second grid

121

17 The regular octagon and n-gons with $n = 2^k$

17.1 The maximum regular octagon

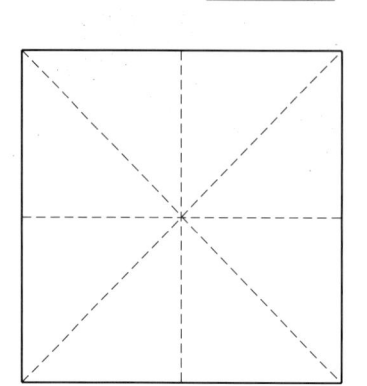

MODEL III MAXIMUM REGULAR OCTAGON

1 fold edge to edge and unfold twice; fold both diagonals and unfold

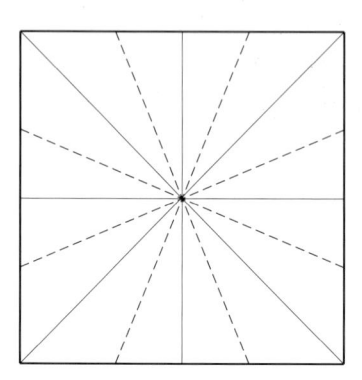

2 fold each crease from step 1 to each neighboring crease and unfold

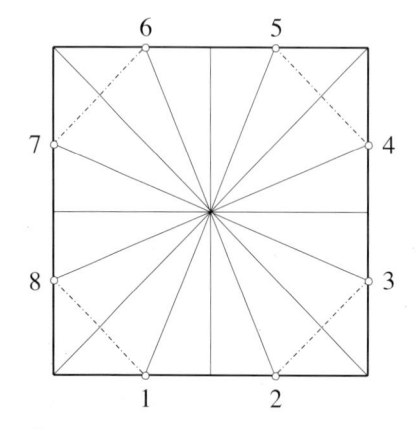

3 fold back lines 2 3, 4 5, 6 7 and 8 1

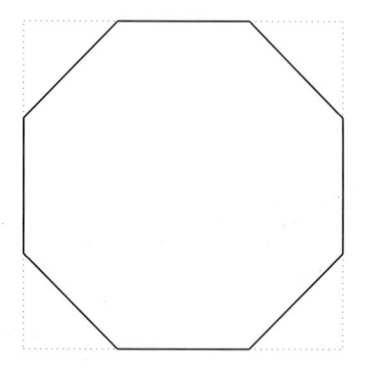

4 the maximum regular octagon

The method presented here is a simple application of the fact, shown in chapter 4, that all maximum $4k$-gons have the same incircle as the folding square, and therefore share four sides with the folding square. Steps 1 and 2 produce the diagonals of the folding square along with their angle bisectors and the crease bisecting the angles between these. Any two adjoining creases illustrated in step 2 meet at an angle of $22\frac{1}{2}°$, and folding the "new" edges 2 3, 4 5, 6 7 and 8 1 therefore yields the maximum regular octagon from the folding square, which was of course already the maximum 4-gon, or square.

17 The regular octagon and n-gons with $n = 2^k$

17.2 Maximum regular $8k$-gons

This method can in fact be used to fold any maximum regular $8k$-gon if we have already determined the maximum regular $4k$-gon (Figure 5.6).

We first fold all diagonals of the $4k$-gon and all perpendicular bisectors of its sides, which yields $4k$ creases in all. The angle bisector of any two neighboring creases then intersects the respective side of the $4k$-gon in a vertex of the maximum $8k$-gon. This is because these points are vertices of the $8k$-gon with $4k$ sides in common with the pre-determined maximum regular $4k$-gon, and therefore with the same incircle as the $4k$-gon. In Figure 5.6, j, $j + 1$ and $j + 2$ are vertices of the $4k$-gon, and $(2j - 1)$, $(2j)$, $(2j + 1)$ and $(2j + 2)$ are vertices of the resulting $8k$-gon, with $(2j - 1)$ and $(2j)$ on the side joining j and $j + 1$, and $(2j + 1)$ and $(2j + 2)$ on the side joining $j + 1$ and $j + 2$.

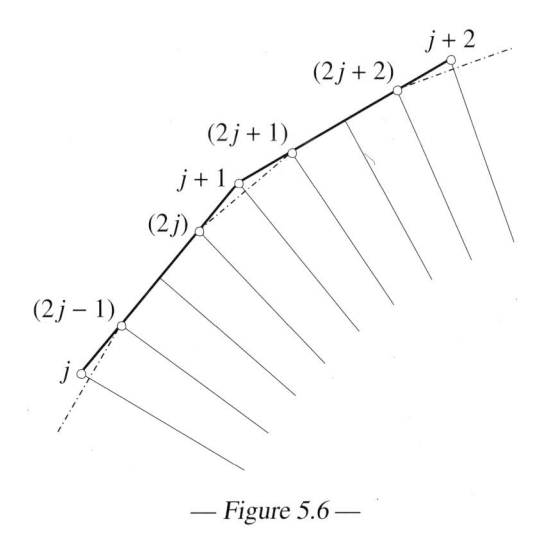

— Figure 5.6 —

In Model IV, we see how this idea helps us derive the maximum regular 16-gon from the maximum regular octagon.

Chapter 5 — Triangles, Squares and More

MODEL IV — MAXIMUM REGULAR 16-GON

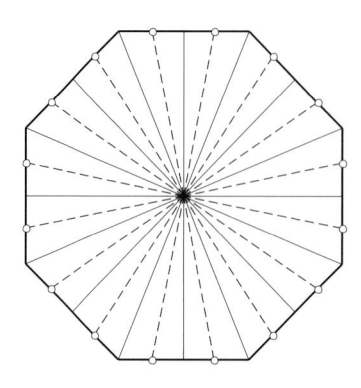

1 starting with the maximum regular octagon from Model III, fold each crease to its neighbors and unfold

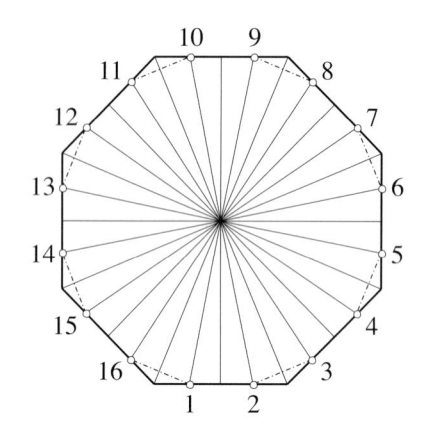

2 fold back 2 3, 4 5, ..., 16 1

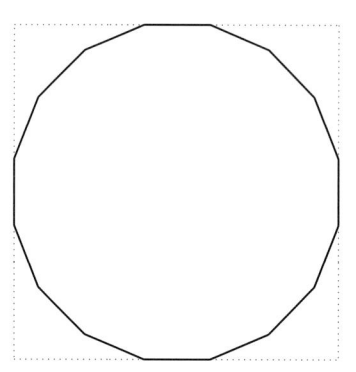

3 the maximum regular 16-gon

This method can be adapted to find a method of folding the maximum $12k$-gon from the maximum $4k$-gon. All this means is replacing the angle bisectors by creases trisecting the angles, and this can be done by applying methods presented in section 10, page 33. The practical use of this idea is very limited, however. There is a much easier method of folding the maximum 12-gon, as we shall see in section 18.2, page 127. Since the maximum 24-gon can be derived from the 12-gon, 3 is the smallest value for k for which the $12k$-gon would reasonably be folded in this way, and the 36-gon is already quite close to a circle, and therefore useless for practical purposes.

18 The regular hexagon and n-gons with $n = 3 \cdot 2^k$

18.1 The maximum regular hexagon

MODEL V   MAXIMUM REGULAR HEXAGON

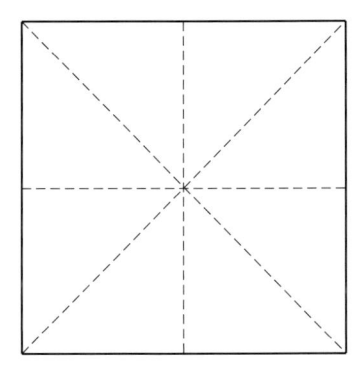

1) fold edge to edge and unfold twice; fold both diagonals and unfold

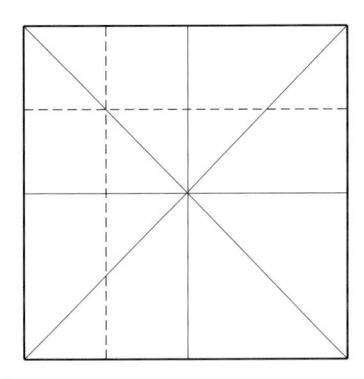

2) fold edge to crease and unfold twice

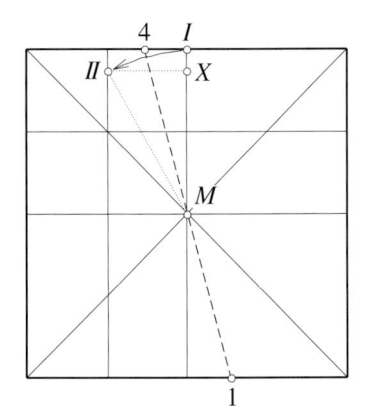

3) fold I onto II such that crease passes through M and unfold; 1 and 4 are vertices of the hexagon

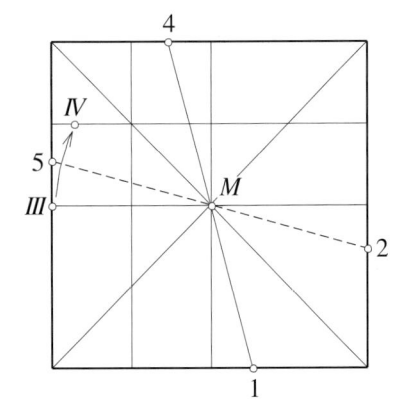

4) fold III onto IV such that crease passes through M; 2 and 5 are vertices of the hexagon

125

| Chapter 5 | Triangles, Squares and More |

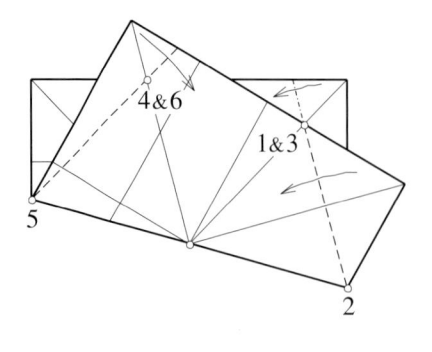

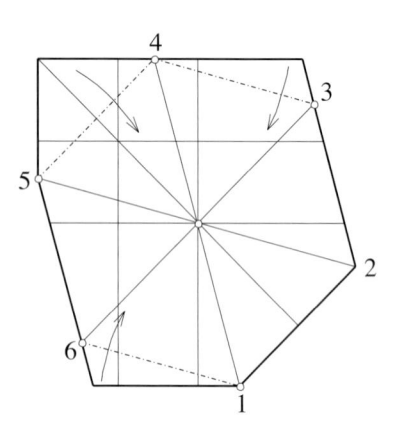

5| vertices 1 and 4 determine vertices 3 and 6; fold edges 1 2, 1 3 and 5 6 and unfold

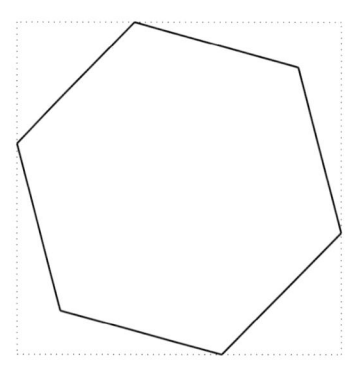

6| fold remaining edges

7| the maximum regular hexagon

Why does this method work? As we know from chapter 4, the maximum regular hexagon has a vertex on each side of the folding square. It has both diagonals of the square as axes of symmetry, and therefore shares its mid-point M with the square.

Since the angle subtended at the center of a regular hexagon is $\frac{360°}{6} = 60°$, one diagonal of the folding square (BD in step 3) has to meet the line joining M with a vertex of the hexagon (4 in step 3) at an angle of $\frac{1}{2} \cdot 60° = 30°$. This means that $\angle 4MI$ has to be equal to 15°, where I is the point on the edge CD with $CD \perp MI$. Due to the way they are determined, points II, M and X (again, in step 3) are the vertices of a right triangle with side XII one quarter the length of the side of the folding square, and hypotenuse MII the same length as MI, that is, half the length of the side of the square. Since MII is therefore twice the length of XII, we have

$$\angle II MX = 30°,$$

18 The regular hexagon and n-gons with $n = 3 \cdot 2^k$

and therefore
$$\angle 4MX = \angle 4MI = 15°.$$

Hence 4 is a vertex of the maximum regular hexagon. For reasons of symmetry, the same holds for 1 in step 3 and 2 and 5 in step 4. Steps 5 and 6 simply complete the regular hexagon, again for reasons of symmetry.

18.2 The maximum regular dodecagon

Since $12 = 4 \cdot 3$, the maximum regular dodecagon has four sides in common with the folding square (Figure 5.7).

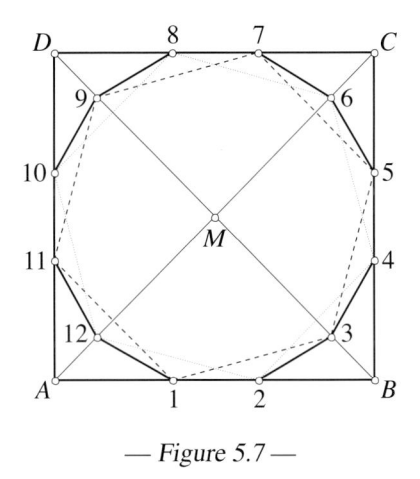

— *Figure 5.7* —

Both diagonals AC and BD of the folding square are axes of symmetry of the dodecagon. It follows that both 2 4 6 8 10 12 and 1 3 5 7 9 11 are maximum regular hexagons. We can therefore fold the maximum regular dodecagon by folding a maximum regular hexagon (for instance 2 4 6 8 10 12), and then determining the points symmetric to its vertices with respect to the vertical line through M. This idea is applied in Model VI.

Chapter 5 — Triangles, Squares and More

Model VI — Maximum Regular Dodecagon

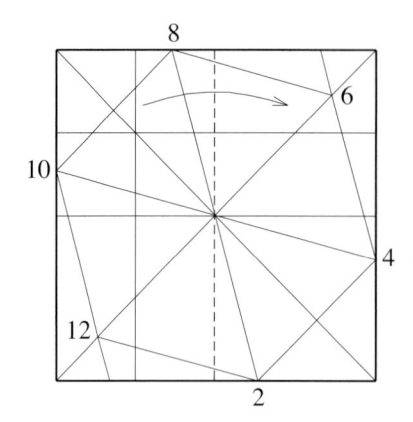

1 starting with the maximum regular hexagon from Model V pre-folded (vertices of the regular hexagon are vertices 2, 4, ..., 12 of the dodecagon), refold edge to edge

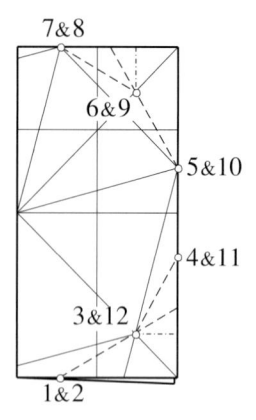

2 fold creases 2 3, 3 4, 4 5, 5 6 and 6 7; turn over and fold 8 9, 9 10, 10 11, 11 12 and 12 1; unfold center crease

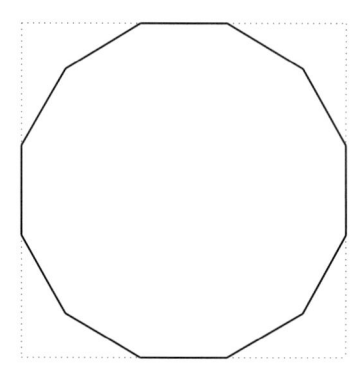

3 the maximum regular dodecagon

Chapter 6

The Regular Pentagon and its Cousins

19 Regular pentagons and the golden section

No discussion of regular pentagons can be complete without a few words on the golden section, and so, here they are.

The golden section results from dividing a line segment into two pieces such that the larger piece and the smaller piece are in the same ratio as the entire original line segment and the larger piece.

— Figure 6.1 —

In other words (Figure 6.1), if the two sections of the line segment are of lengths a and b, we have
$$\frac{b}{a} = \frac{a+b}{b}.$$
(If the length of the whole line segment is assumed to be equal to the unit length and b is the length of the larger section, this is equivalent to $\frac{b}{1-b} = \frac{1}{b}$.) This ratio is called the "golden ratio", and is commonly denoted by ϕ. The numerical value of ϕ is easy to determine, since we have

$$\frac{b}{a} = \frac{a+b}{b} \Leftrightarrow b^2 = a^2 + ab$$
$$\Leftrightarrow b^2 - ab - a^2 = 0$$
$$\Leftrightarrow \left(\frac{b}{a}\right)^2 - \frac{b}{a} - 1 = 0$$
$$\Leftrightarrow \phi^2 - \phi - 1 = 0$$
$$\Leftrightarrow \phi = \frac{\sqrt{5}+1}{2}.$$

(Note that the solution $\frac{1-\sqrt{5}}{2}$ of the quadratic equation is not a possible value of ϕ, since a ratio of the lengths of line segments has to be positive.) The reciprocal of ϕ, that is, the ratio of the smaller piece and the larger piece, is often referred to as $\overline{\phi}$. Its numerical value is obtained as

$$\begin{aligned}\overline{\phi} &= \frac{1}{\phi} \\ &= \frac{2}{\sqrt{5}+1} \\ &= \frac{2(\sqrt{5}-1)}{(\sqrt{5}+1)(\sqrt{5}-1)} \\ &= \frac{2(\sqrt{5}-1)}{4} \\ &= \frac{\sqrt{5}-1}{2}.\end{aligned}$$

While it is interesting to note that ϕ therefore has the curious quality of being "almost" equal to its own reciprocal (with only the sign of the operation in the numerator being different), this is far from being the only remarkable thing about this number. While we shall only mention a few of the more startling properties of the golden ratio here, much more on the subject can be found in numerous publications such as [12]. In fact, there exists a whole cult surrounding the number ϕ, and many almost mystic qualities have been ascribed to it over the centuries. Much interesting information on this aspect of ϕ, and specifically on the many fallacies connected with it, can be found in [47], where we also find a quite extensive list of publications on the subject.

One place the number ϕ turns up surprisingly often is in connection with any number of processes associated with the so-called "Fibonacci" numbers. These are the numbers f_n in the sequence defined recursively by

$$f_1 = f_2 = 1$$

and
$$f_n = f_{n-1} + f_{n-2} \quad \text{for } n \geq 3.$$

Among other things, these numbers play a part in the growth of certain types of plants, the development of some sea-shells, and in the dynamics of certain models of population growth. (In fact, they were first mentioned in the mathematical literature in connection with a population of rabbits in a highly specialized environment.) The Fibonacci sequence has inspired a cult of sorts of its own, and there is even a mathematical periodical devoted solely to results pertaining to the Fibonacci sequence in some way.

It transpires that we can write the n-th Fibonacci number f_n as

$$f_n = \frac{1}{\sqrt{5}} \cdot \left(\phi^n - \left(-\overline{\phi}\right)^n\right),$$

19 Regular pentagons and the golden section

and many natural processes are thus intimately linked with the golden ratio in a subtle way.

Many people believe that there is also an important aesthetic property associated in some unfathomable way with the golden rectangle, that is, the rectangle with sides of length a and $\phi \cdot a$. They point to the common occurrence of (approximately) golden rectangles in artistic endeavors of all sorts, be they in the realms of architecture, painting or sculpture. Although this is sometimes intentional, these rectangles also show up in places where artists seem to have placed them for purely emotional, rather than intellectual reasons, leading to much speculation about the "natural" aesthetic superiority of the golden rectangle. Unfortunately for believers in the mystic properties of numbers, much (if not all) of this speculation seems to be groundless, as explained at length in [47].

As we shall now see, in a regular pentagon the golden ratio is intrinsic, since ϕ is the ratio of its diagonal to its side (Figure 6.2).

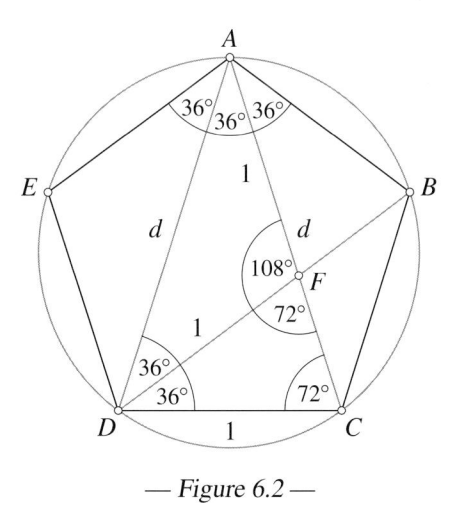

— *Figure 6.2* —

Let us assume that the sides of the regular pentagon $ABCDE$ are of unit length. Since the pentagon can be cut into three triangles $\triangle AED$, $\triangle ADC$ and $\triangle ACB$, each of which has angles that sum to $180°$, the interior angles of the pentagon sum to $3 \cdot 180° = 540°$, and since all five are equal, each is equal to $\frac{540°}{5} = 108°$.

The regular pentagon has a circumcircle, and so the angles $\angle EAD$, $\angle DAC$ and $\angle CAB$ are all equal, since they are angles subtended over chords of the same length in the same circle. Each of these angles is therefore equal to $\frac{108°}{3} = 36°$, and since the same holds for $\angle EDA$, $\angle ADB$ and $\angle BDC$, these angles are also all equal to $36°$.

Triangle $\triangle ADC$ is isosceles, since $AD = AC = d$, and we therefore have

$$\angle ACD = \angle ADC$$
$$= \angle ADB + \angle BDC$$
$$= 72°.$$

131

Letting F denote the point of intersection of AC and BD, we see that triangles $\triangle ADC$ and $\triangle DCF$ are similar, since they have two equal pairs of corresponding angles with

$$\angle ACD = \angle DCF = 72°$$
and
$$\angle CDF = \angle DAC = 36°.$$

It therefore follows that $\triangle DCF$ is also isosceles, and

$$DF = DC = 1.$$

Triangle $\triangle ADF$ is also isosceles, however, since we have

$$\angle FDA = \angle DAF = 36°.$$

It therefore follows that
$$FA = DF = 1$$
also holds.

Since the triangles $\triangle ADC$ and $\triangle DCF$ are similar, we have

$$\frac{DC}{FC} = \frac{AC}{DC}$$

or
$$\frac{1}{d-1} = \frac{d}{1}.$$

This is precisely the defining property of ϕ as shown in Figure 6.1 (page 129) with $b = 1$ and $a = d - 1$, and can be written equivalently as

$$d^2 - d - 1 = 0.$$

We see that d is of length ϕ, and that the ratio of diagonal and side in the regular pentagon is precisely the golden ratio, as claimed.

Taking a closer look at triangle $\triangle ADF$, we can now derive some trigonometric relationships that will prove useful in section 21 (Figure 6.3).

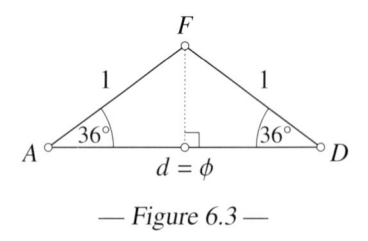

— Figure 6.3 —

Since $\triangle ADF$ is isosceles with $AF = DF = 1$ and $AD = \phi$, and $\angle FAD = \angle FDA = 36°$, the altitude of $\triangle ADF$ through F divides $\triangle ADF$ into two right triangles with a side of length $\frac{\phi}{2}$ and hypotenuse of length 1.

132

We therefore have

$$\cos 36° = \frac{\phi}{2} = \frac{\sqrt{5}+1}{4},$$

and since

$$\sin \frac{x}{2} = \sqrt{\frac{1-\cos x}{2}},$$

it follows that

$$\sin 18° = \sqrt{\frac{1 - \frac{\sqrt{5}+1}{4}}{2}}$$

$$= \frac{\sqrt{5}-1}{4}$$

$$= \frac{\overline{\phi}}{2}.$$

20 Some precise methods for folding a regular pentagon

With all of the above at our disposal, we now turn our attention to actually folding regular pentagons. A first, relatively simple method of folding a regular pentagon can be derived from the fact that the length of the diagonal is ϕ times the length of the side. We assume that the folding square has unit edge length, and that the pentagon is inscribed in the square such that a diagonal is parallel to a side of the folding square, and one vertex of the pentagon is the mid-point of a side of the square (Figure 6.4).

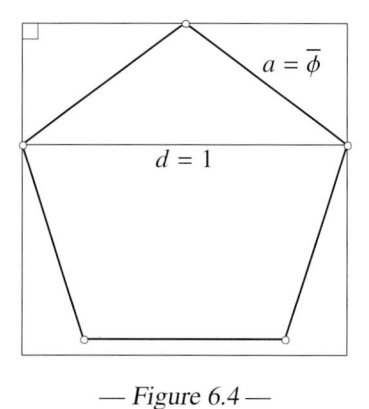

— Figure 6.4 —

The sides of the pentagon then have length

$$\frac{1}{\phi} = \overline{\phi} = \frac{\sqrt{5}-1}{2}.$$

Application of this fact yields the following model.

Chapter 6 | The Regular Pentagon and its Cousins

Model VII Easy Regular Pentagon

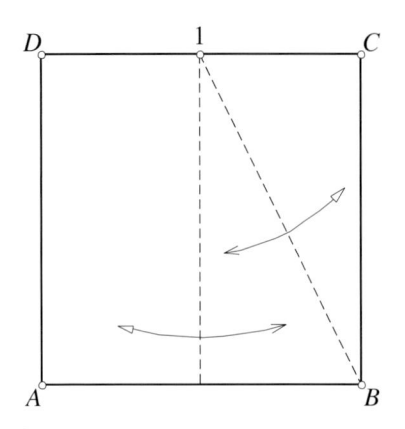

1 fold edge to edge and unfold; fold such that crease joins mid-point 1 of top edge and bottom right-hand corner; unfold

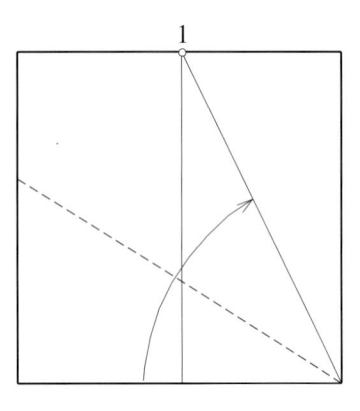

2 fold bottom edge to crease

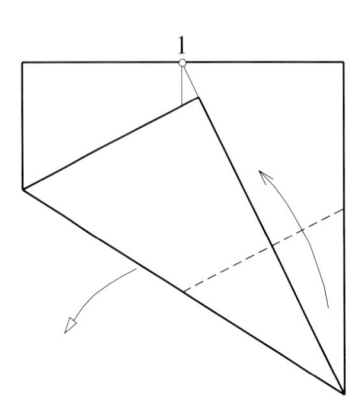

3 fold using crease as guideline; unfold everything

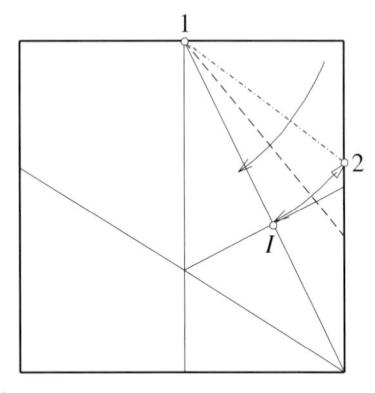

4 fold such that crease contains 1 and point 2 on right-hand edge comes to lie on I; fold back 1 2 using $1I$ as guideline; unfold first fold (1 and 2 are vertices of pentagon)

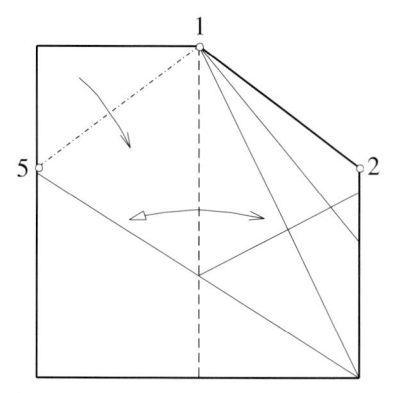

20 Some precise methods for folding a regular pentagon

5| refold edge to edge; fold side 1 5 of pentagon using 1 2 as guideline; unfold first fold

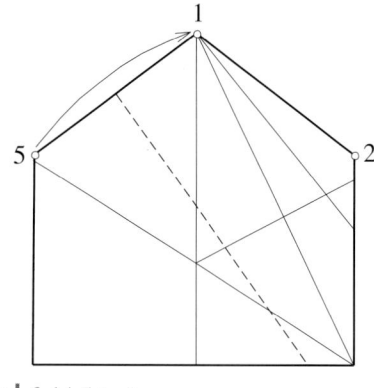

6| fold 5 to 1

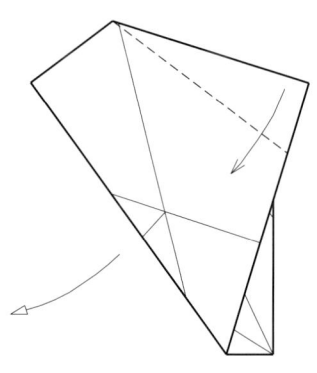

7| fold edge 4 5 using 1 2 as guideline; unfold fold from step 6; repeat steps 6 and 7 folding 2 to 1 instead of 5 to 1 also folding 3 4 using 4 5 as guideline; unfold first fold

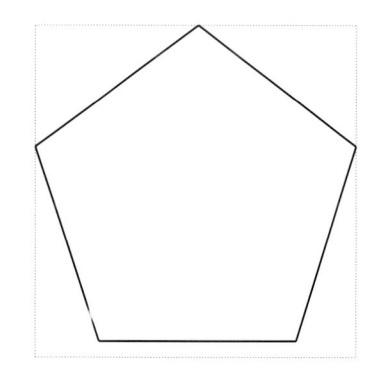

8| finished pentagon

In step 1, triangle $\triangle BC1$ is a right triangle whose sides are of length 1 and $\frac{1}{2}$ respectively. Hypotenuse $1B$ is therefore of length $\frac{\sqrt{5}}{2}$. Transferring a line segment of length $\frac{1}{2}$ onto $1B$ in steps 2 and 3 means that $1I$ in step 4 is of length $\frac{\sqrt{5}-1}{2} = \overline{\phi}$. This also holds for 1 2, and since 1 was chosen as the mid-point of CD, it follows that 1 2 is an edge of the pentagon. Steps 5 through 7 then simply complete the pentagon by utilizing its various symmetries.

Chapter 6 — The Regular Pentagon and its Cousins

Whilst the previous method yields a quite useful pentagon for practical purposes, at this point the question of folding a maximum regular pentagon poses itself quite naturally. This problem was first solved by Roberto Morassi in [51], and a similar but more streamlined method was developed independently by David Dureisseix in [7]. The following method is essentially Dureisseix's version.

MODEL VIII   MAXIMUM REGULAR PENTAGON

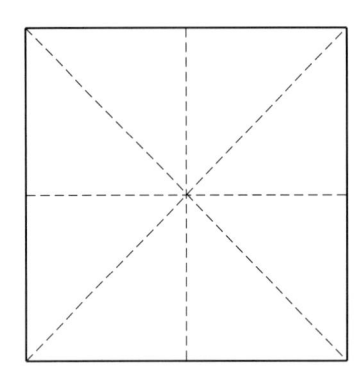

1| fold edge to edge and unfold twice; fold both diagonals and unfold

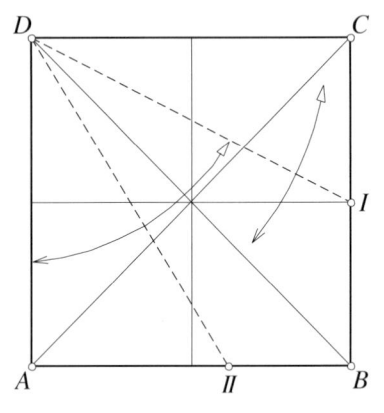

2| fold crease ID and unfold; fold DI to DA and unfold; resulting crease intersects AB in II

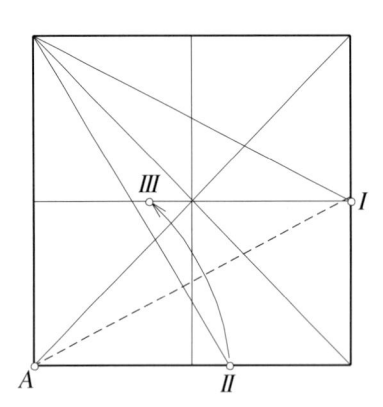

3| fold II to III on horizontal crease through I, such that crease passes through A

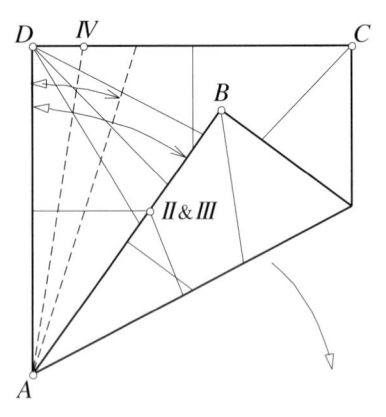

4| fold AD to AB and unfold; then fold AD to resulting crease and open everything

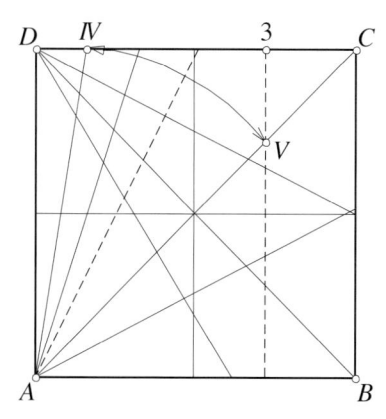

20 Some precise methods for folding a regular pentagon

5| fold *IV* onto *AC* such that crease passes through *A*; fold vertical crease through resulting point *V*; unfold everything; 3 is a vertex of the pentagon

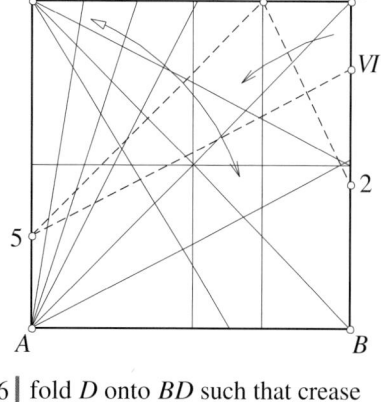

6| fold *D* onto *BD* such that crease passes through 3 and unfold; fold 3 onto *BC* such that crease passes through 5 yielding vertex 2; fold crease through 2 perpendicular to 5*VI*; unfold everything

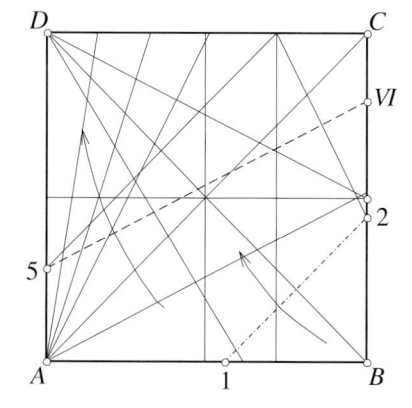

7| fold back 1 2 perpendicular to *BD*; refold crease 5*VI*

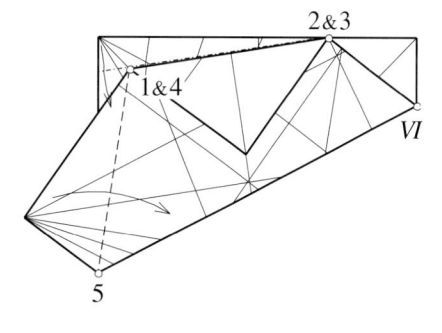

8| fold edges 5 1 and 3 4; unfold 5*VI*

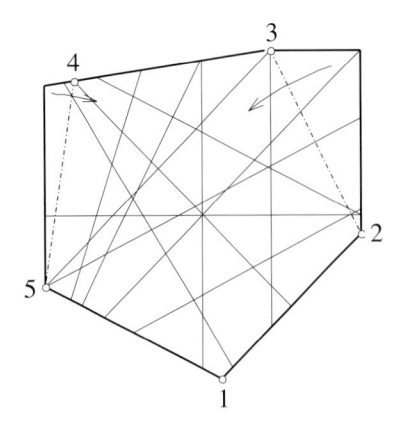

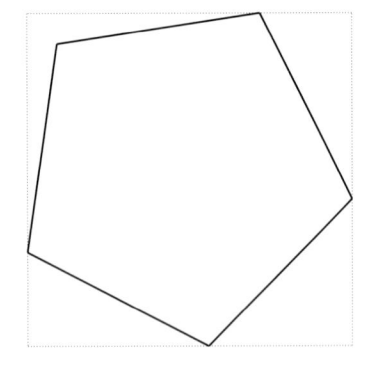

9 fold back remaining edges

10 the maximum regular pentagon

The explanation of this model is a good deal more involved than the last one. First of all, we note that the line segment AII in step 2 is of length $\overline{\phi} = \frac{\sqrt{5}-1}{2}$. Naming $\angle ADI = \alpha$, this follows from the fact that

$$\cos \alpha = \frac{1}{\sqrt{5}} \quad \text{and} \quad AII = \tan \frac{\alpha}{2}.$$

Since

$$\tan \frac{\alpha}{2} = \sqrt{\frac{1 - \cos \alpha}{1 + \cos \alpha}},$$

we have

$$AII = \sqrt{\frac{1 - \frac{1}{\sqrt{5}}}{1 + \frac{1}{\sqrt{5}}}} = \frac{\sqrt{5} - 1}{2}$$

as claimed.

Next, we note that step 4 yields $\angle DAIII = 36°$, and therefore $\angle DAIV = 9°$. Since $AIII = AII = \frac{\sqrt{5}-1}{2}$, this follows from the fact that

$$\cos \angle DAIII = \frac{\frac{1}{2}}{\frac{\sqrt{5}-1}{2}} = \frac{\sqrt{5}+1}{4},$$

as shown in section 19 on page 133.

Since $\angle DAIV = 9°$, it follows that

$$\cos 9° = \frac{1}{AIV},$$

and therefore

$$AIV = \frac{1}{\cos 9°}.$$

138

21 The regular n-gon with $n = 5 \cdot 2^k \cdot 3^l$

— Figure 6.5 —

This is precisely the length of the diagonals d of the maximum regular pentagon inscribed in the unit square, as we can see in Figure 6.5.

Now $\angle 21B = 45°$ and $\angle 312 = 36°$, so we have

$$\angle X13 = \angle X1B - \angle 312 - \angle 21B$$
$$= 90° - 36° - 45°$$
$$= 9°,$$

and therefore

$$d = 1\,3 = \frac{1}{\cos 9°}.$$

It follows that AV in step 5 is therefore also of length $\frac{1}{\cos 9°}$, as is $5\,3$ in step 6, and since $5\,3$ is perpendicular to BD, and 3 lies on CD and 5 on DA, 3 and 5 are vertices of the maximum regular pentagon.

Steps 6 through 9 are then simply the completion of the construction, since both $5VI$ and BD are axes of symmetry of the pentagon.

21 The regular n-gon with $n = 5 \cdot 2^k \cdot 3^l$

Since we can now fold regular pentagons, we also know methods of folding regular n-gons with $n = 5 \cdot 2^k \cdot 3^l$, at least in principle. Being able to fold a regular pentagon means that we can fold an angle of $\frac{360°}{5} = 72°$, since this is the angle $\angle AMB$ subtended over a side at the center of a regular pentagon (M being the mid-point and A and B neighboring vertices of the pentagon). The angle

$$\frac{360°}{n} = \frac{360°}{5 \cdot 2^k \cdot 3^l} = \frac{72°}{2^k \cdot 3^l}$$

subtended over a side at the center of a regular *n*-gon for $n = 5 \cdot 2^k \cdot 3^l$ can therefore be obtained be successive operations of bisecting and trisecting angles, starting with 72°. Folding *n* successive such angles (really just *n*−1) with a common vertex, and transferring the same line segment onto each of the arms with a common end-point in the common vertex yields all *n* vertices of the regular *n*-gon in question.

The simplest such *n*-gon is the regular decagon, and we shall now go on to consider a method for folding the maximum regular decagon.

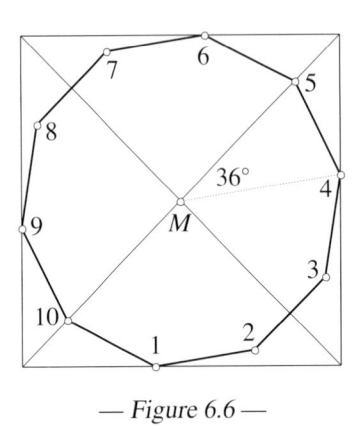

As we know from chapter 4, since 10 is even but not divisible by four, the maximum regular 10-gon has one (and only one) vertex on each side of the folding square, and the diagonals of the square are axes of symmetry of the decagon, with the mid-point of the decagon therefore lying in the mid-point of the folding square (Figure 6.6).

The angle ∠5*M*4 in Figure 6.6 is equal to $\frac{360°}{10} = 36°$, and folding an appropriately placed angle of 36° will therefore yield the maximum regular decagon. At the end of section 19, on page 133, we noted that $\cos 36° = \frac{\sqrt{5}+1}{4}$, and this fact is applied in the following model.

— *Figure 6.6* —

| MODEL IX | MAXIMUM REGULAR DECAGON |

1 fold both diagonals and unfold; fold all four corners to mid-point and unfold

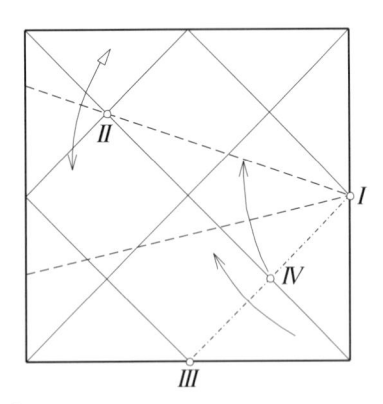

2 fold crease *III* and unfold; fold back *IIII* and fold *IIII* to *III*

140

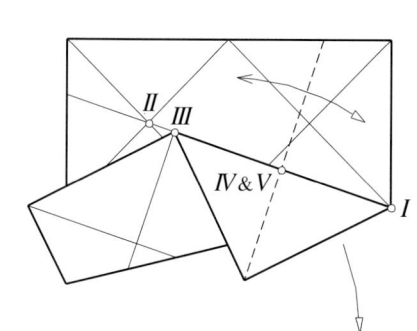

21 The regular n-gon with $n = 5 \cdot 2^k \cdot 3^l$

3| fold I onto III through IV & V and unfold everything

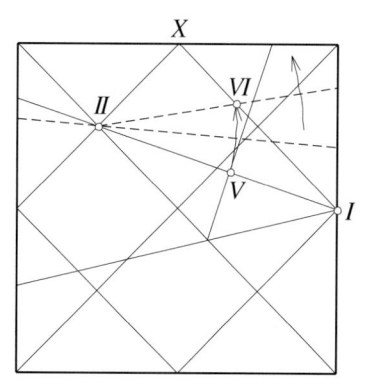

4| fold V onto VI on crease from step 1 such that crease passes through II (folding back IX first makes this easier); fold crease $II\,VI$ using III as guide; unfold everything

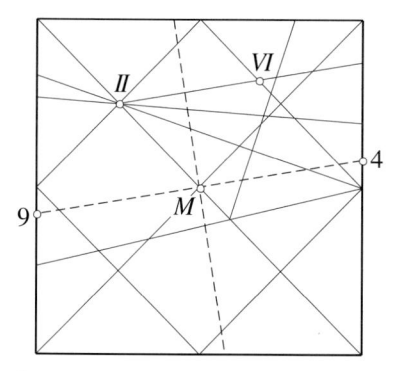

5| fold $II\,VI$ onto itself such that crease passes through M (first continuing crease $II\,VI$ to edge of paper makes this easier) and unfold; fold this crease onto itself through M and unfold; 4 and 9 are vertices of decagon

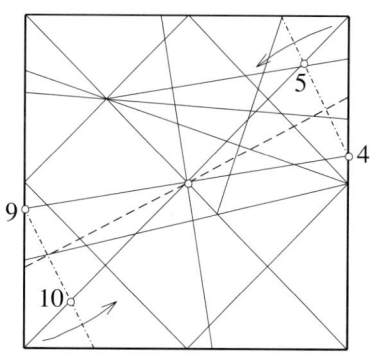

6| fold 4 9 onto diagonal and unfold; fold back perpendicular to resulting crease through 4 and 9; 5 and 10 are further vertices

141

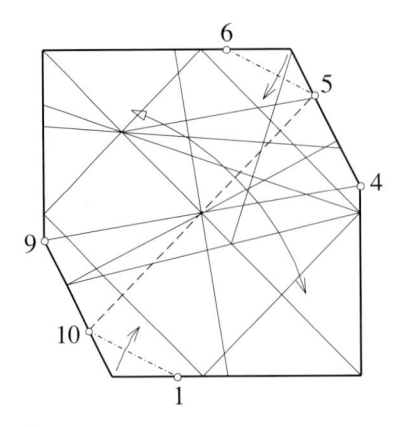

7 refold 5 10; fold back 5 6 and 10 1 using 4 5 and 9 10 as guidelines respectively; unfold 5 10

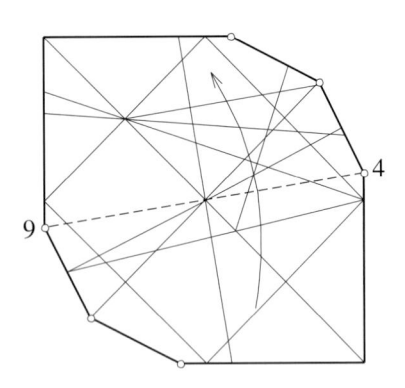

8 refold 4 9

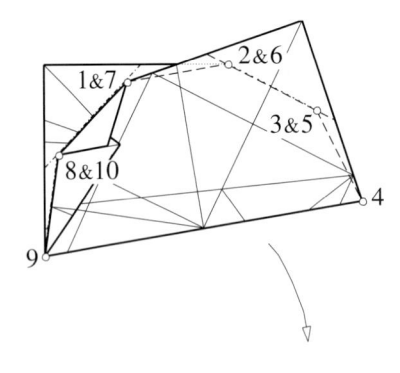

9 fold all remaining edges using 4 5, 5 6, 1 6, 10 1 and 9 10 as guidelines; unfold 4 9

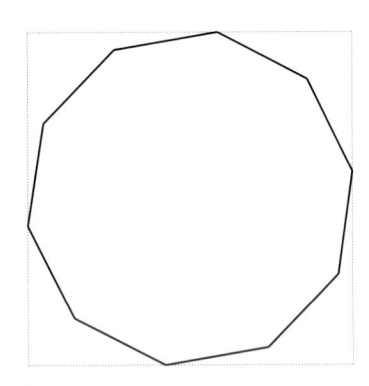

10 the maximum regular decagon

In steps 1 and 2, points *I*, *II* and *IV* are produced. Assuming that the folding square is a unit square, we have

$$I\,IV = \frac{\sqrt{2}}{4}$$

and

$$I\,II = \sqrt{\left(\frac{\sqrt{2}}{4}\right)^2 + \left(\frac{\sqrt{2}}{2}\right)^2} = \frac{\sqrt{10}}{4}.$$

Steps 3 and 4 then yield points *V* and *VI* such that

$$II\,IV = II\,V$$
$$= I\,II - I\,V$$

142

21 The regular n-gon with $n = 5 \cdot 2^k \cdot 3^l$

$$= \frac{\sqrt{10}}{4} - \frac{\sqrt{2}}{4},$$

and since $IIX = \frac{\sqrt{2}}{4}$ in step 4, we have

$$\cos \angle XIIVI = \frac{IIX}{IIVI}$$

$$= \frac{\frac{\sqrt{2}}{4}}{\frac{\sqrt{10}}{4} - \frac{\sqrt{2}}{4}}$$

$$= \frac{1}{\sqrt{5} - 1}$$

$$= \frac{\sqrt{5} + 1}{4},$$

and it therefore follows that $\angle XIIVI = 36°$. Since IIX is parallel to $M5$, it also follows that $\angle 5M4 = 36°$, and 4 is therefore indeed a vertex of the maximum regular decagon as required.

Step 5 yields vertex 9 concurrently with 4, and step 6 transfers 4 and 9 onto the diagonal of the folding square, yielding vertices 5 and 10.

Finally, steps 7, 8 and 9 make use of the axes of symmetry 5 10 and 4 9 of the decagon, completing the model.

Chapter 7

The Regular Heptagon Family

22 The cubic equation

The problem of constructing regular n-gons with straight-edge and compass was, as we have already discussed, one of the classic mathematical problems of Greek antiquity. The smallest n for which the Greeks were unable to find a theoretically precise construction was 7, and this was with good reason. Although they did not realize it at the time, such a construction could not be found for the (not so) simple reason that no such construction is possible. Of course, it took centuries of research to finally prove this, but as it turned out, the construction of the regular heptagon by Euclidean methods is impossible for the same reason that angle trisection and doubling the cube are. Each of these problems requires the graphic solution of an irreducible cubic equation in its algebraic representation, and straight-edge and compass constructions allow only solutions to linear and quadratic problems.

As we saw in section 9 (page 30), solving cubic equations is possible with origami methods. It is therefore not unreasonable to expect that we can fold regular heptagons, despite the fact that we cannot draw them using straight-edge and compass.

One such method was presented by Benedetto Scimemi in [60], and another in [15]. The latter method, presented here as Model X, was later modified by David Dureisseix in [8], yielding a method of folding the maximum regular heptagon. This is essentially the method we shall see as Model XI.

First however, we must familiarize ourselves with some theoretical aspects of the problem. For the first time in this book, we shall consider the folding square as embedded in the complex plane; a method we shall also use in the sections to follow.

The seven corners of a regular heptagon can be thought of as the seven solutions of the equation

(7.1) $$z^7 - 1 = 0$$

Chapter 7   The Regular Heptagon Family

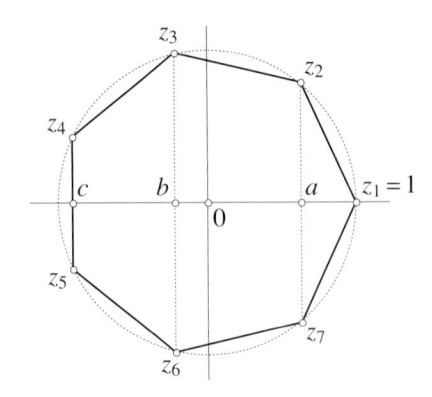

[Figure: regular heptagon with vertices $z_1, \ldots, z_7$ on unit circle, with points a, b, c on real axis]

$z_1 = 1 + i \cdot 0$;

$z_2 = \cos \frac{2\pi}{7} + i \cdot \sin \frac{2\pi}{7}$; $z_3 = \cos \frac{4\pi}{7} + i \cdot \sin \frac{4\pi}{7}$; $z_4 = \cos \frac{6\pi}{7} + i \cdot \sin \frac{6\pi}{7}$;

$z_7 = \overline{z_2}$ $z_6 = \overline{z_3}$ $z_5 = \overline{z_4}$
$= \cos \frac{12\pi}{7} + i \cdot \sin \frac{12\pi}{7}$; $= \cos \frac{10\pi}{7} + i \cdot \sin \frac{10\pi}{7}$; $= \cos \frac{8\pi}{7} + i \cdot \sin \frac{8\pi}{7}$;

$a = \text{Re } z_2 = \text{Re } z_7$ $b = \text{Re } z_3 = \text{Re } z_6$ $c = \text{Re } z_4 = \text{Re } z_5$
$= \cos \frac{2\pi}{7}$; $= \cos \frac{4\pi}{7}$; $= \cos \frac{6\pi}{7}$.

— Figure 7.1 —

in the complex plane. This implies that the unit circle is the circumcircle of the heptagon, and that one corner of the heptagon is the point $z_1 = 1$ on the real axis (Figure 7.1). Since one solution of equation (7.1) is known, the other six are the roots of

(7.2) $$\frac{z^7 - 1}{z - 1} \equiv z^6 + z^5 + z^4 + z^3 + z^2 + z^1 + 1 = 0.$$

For any specific z satisfying this equation, the conjugate $\bar{z}$ is also a solution, since the real axis is an axis of symmetry of the regular heptagon. Also, since

$$|z| = |\bar{z}| = 1,$$

we have $\bar{z} = \frac{1}{z}$. Therefore we can define

(7.3) $$\zeta = z + \frac{1}{z} = z + \bar{z} = 2 \cdot \text{Re } z.$$

Dividing by z^3, we see that equation (7.2) is equivalent to

$$z^3 + z^2 + z + 1 + \frac{1}{z} + \frac{1}{z^2} + \frac{1}{z^3} = 0$$

since 0 is not a root, and since

$$\zeta^3 = \left(z + \frac{1}{z}\right)^3$$

146

22 The cubic equation

$$= z^3 + 3z + \frac{3}{z} + \frac{1}{z^3}$$

$$= z^3 + \frac{1}{z^3} + 3\left(z + \frac{1}{z}\right)$$

$$= z^3 + \frac{1}{z^3} + 3\zeta$$

$$\Leftrightarrow \zeta^3 - 3\zeta = z^3 + \frac{1}{z^3}$$

and

$$\zeta^2 = \left(z + \frac{1}{z}\right)^2$$

$$= z^2 + 2 + \frac{1}{z^2}$$

$$\Leftrightarrow \zeta^2 - 2 = z^2 + \frac{1}{z^2},$$

substituting yields

$$\left(z^3 + \frac{1}{z^3}\right) + \left(z^2 + \frac{1}{z^2}\right) + \left(z + \frac{1}{z}\right) + 1 = 0 \quad \Leftrightarrow \quad \zeta^3 - 3\zeta + \zeta^2 - 2 + \zeta + 1 = 0$$

$$\Leftrightarrow \quad \zeta^3 + \zeta^2 - 2\zeta - 1 = 0.$$

From equation (7.3), we see that each root of the equation

(7.4) $$\zeta^3 + \zeta^2 - 2\zeta - 1 = 0$$

is real, and is equal to twice the common real component of two conjugate complex solutions of equation (7.1). It is therefore possible to find the six complex roots of equation (7.1) in the complex plane by finding the roots of equation (7.4), taking half their values, finding the straight lines parallel to the imaginary axis and at precisely these distances from it, and finally finding the points of intersection of these parallel lines with the unit circle.

We shall now proceed to utilize these steps in folding the regular heptagon.

23 The "easy" regular heptagon and the regular 14-gon

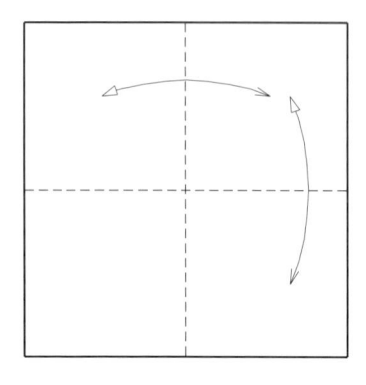

| MODEL X | EASY REGULAR HEPTAGON |

1. fold and unfold twice

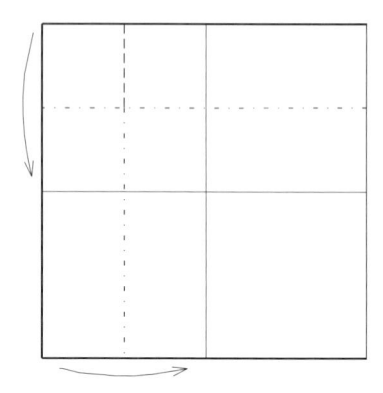

2. fold back twice

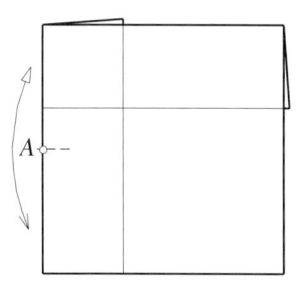

3. fold and unfold, making a crease mark at point A (bisecting the side)

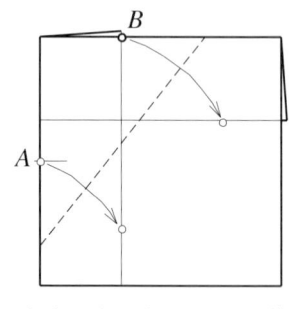

4. fold such that A and B come to lie on the creases

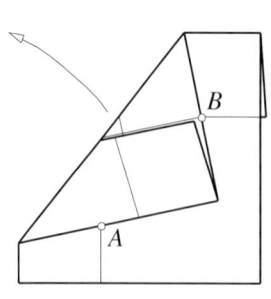

5. unfold everything

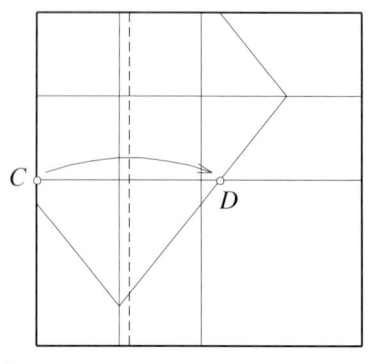

6. fold C to D

23 The "easy" regular heptagon and the regular 14-gon

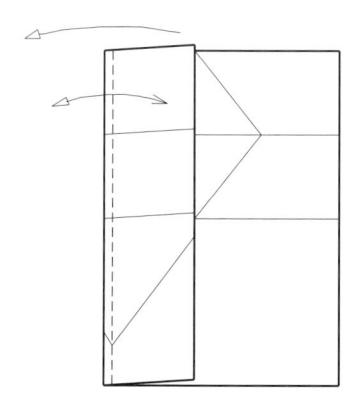

7| fold and unfold both layers at crease through A, then unfold everything

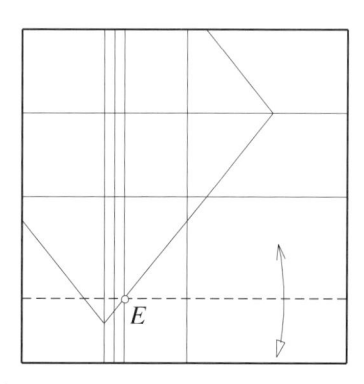

8| fold horizontally through E, then unfold

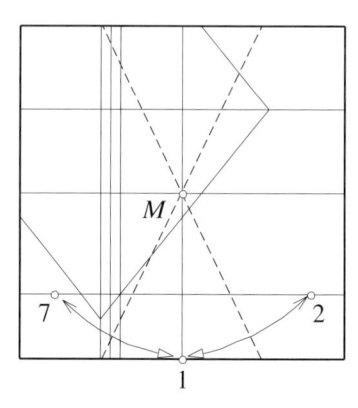

9| fold through M such that 1 lies on crease, resulting in 2 and 7; point M is mid-point of heptagon, points 1, 2 and 7 are corners

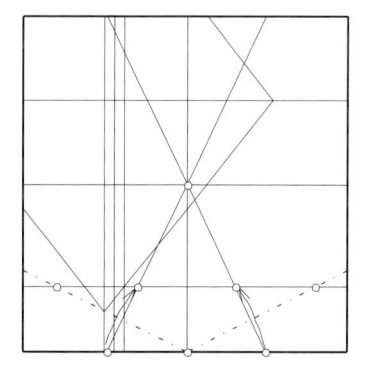

10| fold back twice, so that marked points come to lie on one another; resulting folds are first two sides of heptagon

| Chapter 7 | The Regular Heptagon Family |

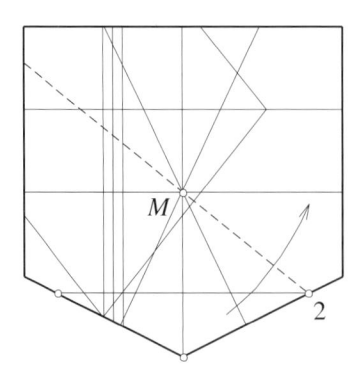

11| fold through M and 2

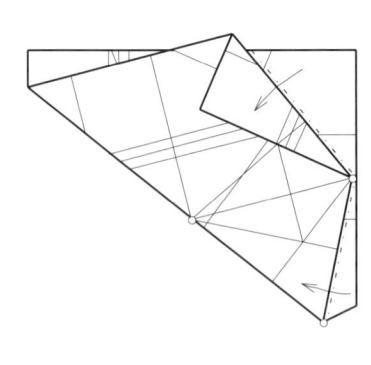

12| fold back lower layer using edges of upper layer as guidelines; resulting folds are two more sides of heptagon; open up fold from step 11 and repeat steps 11 and 12 on left side

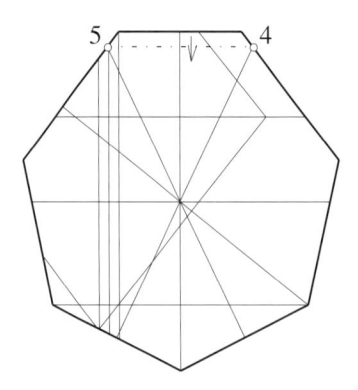

13| fold back final edge of heptagon through 4 and 5

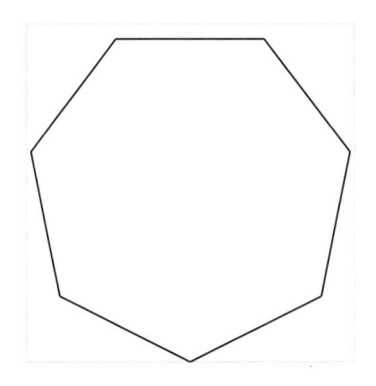

14| finished heptagon

In this model, we assume a square of paper to be given with the edge-to-edge folds in step 1 as the *x*- and *y*-axes of a system of cartesian coordinates, and the edge-length of the given square as four units. The mid-point of the square is then the origin $M(0, 0)$, and the end-points of the folds have the coordinates $(-2, 0)$ and $(2, 0)$, and $(0, -2)$ and $(0, 2)$ respectively.

As shown in section 9 on page 30, the solutions of the cubic equation

$$x^3 + px^2 + qx + r = 0$$

are the slopes of the common tangents of the parabolas p_1 and p_2 with foci

$$F_1\left(-\frac{p}{2} + \frac{r}{2}, \frac{q}{2}\right) \quad \text{and} \quad F_2\left(0, \frac{1}{2}\right)$$

23 The "easy" regular heptagon and the regular 14-gon

and directrices

$$l_1 : x = -\frac{p}{2} - \frac{r}{2} \quad \text{and} \quad l_2 : y = -\frac{1}{2}$$

respectively.

The solutions of equation (7.4) can therefore be obtained by finding the common tangents of the parabolas with foci

$$F_1(-1, -1) \quad \text{and} \quad F_2\left(0, \frac{1}{2}\right)$$

and directrices

$$l_1 : x = 0 \quad \text{and} \quad l_2 : y = -\frac{1}{2}$$

respectively. Since the slope of the common tangents is not altered by translating the parabolas parallel to the y-axis we can, for convenience, use

$$F_1\left(-1, -\frac{1}{2}\right) \quad \text{and} \quad F_2(0, 1)$$

and

$$l_1 : x = 0 \quad \text{and} \quad l_2 : y = 0.$$

This is precisely what is done in steps 2 to 5, where F_1 is the point A, and F_2 is the point B. The fold in step 4 is then the only common tangent of the parabolas with positive slope, and thus twice the real component of the solutions of equation (7.1) which lie to the right of the imaginary axis and are not equal to 1. In other words, the slope of this fold is $2 \cdot \cos \frac{360°}{7}$. Step 4, by the way, is the only step that cannot be replaced by a straight-edge and compass construction.

In steps 6 to 8, the unit-length is then transferred in such a way that point E in step 8 has y-coordinate $-2 \cdot \cos \frac{360°}{7}$. Since the distance from M to point 1 in step 9 is 2 units, the distances from M to points 2 and 7 are also 2 units, and so points 7, 1 and 2 are three consecutive corners of the regular heptagon. (We assume that point 1 with coordinates $(0, -2)$ is the first corner, and continue counter-clockwise from there.)

Step 10 thus yields two sides of the heptagon, and steps 11 to 13 yield the remaining sides of the heptagon by making use of its radial symmetry, until finally step 14 shows us the completed regular heptagon.

This method can easily be modified to yield the maximum regular 14-gon (Figure 7.2 on the following page).

Letting A, B, C and D be the corners and M the mid-point of the folding square, $1, 2, \ldots, 7$ the vertices of the heptagon from Model X, and $(1), (2), \ldots, (14)$ the vertices of the maximum regular 14-gon, we see that $\angle BM1 = 45°$. Since that maximum regular 14-gon has both diagonals of the folding square as axes of symmetry, we also have

$$\angle BM(1) = \frac{3}{2} \cdot \frac{360°}{14} = \frac{270°}{7},$$

151

Figure 7.2

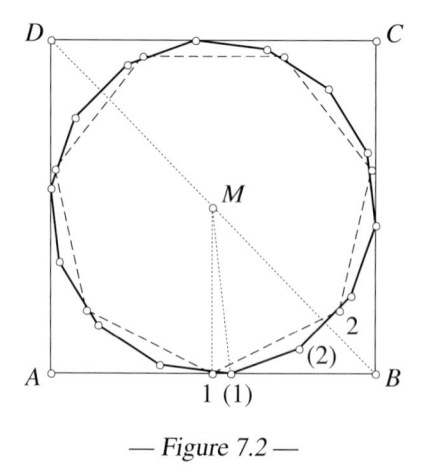

and therefore

$$\angle(1)M1 = \angle BM1 - \angle BM(1)$$
$$= 45° - \frac{270°}{7}$$
$$= \frac{45°}{7}.$$

Since Model X yields a regular heptagon, we have

$$\angle 2M1 = \frac{360°}{7},$$

and since

$$\frac{45°}{7} = \frac{360°}{7} \cdot \frac{1}{2} \cdot \frac{1}{2} \cdot \frac{1}{2},$$

we obtain vertex (1) by bisecting $\angle 2M1$ three consecutive times. This operation also yields vertex (8), and the other vertices are obtained by applying the symmetries of the regular 14-gon.

As was the case starting from the regular pentagon, we can, of course, also obtain any regular n-gon with $n = 7 \cdot 2^k \cdot 3^l$ by applying successive bisections and trisections to the heptagon.

24 The maximum regular heptagon

Since the maximum regular heptagon will have a diagonal of the folding square as an axis of symmetry and vertices on all four sides of the folding square, it must be placed as shown in Figure 7.3.

We again name the corners of the folding square A, B, C and D, the mid-point of the folding square M, and the vertices of the heptagon $1, 2, \ldots, 7$. Assuming that the edges

24 The maximum regular heptagon

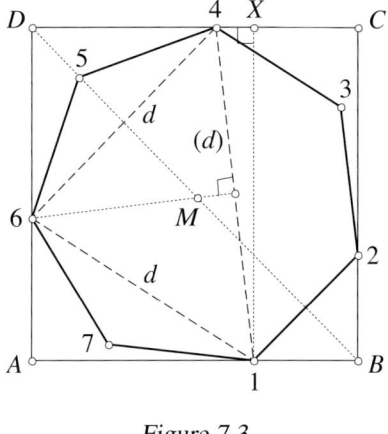

— Figure 7.3 —

of the folding square are again of unit length, we can determine the lengths of the large diagonal $(d) = 1\,4$ and the small diagonal $d = 4\,6$ of the heptagon.

Since the regular heptagon has a circumcircle and the angle subtended over any side of the heptagon at the mid-point is equal to $\frac{360°}{7}$, the angle subtended over any side of the heptagon at a vertex is half this angle, that is, $\frac{180°}{7}$. We note that 4 and 6 are symmetric with respect to BD, and therefore we have $\angle 64D = 45°$. Since

$$\angle 647 = \angle 741 = \frac{180°}{7},$$

it follows that

$$\angle 14C = 180° - \angle 64D - \angle 647 - \angle 741$$
$$= 180° - 45° - \frac{180°}{7} - \frac{180°}{7}$$
$$= \frac{585°}{7}$$

holds. Letting X denote the foot of 1 on CD, we have $1X = BC = 1$, and therefore

$$\sin \angle 14C = \frac{1X}{14} = \frac{1}{(d)},$$

or

$$(d) = \frac{1}{\sin \angle 14C}$$
$$= \frac{1}{\sin \frac{585°}{7}}$$
$$= \frac{1}{\cos \frac{45°}{7}}.$$

153

We now note that △146 is isosceles with $46 = 16 = d$ and $14 = (d)$. Furthermore, we already know that $\angle 641 = \frac{360°}{7}$, and so it follows that

$$\cos \angle 641 = \frac{\frac{(d)}{2}}{d}.$$

We therefore have

$$\begin{aligned} d &= \frac{(d)}{2 \cdot \cos \angle 641} \\ &= \frac{(d)}{2 \cdot \cos \frac{360°}{7}} \\ &= \frac{1}{2 \cdot \cos \frac{45°}{7} \cdot \cos \frac{360°}{7}}, \end{aligned}$$

and the lengths of (d) and d are ready to be applied in Model XI.

MODEL XI MAXIMUM REGULAR HEPTAGON

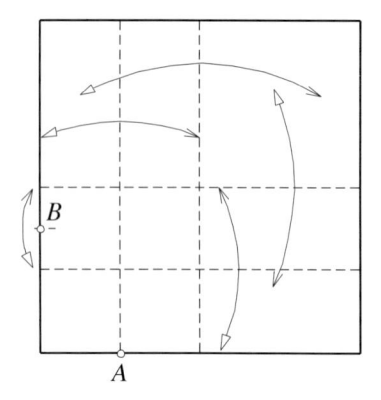

1| fold edge to edge and unfold twice; fold left edge to crease yielding A and unfold; fold bottom edge to crease and unfold; fold crease to crease yielding B and unfold

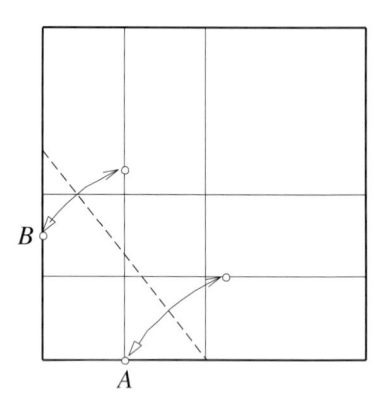

2| fold A and B onto respective creases simultaneously and unfold; end-points of resulting crease are C and D

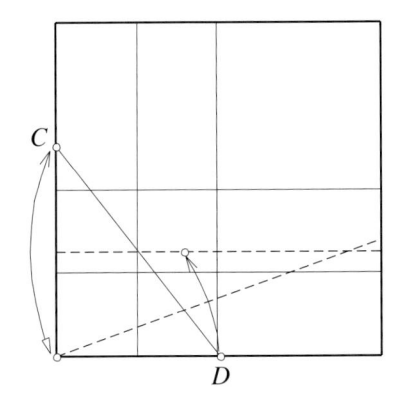

24 The maximum regular heptagon

3 fold corner to C and unfold; fold D onto resulting crease such that new crease passes through corner of square

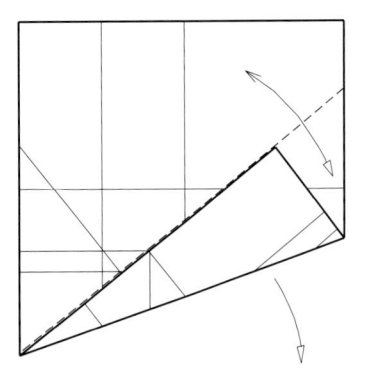

4 fold using edge as guide; unfold everything; resulting crease intersects horizontal center crease in E

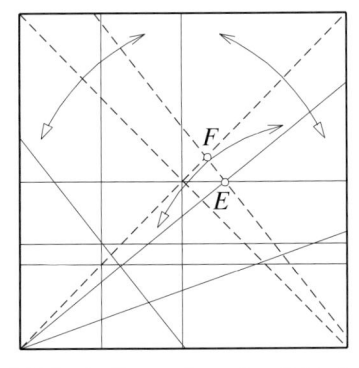

5 fold both diagonals and unfold; fold crease from step 4 onto itself through E and unfold; resulting crease intersects diagonal in F

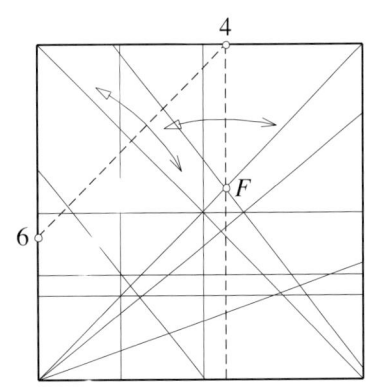

6 fold vertical crease through F and unfold; top end-point of resulting crease is vertex 4 of heptagon; fold crease through 4 perpendicular to diagonal and unfold

| Chapter 7 | The Regular Heptagon Family |

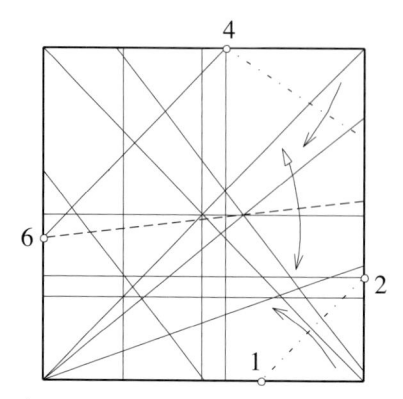

7 fold 4 onto bottom edge of square such that crease passes through 6; 4 comes to lie on 1; fold back 1 2 perpendicular to diagonal of square and fold crease through 4 using 1, 2 as guide; unfold first fold

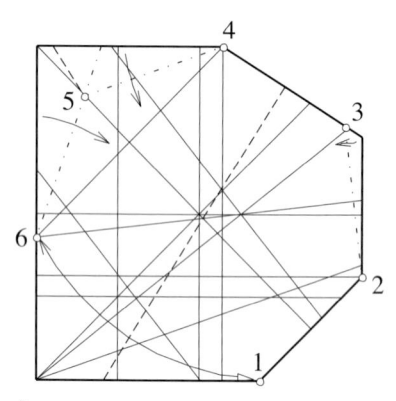

8 fold 1 onto 6; fold 5, 6 using 1, 2 as guide; then fold back 4, 5; finally, fold 2, 3 using 4, 5 as guide; unfold first fold

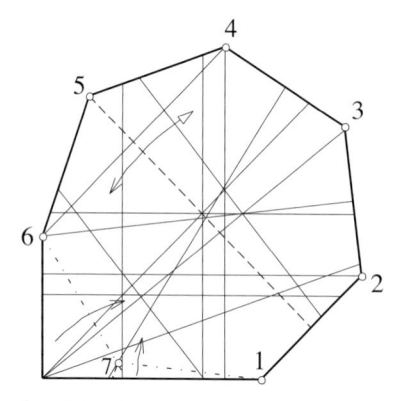

9 refold diagonal of square through 5; fold back 6, 7 and 7, 1 using 3, 4 and 2, 3 as guides; unfold first fold

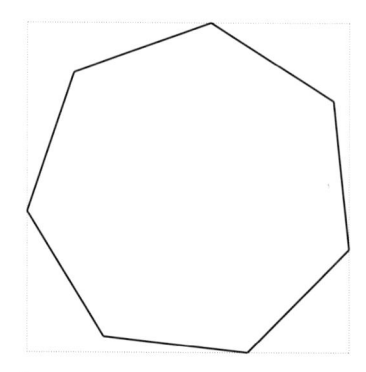

10 the maximum regular heptagon

In order to show the validity of this method, we need only show that the length of 4 6 is indeed equal to

$$d = \frac{1}{2 \cdot \cos \frac{45°}{7} \cdot \cos \frac{360°}{7}}.$$

Comparing points A and B in step 2 with points B and A in step 4 of Model X, we see that the slope of the crease in step 2 is the same as that of the crease from step 4 of Model X with the sign reversed, that is, $-2 \cdot \cos \frac{360°}{7}$. Now, let us look at the relative positions of points C and D in step 3 (Figure 7.4).

Letting (A) denote the bottom left corner of the folding square, we say that D is folded

24 The maximum regular heptagon

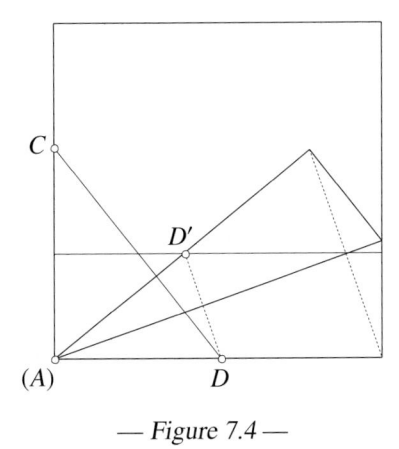

— Figure 7.4 —

onto the point D' on the perpendicular bisector of $(A)C$ in step 3. Since the slope of CD is equal to $-2 \cdot \cos \frac{360°}{7}$, we have

$$\frac{(A)C}{(A)D} = 2 \cdot \cos \frac{360°}{7},$$

and therefore

$$\cos \angle C(A)D' = \frac{\frac{1}{2} \cdot (A)C}{(A)D'}$$

$$= \frac{1}{2} \cdot \frac{(A)C}{(A)D}$$

$$= \frac{1}{2} \cdot 2 \cdot \cos \frac{360°}{7}$$

$$= \cos \frac{360°}{7}.$$

It follows that

$$\angle C(A)D' = \frac{360°}{7}.$$

What about points E and F in steps 4 and 5 (Figure 7.5 on the next page)?

Naming the corners of the folding square (A), (B), (C) and (D), we have $\angle(D)(A)E = \frac{360°}{7}$, and since Y is the mid-point of $(A)(D)$, we have

$$\frac{(A)Y}{(A)E} = \cos \frac{360°}{7},$$

and therefore

$$\frac{\frac{1}{2}}{(A)E} = \cos \frac{360°}{7}$$

or

$$(A)E = \frac{1}{2 \cdot \cos \frac{360°}{7}}.$$

157

— Figure 7.5 —

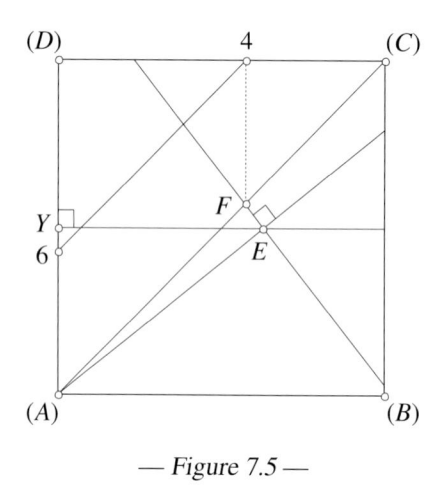

Since
$$\angle F(A)E = \angle(D)(A)E - \angle(D)(A)F$$
$$= \frac{360°}{7} - 45°$$
$$= \frac{45°}{7},$$

it then follows that
$$\frac{(A)E}{(A)F} = \cos\frac{45°}{7},$$

and so we have
$$(A)F = \frac{(A)E}{\cos\frac{45°}{7}}$$
$$= \frac{1}{2 \cdot \cos\frac{45°}{7} \cdot \cos\frac{360°}{7}}.$$

Noting that $4\,6$ results by translation of $F(A)$, we have shown that the length of $4\,6$ is indeed equal to
$$\frac{1}{2 \cdot \cos\frac{45°}{7} \cdot \cos\frac{360°}{7}},$$
as required. Steps 7 through 9 then simply serve to complete the heptagon by application of its various symmetries.

The method used here to fold the maximum regular heptagon was derived from a method of folding an angle of $\frac{360°}{7}$. This idea can be modified to give a method for folding a maximum regular n-gon for any odd n, assuming that we can find a method of folding an angle of $\frac{360°}{n}$. Since these methods tend to become a bit involved, we will not include any more maximum regular n-gons in the sections to come, but will remain content with folding the simplest possible cases. Modifying these methods in order to fold the maximum n-gons in each case is left as an exercise for the interested reader.

158

Chapter 8

A Few More Polygons

25 The regular nonagon

In the last two sections, we mentioned that being able to fold a regular n-gon means that it is also possible, at least in theory, to fold any regular $(n \cdot 2^k \cdot 3^l)$-gon. Since the angle subtended over a side at the center of a regular n-gon is equal to $\alpha_n = \frac{360°}{n}$, the angle subtended over a side at the center of a regular $(n \cdot 2^k \cdot 3^l)$-gon, namely

$$\frac{360°}{n \cdot 2^k \cdot 3^l} = \frac{360°}{n} \cdot \frac{1}{2^k} \cdot \frac{1}{3^l},$$

results from α_n by successive operations of bisection and trisection.

In chapter 5, we have already taken a look at methods of folding regular n-gons with $n = 2^k \cdot 3^l$ and $k \geq 1$, but what about the case $n = 3^l$? For $l = 1$, this is simply the equilateral triangle, which is quite straight forward to fold. One method of folding 3^l-gons is therefore given by first folding an equilateral triangle and then trisecting the angle subtended over its side at the center $l - 1$ successive times. This is essentially the method presented here for the nonagon, that is, the case $l = 2$. (An interesting variant of this idea is presented in [40].)

As illustrated in Figure 8.1 on the following page, the angle subtended over the side of an equilateral triangle at its center is equal to

$$\alpha_3 = \frac{360°}{3} = 120°.$$

The corresponding angle for the nonagon is equal to

$$\alpha_9 = \frac{360°}{9} = 40° = \frac{\alpha_3}{3},$$

and folding the regular nonagon therefore involves the trisection of $120°$. As was shown in section 10 (page 33), angle trisection involves the irreducible cubic equation

$$x^3 - \frac{3}{4} \cdot x - \frac{1}{4} \cdot \cos 3\alpha = 0,$$

Chapter 8 — A Few More Polygons

which derives from the fact that

$$\cos 3\alpha = 4\cos^3 \alpha - 3\cos \alpha.$$

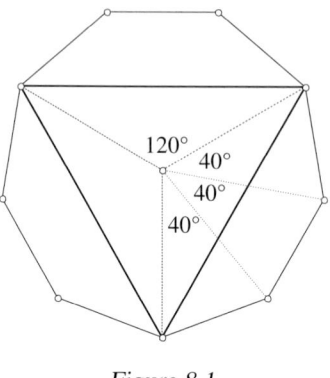

— Figure 8.1 —

For the specific case at hand, where $3\alpha = 120°$, the cubic equation in question is

$$x^3 - \frac{3}{4} \cdot x + \frac{1}{8} = 0.$$

From section 9 (page 30) we know that the solutions of this equation are the slopes of the common tangents of the parabolas p_1 and p_2, whereby p_1 is defined by its focus

$$F_1\left(\frac{1}{16}, -\frac{3}{8}\right)$$

and its directrix

$$\ell_1 : x = -\frac{1}{16},$$

and p_2 is defined by its focus

$$F_2\left(0, \frac{1}{2}\right)$$

and its directrix

$$\ell_2 : y = -\frac{1}{2}.$$

This is precisely the method used to derive Model XII.

25 The regular nonagon

MODEL XII   **REGULAR NONAGON**

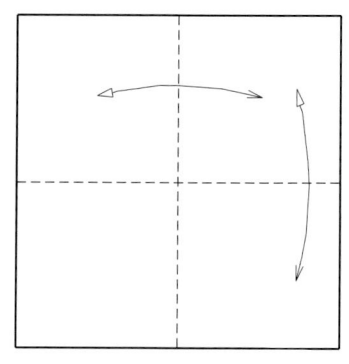

1. fold and unfold twice

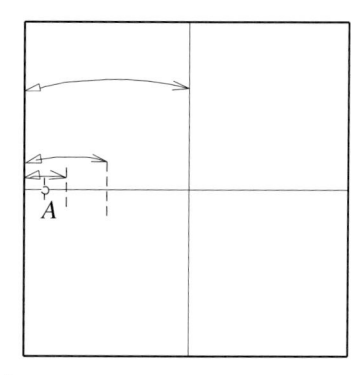

2. fold and unfold three times, making crease marks each time; final crease yields point *A*

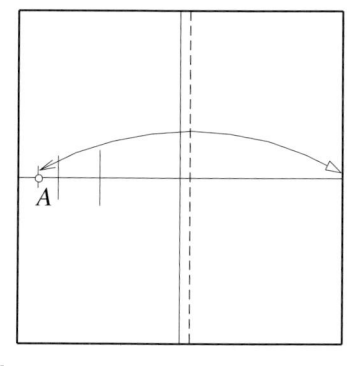

3. fold edge to point *A* and unfold

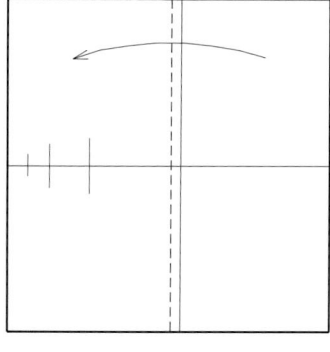

4. refold edge to edge

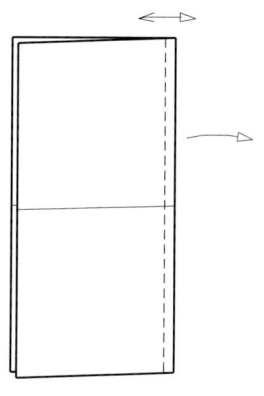

5. fold and unfold both layers at crease, then unfold

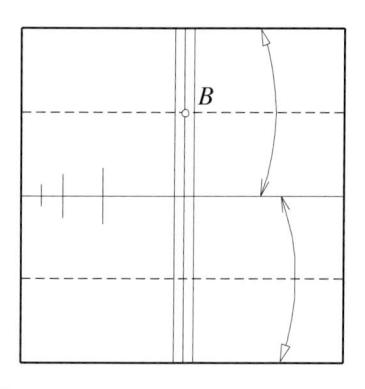

6. fold and unfold twice, marking point *B*

Chapter 8 | A Few More Polygons

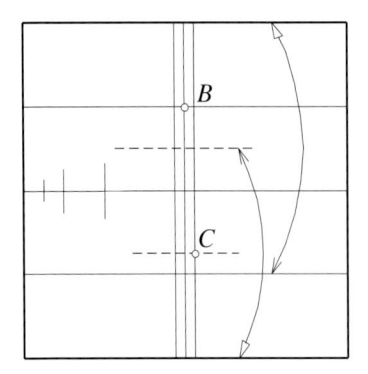

7| fold upper edge to crease, unfold, then fold lower edge to new crease, making crease mark at point C

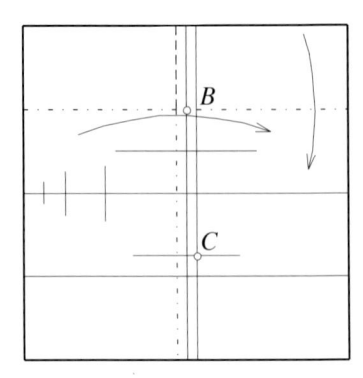

8| mountain fold along creases

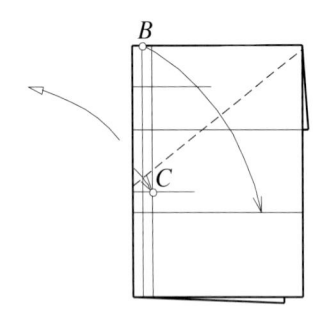

9| fold so that B comes to lie on crease, and vertical fold from step 8 comes to lie on C; unfold everything

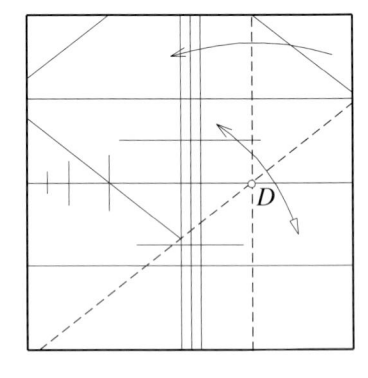

10| fold along crease and unfold, then fold vertically through point D

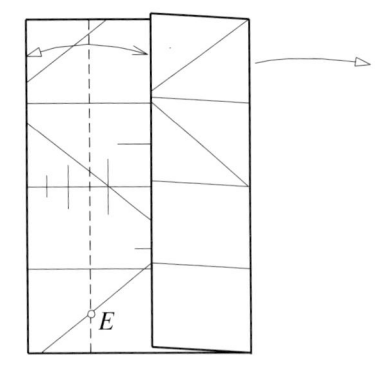

11| fold edge to edge and unfold everything

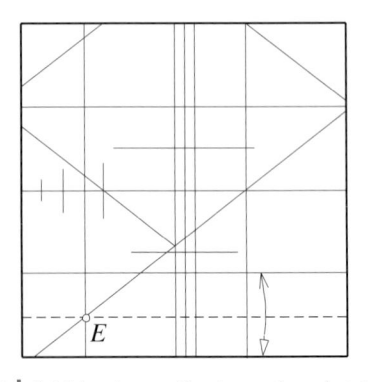

12| fold horizontally through point E and unfold

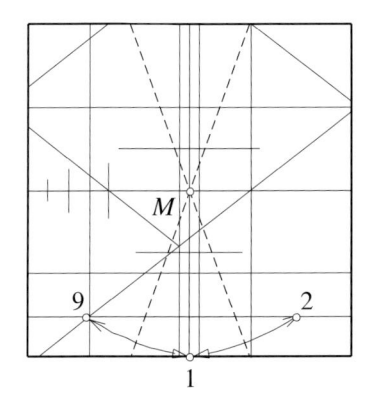

25 The regular nonagon

13 fold through M such that point 1 lies on crease, unfold and repeat on other side (points 1, 2, 9 are corners of nonagon)

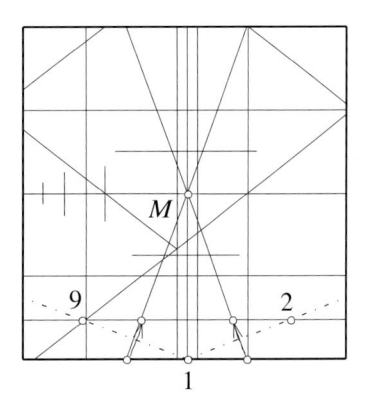

14 fold back twice such that marked points come to lie on each other, resulting folds are sides of nonagon

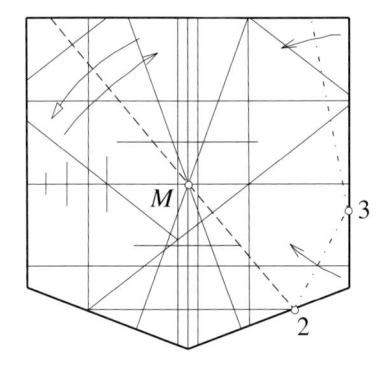

15 fold through M and 2; mountain fold lower layer using edges of upper layer as guide lines; resulting folds are two more sides of nonagon; open up fold $M\,2$ and repeat on left side, then fold through M and 2 once more; new edges are new guide lines; repeating process completes nonagon

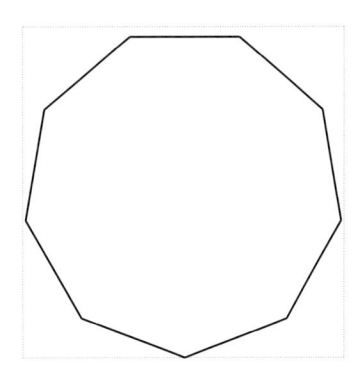

16 finished nonagon

We consider the edge-to-edge folds in step 1 as the x- and y-axes of a system of cartesian coordinates, and the edge-length of the given square as two units. The mid-point of the square is then the origin $M(0,0)$, and the end-points of the folds have the coordinates $(-1, 0)$ and $(1, 0)$, and $(0, -1)$ and $(0, 1)$, respectively.

Steps 1 through 8 yield the foci and directrices of the parabolas as discussed. The point

163

C is the focus F_1 of parabola p_1, point B is the focus F_2 of parabola p_2, and the creases onto which these two points are folded in step 9 are the directrices ℓ_1 and ℓ_2. Since the coordinates involved are all arrived at by halving certain line segments, it is quite easy to see that this is indeed the case.

The fold made in step 9 is then a common tangent of the parabolas, and its slope is therefore $\cos 40°$. Steps 10 to 12 then yield the horizontal line represented by the equation $y = -\cos 40°$. This is the horizontal fold through point E, as the distance between the vertical folds through points D and E is equal to 1.

We then obtain vertices 2 and 9 of the nonagon (assuming the point with coordinates $(0, -1)$ to be vertex 1) on this horizontal line by folding the unit length onto this line from mid-point M in step 13. Step 14 therefore yields the first two sides of the nonagon, and step 15 completes the model, making use of both the radial symmetry of the figure, and its axial symmetry with respect to the vertical line $M1$. Step 16, finally, shows us the completed regular nonagon.

If we wish, we can now fold the regular 27-gon by trisecting the angle of $40°$, and so on, in principle yielding the entire class of regular 3^l-gons.

26 The regular triskaidekagon

As we all know, the number 13 is considered special in some way by many people. Specifically, in many European cultures, it is considered especially unlucky (or especially lucky, as the case may be). This goes so far that there is actually a word for the pathological fear of the number 13, namely *triskaidekaphobia*. Although the regular 13-gon cannot be drawn by euclidean methods because of the cubic equation involved in its algebraic representation, we need not fear it when using origami methods, as we shall see in this section.

As we did for the regular heptagon (section 22, page 145), we think of the corners of the regular triskaidekagon as the solutions in the complex plane of a simple polynomial equation, specifically

$$z^{13} - 1 = 0.$$

The unit circle is then the circumcircle of the triskaidekagon, and the point $z_1 = 1$ on the real axis is one corner. The other twelve corners are the twelve roots of the cyclotomic equation

(8.1) $$\frac{z^{13} - 1}{z - 1} \equiv z^{12} + z^{11} + \ldots + z + 1 = 0.$$

These roots can be written in polar coordinates as

$$z_n = \left(1; \frac{2\pi(n-1)}{13}\right) = \cos\frac{2\pi(n-1)}{13} + i \cdot \sin\frac{2\pi(n-1)}{13}$$

26 The regular triskaidekagon

for $n = 2, 3, \ldots, 13$, and taking $z_2 =: \zeta$, we have

$$z_n = \zeta^{n-1} \quad \text{for} \quad n = 2, 3, \ldots, 13.$$

In order to develop a folding process for the regular triskaidekagon, we shall now proceed to determine $\operatorname{Re} \zeta = \cos \frac{2\pi}{13}$.

We define variables y_1 and y_2 as

$$y_1 = \zeta + \zeta^4 + \zeta^3 + \zeta^{12} + \zeta^9 + \zeta^{10}$$

and

$$y_2 = \zeta^2 + \zeta^8 + \zeta^6 + \zeta^{11} + \zeta^5 + \zeta^7.$$

(The reason for this choice lies in the fact that successive squaring of the roots of equation (8.1), starting with ζ, yields the roots in the order

$$\zeta, \zeta^2, \zeta^4, \zeta^8, \zeta^3, \zeta^6, \zeta^{12}, \zeta^{11}, \zeta^9, \zeta^5, \zeta^{10}, \zeta^7, \zeta, \ldots.$$

Choosing alternate elements of the series in each sum then yields y_1 and y_2.) We then have

$$y_1 + y_2 = \zeta + \zeta^2 + \zeta^3 + \cdots + \zeta^{12}$$
$$= -1$$

and

$$y_1 \cdot y_2 = 3 \cdot \left(\zeta + \zeta^2 + \zeta^3 + \cdots + \zeta^{12}\right)$$
$$= -3,$$

and so y_1 and y_2 are the solutions of the quadratic equation

$$y^2 + y - 3 = 0.$$

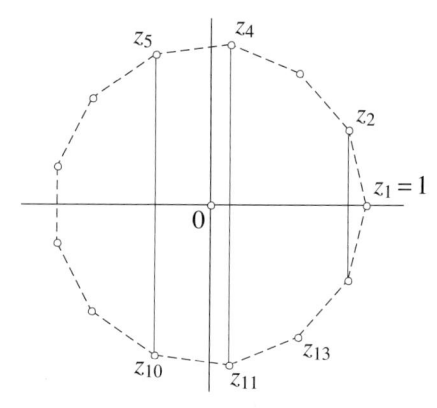

$z_2 = \zeta \quad z_4 = \zeta^3 \quad z_5 = \zeta^4 \quad z_{10} = \zeta^9 \quad z_{11} = \zeta^{10}$

— Figure 8.2 —

We now note that y_1 is certainly positive, and therefore y_2 negative, since the sum of y_1 and y_2 is negative. We see this by glancing at Figure 8.2.

Since we have
$$\zeta^{13} = 1,$$
it follows that
$$\zeta^{12} = \frac{1}{\zeta} \cdot \zeta^{13} = \frac{1}{\zeta},$$
and similarly
$$\zeta^{10} = \frac{1}{\zeta^3} \quad \text{and} \quad \zeta^9 = \frac{1}{\zeta^4}.$$
Since
$$|\zeta| = |\zeta^3| = |\zeta^4| = 1,$$
we have
$$\frac{1}{\zeta} = \overline{\zeta}$$
(with $\overline{\zeta}$ denoting the conjugate of ζ), and therefore
$$\zeta + \frac{1}{\zeta} = 2 \cdot \mathrm{Re}\, \zeta.$$
Similarly, we also have
$$\zeta^3 + \frac{1}{\zeta^3} = 2 \cdot \mathrm{Re}\, \zeta^3$$
and
$$\zeta^4 + \frac{1}{\zeta^4} = 2 \cdot \mathrm{Re}\, \zeta^4,$$
and therefore
$$y_1 = \zeta + \zeta^{12} + \zeta^3 + \zeta^{10} + \zeta^4 + \zeta^9$$
$$= \left(\zeta + \frac{1}{\zeta}\right) + \left(\zeta^3 + \frac{1}{\zeta^3}\right) + \left(\zeta^4 + \frac{1}{\zeta^4}\right)$$
$$= 2 \cdot \mathrm{Re}\, \zeta + 2 \cdot \mathrm{Re}\, \zeta^3 + 2 \cdot \mathrm{Re}\, \zeta^4.$$

Since it is quite obvious that $|\mathrm{Re}\, \zeta| > |\mathrm{Re}\, \zeta^4|$ holds, and $\mathrm{Re}\, \zeta^3 > 0$, it certainly follows that $y_1 > 0$.

We have therefore now determined that
$$y_1 = \frac{-1 + \sqrt{13}}{2} \quad \text{and} \quad y_2 = \frac{-1 - \sqrt{13}}{2}$$
hold.

In order to reduce to a cubic equation (which we can solve by the method introduced in section 9, page 30), we define new variables
$$f_1 = \zeta + \zeta^{12}, \quad f_2 = \zeta^3 + \zeta^{10}, \quad \text{and} \quad f_3 = \zeta^4 + \zeta^9.$$

26 The regular triskaidekagon

Noting that

$$f_1 = \zeta + \frac{1}{\zeta} = 2 \cdot \cos \frac{2\pi}{13} > 1,$$

$$f_2 = \zeta^3 + \frac{1}{\zeta^3} = 2 \cdot \cos \frac{6\pi}{13} < 1 \quad (\text{but } f_2 < 0),$$

and

$$f_3 = \zeta^4 + \frac{1}{\zeta^4} = 2 \cdot \cos \frac{8\pi}{13} < 0$$

hold (and therefore $f_1 > f_2 > f_3$), and that

$$f_1 + f_2 + f_3 = y_1$$
$$= \frac{-1 + \sqrt{13}}{2},$$

$$f_1 f_2 + f_2 f_3 + f_3 f_1 = \zeta + \zeta^2 + \zeta^3 + \cdots + \zeta^{12}$$
$$= -1,$$

and

$$f_1 f_2 f_3 = \zeta^2 + \zeta^5 + \zeta^6 + \zeta^7 + \zeta^8 + \zeta^{11} + 2$$
$$= y_2 + 2$$
$$= \frac{-1 - \sqrt{13}}{2} + 2$$
$$= \frac{3 - \sqrt{13}}{2},$$

it follows that $f_1 = 2 \cdot \cos \frac{2\pi}{13}$ is the largest root of the cubic equation

$$f^3 + \frac{1 - \sqrt{13}}{2} \cdot f^2 - f + \frac{-3 + \sqrt{13}}{2} = 0.$$

This is a cubic equation of the form

$$x^3 + px^2 + qx + r = 0,$$

and as we know from section 9 (page 30), the roots of such an equation are the slopes of the creases obtained by simultaneously folding

$$F_1\left(-\frac{p}{2} + \frac{r}{2}, \frac{q}{2}\right)$$

onto the line

$$\ell_1 : x = -\frac{p}{2} - \frac{r}{2},$$

and

$$F_2\left(0, \frac{1}{2}\right)$$

onto the line

$$\ell_2 : y = -\frac{1}{2}.$$

167

Substituting
$$p = \frac{1 - \sqrt{13}}{2}, \quad q = -1 \quad \text{and} \quad r = \frac{-3 + \sqrt{13}}{2},$$
we obtain
$$F_1\left(\frac{-2 + \sqrt{13}}{2}, -\frac{1}{2}\right)$$
and
$$\ell_1 : x = \frac{1}{2}.$$

Applying this yields $f_1 = 2 \cdot \cos \frac{2\pi}{13}$ as the slope of the steepest of the three folds thus obtained. From this we proceed to develop the folding sequence for the regular triskaidekagon.

MODEL XIII   REGULAR TRISKAIDEKAGON

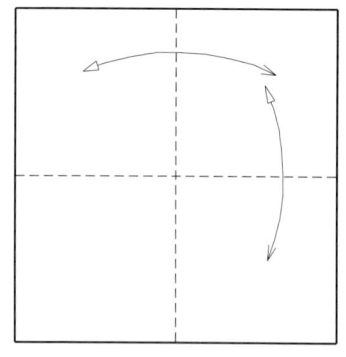

1. fold and unfold twice

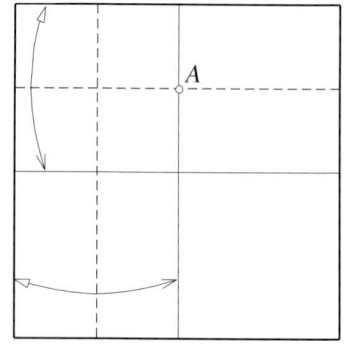

2. fold edge to crease twice and unfold, noting point A

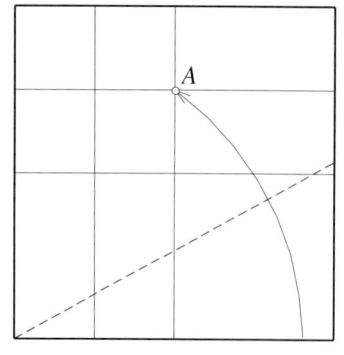

3. fold such that crease goes through corner and edge comes to lie on A

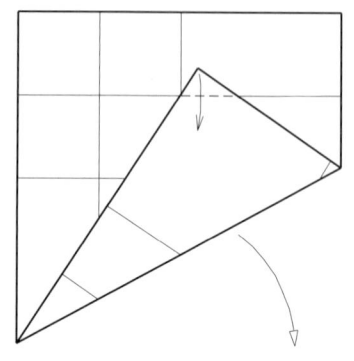

4. fold using lower crease as guide; unfold everything

26   The regular triskaidekagon

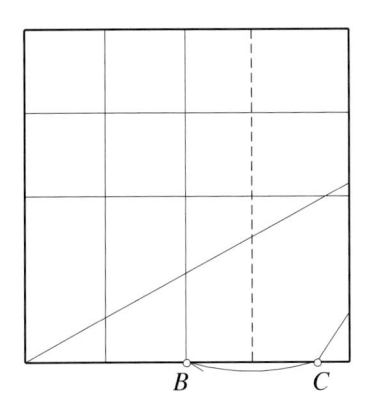

5| fold B to C

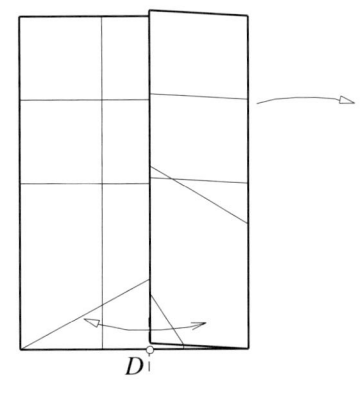

6| fold using edge as guideline, making a crease mark at point D; unfold everything

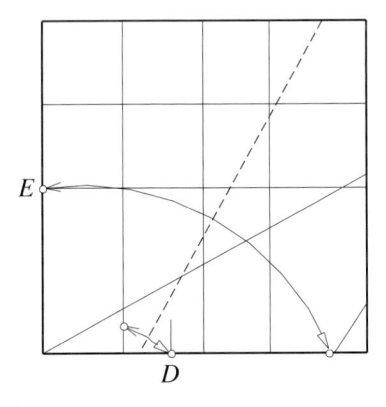

7| fold such that D comes to lie on crease and edge comes to lie on E

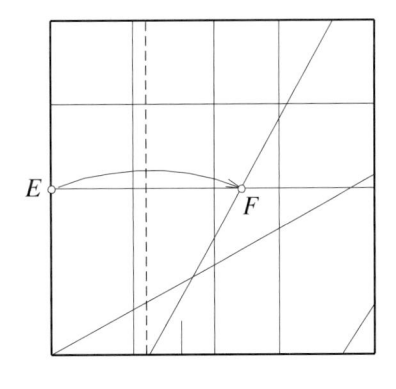

8| unfold; fold E to F

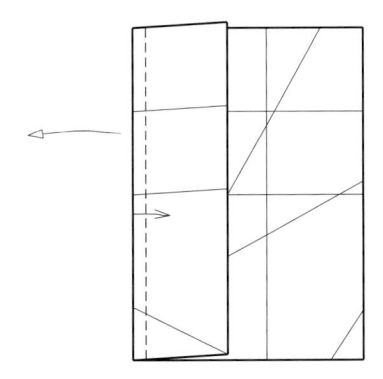

9| fold and unfold both layers at crease, then unfold everything

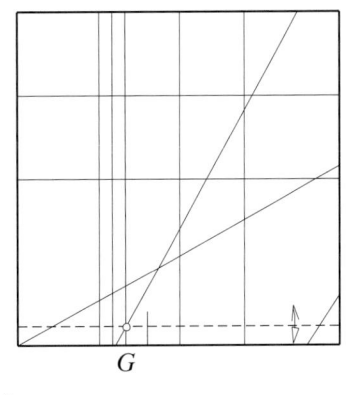

10| fold horizontally through G, then unfold

169

| Chapter 8 | A Few More Polygons |

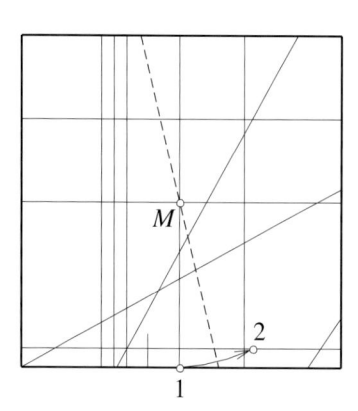

11 fold such that *M* lies on crease and point 1 comes to lie on crease from step 10, resulting in point 2; point *M* is mid-point of 13-gon, points 1 and 2 are corners

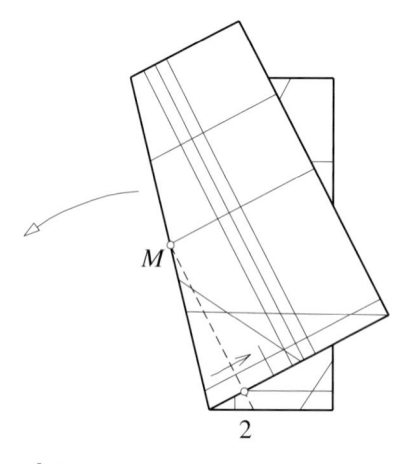

12 fold such that *M* and 2 lie on crease; unfold everything and repeat on left, yielding corner 13 of 13-gon

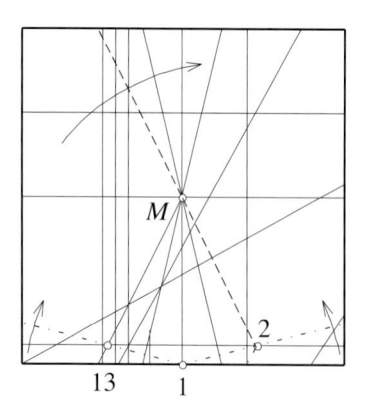

13 fold back twice (resulting folds are two sides of the 13-gon); then fold such that crease connects *M* and 2

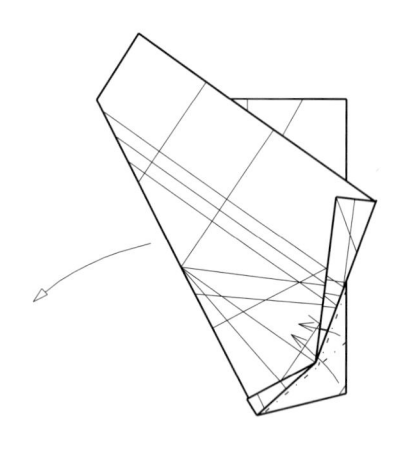

14 fold back twice using edges as guidelines, yielding two more sides of the 13-gon; repeat on left using *M* and 13

26 The regular triskaidekagon

15 fold such that crease connects M and 3; as in step 13, use edges as guidelines to fold back four new edges; repeat on left using M and 12

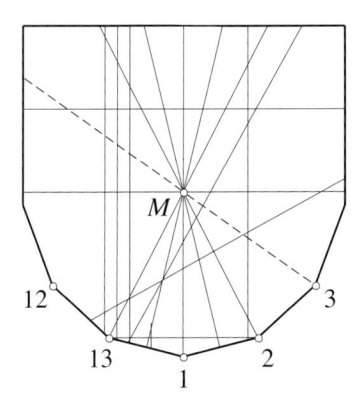

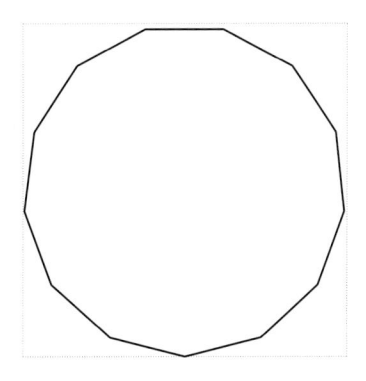

16 the finished triskaidekagon

If we assume that the square we are folding has edges of length 2, the point A in step 2 is 1 unit from the left-hand edge, and $\frac{3}{2}$ units from the bottom edge. This means that point A, and therefore also point B in step 5, are $\frac{1}{2} \cdot \sqrt{13}$ units from the lower left-hand corner of the square. Point D in step 6 is therefore

$$\frac{1}{2} \cdot \sqrt{13} - 1 = \frac{-2 + \sqrt{13}}{2}$$

units from the lower left-hand corner.

Assuming the origin of a system of cartesian coordinates $\frac{1}{2}$ unit above the lower left-hand corner, this point D is therefore the focus

$$F_1\left(\frac{-2 + \sqrt{13}}{2}, -\frac{1}{2}\right)$$

as required. This point has to be folded onto the directrix $\ell_1 : x = \frac{1}{2}$, which is the crease parallel to the left-hand edge of the square as generated in step 2.

Simultaneously, we must fold $F_2\left(0, \frac{1}{2}\right)$ onto $\ell_2 : y = -\frac{1}{2}$, where F_2 is the point E in step 7 (that is, the mid-point of the left-hand edge), and ℓ_2 is the lower edge of the folding square. In step 7, we simultaneously fold F_1 onto ℓ_1 and F_2 onto ℓ_2, taking care to generate the crease with slope greater than 1, as required.

By folding E to F in step 8, and transferring the crease to the bottom layer of the paper in step 9, a right-angled triangle is created, whose hypotenuse lies on the crease with slope $2 \cdot \cos \frac{2\pi}{13}$. Since the side of this triangle through F and parallel to the lower edge of the paper is $\frac{1}{2}$ unit in length, the length of the side parallel to the left-hand edge of the paper is $\cos \frac{2\pi}{13}$, and the horizontal crease through G in step 10 is therefore the line joining

171

Chapter 8   A Few More Polygons

corners 2 and 13 of the 13-gon, taking the mid-point of the bottom edge of the folding square as corner 1.

Steps 12 through 16 then simply complete the 13-gon.

27   The regular 17-gon

Folding a regular 17-gon is of particular interest, since this is one n-gon with prime n that can be drawn with straight-edge and compass, as was shown so brilliantly by the young Gauss in the late eighteenth century. Unlike the 7-gon or the 13-gon, the equations associated with the 17-gon can all be reduced to linear and quadratic problems, making them accessible to Euclidean constructions. Since we can fold any object that can be constructed by Euclidean methods (Theorem 1, page 16), it must be possible to fold a regular 17-gon.

As for the 7-gon and the 13-gon, we once again think of the vertices of the 17-gon and the solutions of a polynomial equation in the complex plane. In this case, the equation in question is

$$z^{17} - 1 = 0.$$

As before, we note that the unit circle is the circumcircle of the 17-gon, and that the point $z_1 = 1$ on the real axis is one vertex. The other 16 vertices are therefore the roots of the equation

$$\frac{z^{17} - 1}{z - 1} \equiv z^{16} + z^{15} + \cdots + z + 1 = 0,$$

and we can write all 17 roots (in polar coordinates) as

$$z_k = \left(1; \frac{2\pi(k-1)}{17}\right) = \cos\frac{2\pi(k-1)}{17} + i \cdot \sin\frac{2\pi(k-1)}{17}$$

for $k = 1, 2, \ldots, 17$.

Naming $z_2 =: \zeta$, we then have

$$z_k = \zeta^{k-1}$$

for $k = 2, 3, \ldots, 17$. As we saw in the previous section for the case of the 13-gon, grouping the powers of ζ in an appropriate way allows us to reduce the solution of the degree 16 equation to the successive solution of a number of equations of lesser degree. Indeed, as we know from Gauss, if we do it correctly, we can expect all of these equations to be of no higher degree than second.

Successive squaring of ζ yields values of z_k in the order

$$\zeta, \zeta^2, \zeta^4, \zeta^8, \zeta^{16}, \zeta^{15}, \zeta^{13}, \zeta^9,$$

and the powers of ζ missing in this sequence are obtained by successive squaring of ζ^3 in the order

$$\zeta^3, \zeta^6, \zeta^{12}, \zeta^7, \zeta^{14}, \zeta^{11}, \zeta^5, \zeta^{10}.$$

27 The regular 17-gon

We define variables y_1 and y_2 as

$$y_1 = \zeta + \zeta^2 + \zeta^4 + \zeta^8 + \zeta^{16} + \zeta^{15} + \zeta^{13} + \zeta^9$$

and

$$y_2 = \zeta^3 + \zeta^6 + \zeta^{12} + \zeta^7 + \zeta^{14} + \zeta^{11} + \zeta^5 + \zeta^{10},$$

and note that we then have

$$y_1 + y_2 = \zeta + \zeta^2 + \zeta^3 + \cdots + \zeta^{16}$$
$$= -1$$

and

$$y_1 \cdot y_2 = 4 \cdot \left(\zeta + \zeta^2 + \zeta^3 + \cdots + \zeta^{16}\right)$$
$$= -4.$$

This means that y_1 and y_2 are the solutions of the equation

$$y^2 + y - 4 = 0.$$

Of these two solutions, y_1 is certainly positive (as we see in Figure 8.3), since $\zeta + \zeta^{16}$, $\zeta^2 + \zeta^{15}$ and $\zeta^4 + \zeta^{13}$ are all positive real numbers and only $\zeta^8 + \zeta^9$ is negative. (Details of this argument are analogous to those used in the case of the 13-gon in section 26.) We therefore see that

$$y_1 = \frac{-1 + \sqrt{17}}{2} \quad \text{and} \quad y_2 = \frac{-1 - \sqrt{17}}{2}.$$

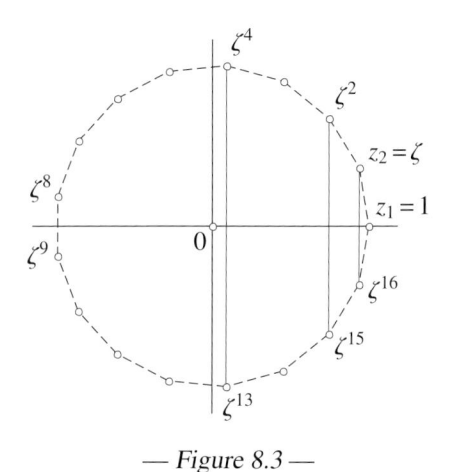

— Figure 8.3 —

Next we define variables n_1 and n_2 by

$$n_1 = \zeta + \zeta^4 + \zeta^{16} + \zeta^{13}$$

and

$$n_2 = \zeta^2 + \zeta^8 + \zeta^{15} + \zeta^9.$$

We have

$$n_1 + n_2 = \zeta + \zeta^2 + \zeta^4 + \zeta^8 + \zeta^{16} + \zeta^{15} + \zeta^{13} + \zeta^9$$
$$= y_1$$

and
$$n_1 \cdot n_2 = \zeta + \zeta^2 + \zeta^3 + \cdots + \zeta^{16}$$
$$= -1.$$

The two numbers n_1 and n_2 are therefore the solutions of the quadratic equation
$$n^2 - y_1 n - 1 = 0,$$
and glancing at Figure 8.3 on the previous page shows us immediately that n_1 is positive (since both $\zeta + \zeta^{16}$ and $\zeta^4 + \zeta^{13}$ are positive) and n_2 is negative (since $\zeta^8 + \zeta^9$ is negative and much nearer to $2 \cdot (-1)$ than $\zeta^2 + \zeta^{15}$ is to $2 \cdot (+1)$).

Furthermore, we define m_1 and m_2 in an analogous way by
$$m_1 = \zeta^3 + \zeta^{12} + \zeta^{14} + \zeta^5$$
and
$$m_2 = \zeta^6 + \zeta^7 + \zeta^{11} + \zeta^{10}.$$

We have
$$m_1 + m_2 = \zeta^3 + \zeta^6 + \zeta^{12} + \zeta^7 + \zeta^{14} + \zeta^{11} + \zeta^5 + \zeta^{10}$$
$$= y_2$$
and
$$m_1 \cdot m_2 = \zeta + \zeta^2 + \zeta^3 + \cdots + \zeta^{16}$$
$$= -1,$$
and the numbers m_1 and m_2 are the solutions of the quadratic equation
$$m^2 - y_2 m - 1 = 0.$$

It is obvious that m_2 is negative, since both $\zeta^6 + \zeta^{11}$ and $\zeta^7 + \zeta^{10}$ are negative real numbers. The other solution m_1 is positive, since $\zeta^3 + \zeta^{14}$ is positive with $\mathrm{Re}\,\zeta^3 > |\mathrm{Re}\,\zeta^5|$.

As a final step, we define variables v_1 and v_2 as
$$v_1 = \zeta^2 + \zeta^{15}$$
and
$$v_2 = \zeta^8 + \zeta^9.$$

Since we have
$$v_1 + v_2 = \zeta^2 + \zeta^8 + \zeta^{15} + \zeta^9$$
$$= n_2$$
and
$$v_1 \cdot v_2 = \zeta^6 + \zeta^7 + \zeta^{11} + \zeta^{10}$$
$$= m_2,$$
the numbers v_1 and v_2 are the solutions of the quadratic equation
$$v^2 - n_2 v + m_2 = 0,$$

27 The regular 17-gon

with
$$v_1 = 2 \cdot \cos \frac{4\pi}{17} > 0$$

and
$$v_2 = 2 \cdot \cos \frac{16\pi}{17} < 0.$$

In Model XIV, we shall determine v_1 and then go on to complete the n-gon by applying the various symmetries inherent to it.

MODEL XIV   REGULAR 17-GON

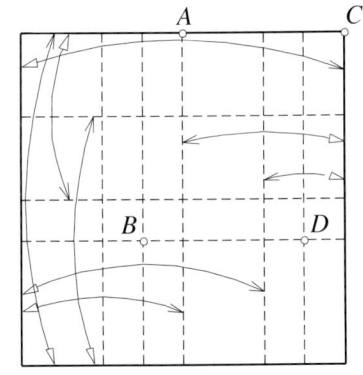

1. fold edge to edge and unfold twice; fold edges to creases and unfold to create 6 more creases

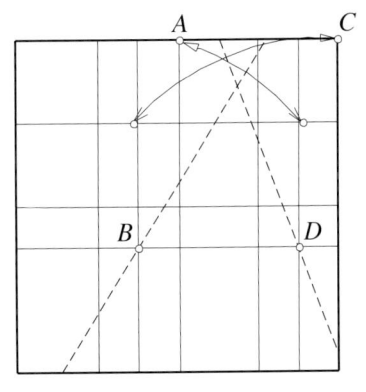

2. fold A to horizontal crease such that resulting crease passes through B and unfold; do same with C such that resulting crease passes through D

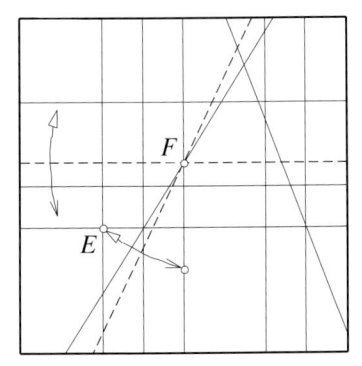

3. fold horizontal crease through F and unfold; fold E onto vertical crease through F such that new crease also passes through F and unfold

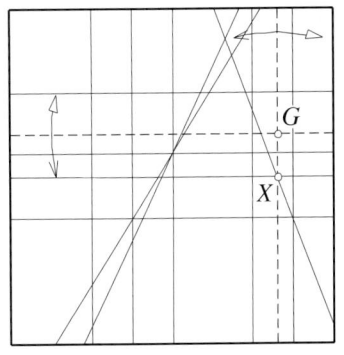

4. fold vertical crease through X and unfold; fold one horizontal crease onto the other and unfold; these two resulting creases intersect in point G

175

Chapter 8 A Few More Polygons

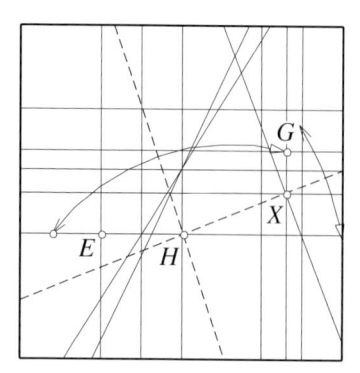

5) fold crease from step 2 through D onto itself through X and unfold; resulting crease intersects horizontal crease through E in point H; fold G onto EH such that crease passes through H and unfold

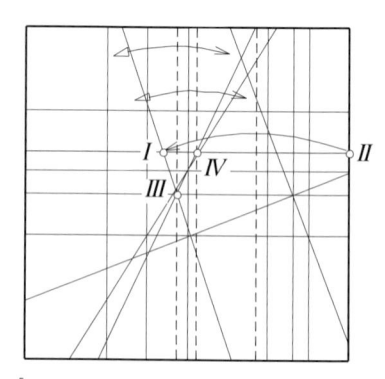

6) IV is on crease from step 3; fold vertical creases through III and IV and unfold; fold II onto I

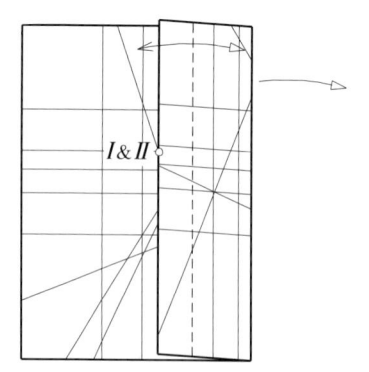

7) fold both layers through crease from step 1 and unfold everything

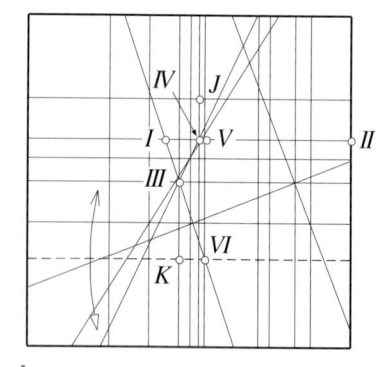

8) fold horizontal crease through VI and unfold

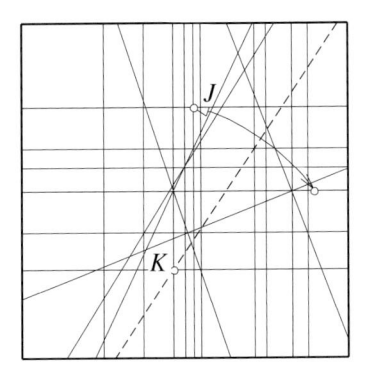

27 The regular 17-gon

9 fold J onto first horizontal crease from step 1 such that crease passes through K and unfold

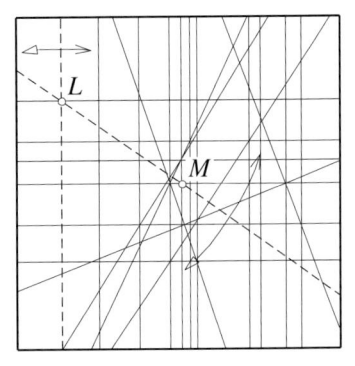

10 fold crease from step 9 onto itself through M and unfold; fold vertical crease through L and unfold

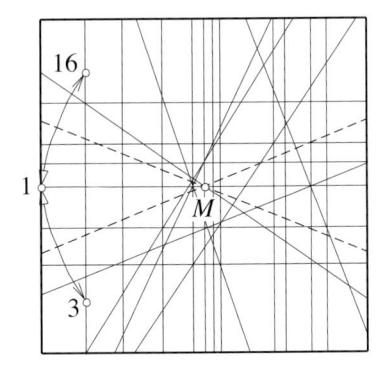

11 fold point 1 onto crease from previous step such that crease passes through M and unfold twice

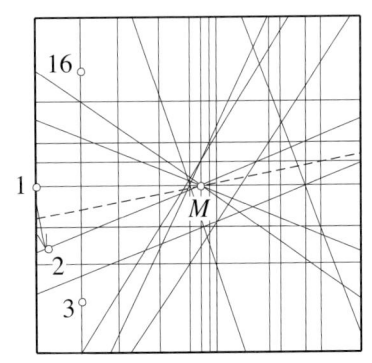

12 fold 1 onto crease from previous step such that crease passes through M

177

Chapter 8   A Few More Polygons

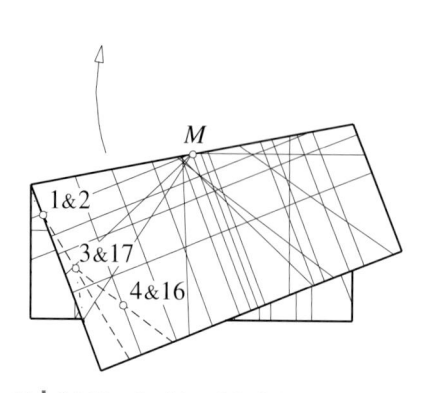

13 | fold back sides 2 3, 3 4, 17 1 and 16 17 of 17-gon using points in both levels as guide; unfold first fold

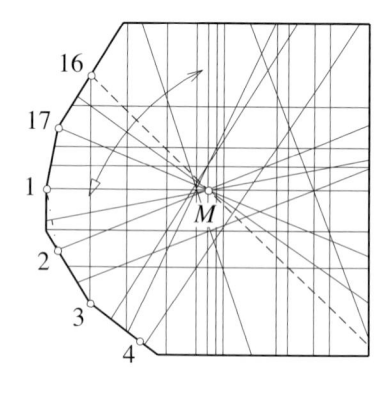

14 | fold back side 1 2; fold crease joining *M* and vertex 16; fold back sides of 17-gon using sides 16 17, 17 1, 1 2, 2 3 and 3 4 as guidelines; unfold first fold

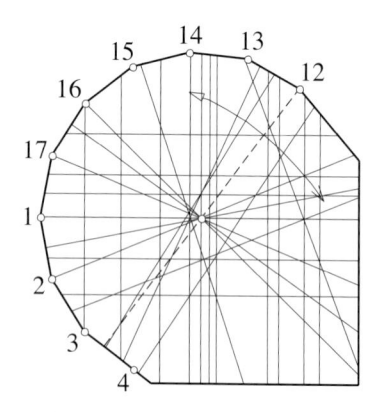

15 | fold crease joining *M* and vertex 12; fold back remaining sides of 17-gon using sides as guidelines; unfold first fold

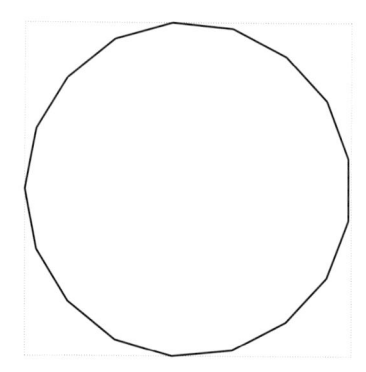

16 | the regular 17-gon

As we know from section 7 (page 23), the solutions of any quadratic equation

$$x^2 + px + q = 0$$

are the slopes of the tangents of the parabola with focus $F(0, 1)$ and directrix $\ell : y = -1$ passing through the point $P(-p, q)$, which we can determine by folding F onto ℓ such that the crease passes through P. In order to determine v_1 as the positive solution of the equation

$$v^2 - n_2 v + m_2 = 0,$$

27 The regular 17-gon

we must first determine the values of n_2 and m_2, so that we can find the point with coordinates (n_2, m_2). We know that n_2 is the negative solution of

$$n^2 - y_1 n - 1 = 0,$$

and that m_2 is the negative solution of

$$m^2 - y_2 m - 1 = 0,$$

and as a first step it is therefore necessary to determine y_1 and y_2 as the solutions of

$$y^2 + y - 4 = 0.$$

This is done in steps 1 and 2. We assume that the folding square has sides of length 8 units, and due to the successive bisections in step 1, we can assume that A has the coordinates $(0, 1)$ and B has the coordinates $(-1, -4)$, whereby we assume that the x-axis is oriented to the right and the y-axis upwards. The line parallel to the upper edge and just below it is then represented by the equation $y = -1$, and folding A onto this line such that the crease passes through B in step 2 yields a crease with slope y_1.

Since the size of the folding square is limited, we cannot fold a crease with slope y_2 in this way, but since points C and D have the same relative position as A and B, we can also assume that C has the coordinates $(0, 1)$ and D has the coordinates $(-1, -4)$, and folding C onto the horizontal line $y = -1$ such that the crease passes through D then yields a crease with slope y_2.

In step 3, we fold a crease with slope n_2. Since n_2 solves the equation $n^2 - y_1 n - 1 = 0$, we must determine points $F(0, 1)$ and $P(y_1, -1)$ relative to some system of coordinates. This is done by assuming the x-axis of such a system oriented upwards and the y-axis oriented to the left. Leaving the unit length as in steps 1 and 2, choice of E in the grid point from step 1 as shown yields a point F whose x-coordinate is larger than that of E by 2 units. We can therefore assume that the coordinates of E relative to the new system are $(0, 1)$, and the coordinates of F in this system are therefore $(y_1, -1)$ as required, since F is one unit to the right of B, and therefore y_1 units higher than EB. Folding E onto the vertical crease through F (the line represented by the equation $y = -1$ in this system of coordinates) then yields a crease with slope n_2 in this system.

In steps 4 and 5, we fold a crease with slope m_2, retaining the orientation and unit length of the system of coordinates as in steps 1 and 2. By first folding the crease with slope y_2 onto itself, we obtain a crease with slope $-\frac{1}{y_2}$. The x-coordinate of the point H is therefore smaller than that of G by $|y_2|$ (recall that y_2 is negative), and since G is located on the horizontal crease two units above that through H, we can assume that G has the coordinates $(0, 1)$ and H has the coordinates $(y_2, 1)$. We know that m_2 is the negative solution of the quadratic equation $m^2 - y_2 m - 1 = 0$, and folding G onto the horizontal crease through H (which is represented by the equation $y = -1$) such that the crease passes through H therefore yields a crease with slope m_2.

We are now ready to determine v_1. Since v_1 is a solution of the quadratic equation $v^2 - n_2 v + m_2 = 0$, it results as the slope of a crease derived by folding $(0, 1)$ onto the line represented by $y = -1$ such that the crease passes through the point (n_2, m_2) in some system of coordinates. This is done is steps 6 through 9.

The horizontal crease three units from the upper edge intersects the crease with slope m_2 in *I* and the right edge of the folding square in *II*. Folding *II* to *I* in step 6 and then re-folding the crease one unit from the edge of the square through both layers in step 7 yields a vertical crease intersecting *III* in *V*, and the crease with slope m_2 in *VI*. Since *I* and *V* are one unit apart, *V* and *VI* are $|m_2|$ units apart, and the horizontal crease in step 8 through *VI* is m_2 units below *III*.

At the same time, *III* intersects the crease with slope n_2 (relative to the rotated system of coordinates) in *IV*. The horizontal line one unit below *III* intersects this crease in *III*, and the vertical creases through *III* and *IV* are therefore $|n_2|$ units apart. It follows that the point *K*, in which the horizontal line through *VI* and the vertical line through *III* intersect, is $|n_2|$ to the left and $|m_2|$ below the point *IV*. Taking *IV* as the origin of a new system of coordinates, once again with the *x*-axis oriented to the right and the *y*-axis oriented upwards, *K* has the coordinates (n_2, m_2). The point *J*, in which the vertical line through *IV* intersects the horizontal line one unit above *III*, has the coordinates $(0, 1)$, and the horizontal line one unit below *III* is represented by the equation $y = -1$. The crease obtained by folding *J* onto this line such that the crease passes through *K* therefore solves the equation, and its slope is

$$v_1 = 2\cos\frac{4\pi}{17}.$$

The crease perpendicular to this one through the mid-point *M* of the folding square in step 10 therefore has the slope $-\frac{1}{2\cos\frac{4\pi}{17}}$. Since we wish the circumcircle of the 17-gon to be the incircle of the folding square, we now assume that the edges of the square are two units in length. The distance between the mid-point *M* of the folding square and the horizontal line through *J* is then one half unit, and this line intersects the crease with slope $-\frac{1}{2\cos\frac{4\pi}{17}}$ in a point *L*, whose distance from the vertical line through the mid-point of the square is $\cos\frac{4\pi}{17}$.

If we assume in step 11 that the point 1 in which the horizontal line through the mid-point of the square intersects the left-hand edge is a vertex of the 17-gon, we obtain vertices 3 and 16 by folding 1 onto the vertical line through *L*. The creases resulting from these folds are *M* 2 and *M* 17.

Steps 12 through 15 then complete the 17-gon by applying its symmetries.

28 The regular 19-gon

In this final section, we shall develop a method of folding a regular 19-gon. The methods used are more or less the same as those applied in the last few sections for regular *n*-gons in the cases $n = 7, 9, 13$ and 17. Cubic equations will once again play an important role, but unlike the cases $n = 7, 9$ and 13, we shall see that the case $n = 19$ involves solving a cubic equation whose coefficients are first determined by solving another cubic equation.

28 The regular 19-gon

This has to do with the fact that the prime number 19 is such that $19 - 1 = 18$ is divisible by 3^2. The next such prime number is 37. An analogous folding method could certainly be developed for this case, but it seems that the actual diagramming of such a method would be prohibitively complex. In fact, after 19, the next prime n for which the regular n-gon can be folded precisely by the methods presented in this book is in fact 37, and so 19 seems to be a logical point to stop.

Analogous to the cases $n = 7$ and 13, we consider the roots of the equation

$$z^{19} - 1 = 0$$

in the complex plane. These roots z_i ($i = 1, 2, \ldots, 19$) are the corners of a regular 19-gon. The roots of the cyclotomic equation

(8.2) $$\frac{z^{19} - 1}{z - 1} \equiv z^{18} + z^{17} + \cdots + z + 1 = 0$$

are then

$$z_n = \left(1; \frac{2\pi(n-1)}{19}\right) = \cos\frac{2\pi(n-1)}{19} + i \cdot \sin\frac{2\pi(n-1)}{19}$$

for $n = 2, 3, \ldots, 19$ (assuming $z_1 = 1$), and with $z_2 =: \zeta$, we have

$$z_n = \zeta^{n-1} \quad \text{for} \quad n = 2, 3, \ldots, 19$$

analogous to the assumptions made for the heptagon and triskaidekagon.

Successively squaring the roots of equation (8.2), starting with ζ, we obtain the sequence

$$\zeta, \zeta^2, \zeta^4, \zeta^8, \zeta^{16}, \zeta^{13}, \zeta^7, \zeta^{14}, \zeta^9, \zeta^{18}, \zeta^{17}, \zeta^{15}, \zeta^{11}, \zeta^3, \zeta^6, \zeta^{12}, \zeta^5, \zeta^{10}, \zeta, \ldots.$$

We now define variables

$$y_1 = \zeta + \zeta^8 + \zeta^7 + \zeta^{18} + \zeta^{11} + \zeta^{12},$$
$$y_2 = \zeta^2 + \zeta^{16} + \zeta^{14} + \zeta^{17} + \zeta^3 + \zeta^5$$

and

$$y_3 = \zeta^4 + \zeta^{13} + \zeta^9 + \zeta^{15} + \zeta^6 + \zeta^{10}.$$

These variables are such that

$$y_1 + y_2 + y_3 = \zeta + \zeta^2 + \cdots + \zeta^{18}$$
$$= -1,$$
$$y_1 y_2 + y_2 y_3 + y_3 y_1 = 6 \cdot \left(\zeta + \zeta^2 + \cdots + \zeta^{18}\right)$$
$$= -6$$

and

$$y_1 y_2 y_3 = 18 + 11 \cdot \left(\zeta + \zeta^2 + \cdots + \zeta^{18}\right)$$
$$= 18 - 11$$
$$= 7,$$

Chapter 8   A Few More Polygons

and y_1, y_2 and y_3 are therefore the roots of the cubic equation

(8.3) $$y^3 + y^2 - 6y - 7 = 0.$$

They are all real, since each y_i is of the form

$$y_i = \zeta^r + \zeta^s + \zeta^t + \zeta^{19-r} + \zeta^{19-s} + \zeta^{19-t},$$

and since

$$\zeta^{19} = 1,$$

and therefore

$$\zeta^{19-r} = \frac{1}{\zeta^r} \cdot \zeta^{19} = \frac{1}{\zeta^r}$$

and

$$|\zeta^r| = \left|\frac{1}{\zeta^r}\right| = 1$$

with

$$\frac{1}{\zeta^r} = \overline{\zeta^r}$$

hold (with $\overline{\zeta^r}$ denoting the conjugate of ζ^r). Each expression of the form

$$\zeta^r + \frac{1}{\zeta^r} = 2 \cdot \operatorname{Re} \zeta^r$$

is therefore real with

$$\zeta^r + \frac{1}{\zeta^r} = 2 \cdot \cos \frac{2\pi(r-1)}{19},$$

and so therefore is each y_i.

We now note by a quick flick of the calculator (or, for purists, a slightly longer inspection of the relative positions of the solutions of the cyclotomic equation and the coordinate axes) that

$$y_1 = 2 \cdot \left(\cos \frac{2\pi}{19} + \cos \frac{14\pi}{19} + \cos \frac{16\pi}{19}\right) \approx -1.22$$

$$y_2 = 2 \cdot \left(\cos \frac{4\pi}{19} + \cos \frac{6\pi}{19} + \cos \frac{10\pi}{19}\right) \approx +2.51$$

and $$y_3 = 2 \cdot \left(\cos \frac{8\pi}{19} + \cos \frac{12\pi}{19} + \cos \frac{18\pi}{19}\right) \approx -2.29$$

holds, and therefore

$$y_2 > 0 > y_1 > y_3.$$

We now define further variables by

$$f_1 = \zeta^4 + \zeta^{15}$$
$$f_2 = \zeta^6 + \zeta^{13}$$
and $$f_3 = \zeta^9 + \zeta^{10}.$$

The variables f_1, f_2 and f_3 are such that the following relations hold:

$$f_1 + f_2 + f_3 = y_3,$$
$$f_1 f_2 + f_2 f_3 + f_3 f_1 = y_2 + y_3,$$

and
$$f_1 f_2 f_3 = 2 + y_1.$$

The three (real) numbers f_1, f_2 and f_3 are therefore the roots of the cubic equation

(8.4) $$f^3 - y_3 \cdot f^2 + (y_2 + y_3) \cdot f - (2 + y_1) = 0.$$

The largest of these roots is

$$f_1 = \zeta^4 + \zeta^{15} = 2 \cdot \cos \frac{8\pi}{19}.$$

(Note that we could have chosen to find the value of $2 \cdot \cos \frac{2\pi}{19}$ by this method by choosing $\zeta + \zeta^{18}$ as a new variable and the others accordingly, but the folding is easier with f_1 as chosen.)

From section 9 (page 30) we know that the solutions of a cubic equation

$$x^3 + px^2 + qx + r = 0$$

are the slopes of the common tangents of the parabolas with foci

$$F_1\left(-\frac{p}{2} + \frac{r}{2}, \frac{q}{2}\right) \quad \text{and} \quad F_2\left(0, \frac{1}{2}\right)$$

and directrices

$$\ell_1 : x = -\frac{p}{2} - \frac{r}{2} \quad \text{and} \quad \ell_2 : y = -\frac{1}{2}$$

respectively. These common tangents are immediately obtained by simultaneously folding F_1 onto ℓ_1 and F_2 onto ℓ_2.

Applying this to equation (8.3) means that we must fold $F_1(-4, -3)$ onto $\ell_1 : x = 3$ and $F_2\left(0, \frac{1}{2}\right)$ onto $\ell_2 : y = -\frac{1}{2}$ simultaneously in order to obtain creases with slopes y_1, y_2 and y_3, whereby y_2 is the positive slope value obtained, and y_3 the lesser of the two negative slope values.

Once we know y_1, y_2 and y_3, we can solve equation (8.4) in this way as well. Here, we must fold

$$F_1\left(\frac{y_3 - y_1}{2} - 1, \frac{y_2 + y_3}{2}\right)$$

onto

$$\ell_1 : x = \frac{y_1 + y_3}{2} + 1$$

and $F_2\left(0, \frac{1}{2}\right)$ onto $\ell_2 : y = -\frac{1}{2}$ simultaneously to obtain f_1, f_2 and f_3. Since f_1 is the largest of these, it is sufficient to find the steepest crease (with positive slope) obtained in this way. With

$$f_1 = 2 \cdot \cos \frac{8\pi}{19}$$

we then have all we need to fold the regular 19-gon.

Chapter 8

A Few More Polygons

MODEL XV   REGULAR 19-GON

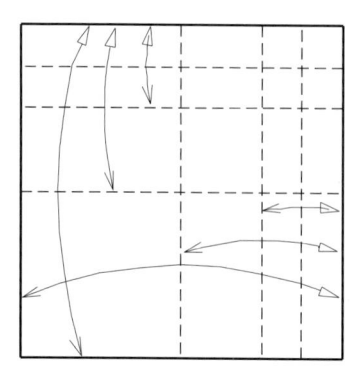

1. fold edge to edge twice and unfold; then fold edge to middle twice and unfold; fold edge to crease twice and unfold

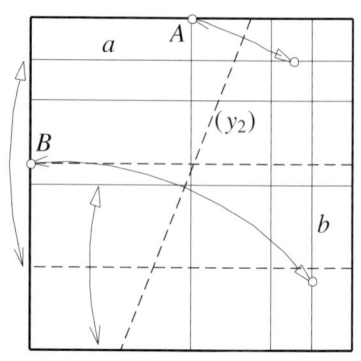

2. fold edge to middle horizontally and unfold; then fold crease to crease a and unfold; folding point A to crease a and point B to crease b simultaneously yields crease with slope y_2; unfold

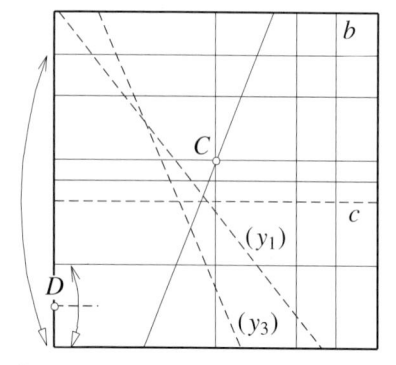

3. fold edge to crease a, yielding crease c and unfold; fold edge to first crease from step 2, marking point D and unfold; folding point C to crease c and point D to crease b simultaneously yields two folds with slopes y_1 and y_3 respectively

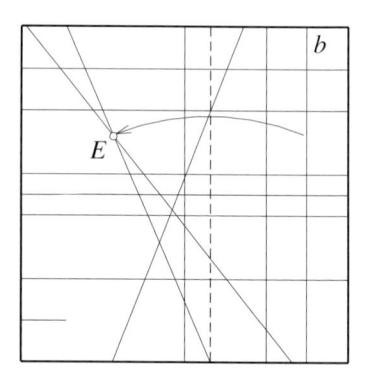

4. fold vertically, such that crease b comes to lie on point E

184

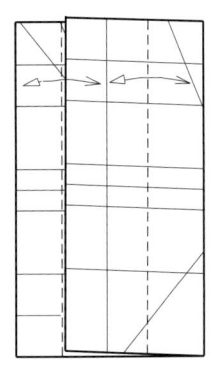

28 The regular 19-gon

5| fold twice using edge and crease as guidelines; unfold everything

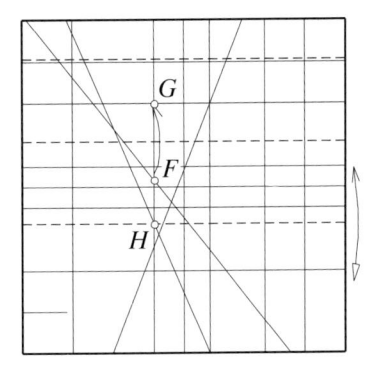

6| fold F to G; then fold both layers horizontally through point H; unfold everything

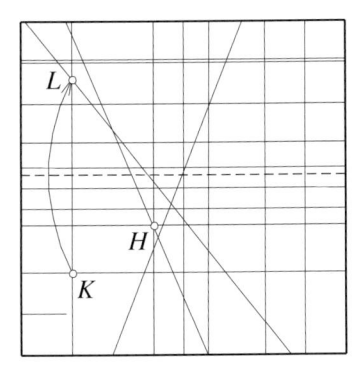

7| fold K to L, noting location of H on back side

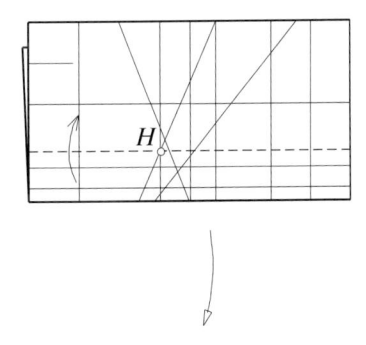

8| fold both layers horizontally through H; unfold everything (resulting crease in lower layer is crease q)

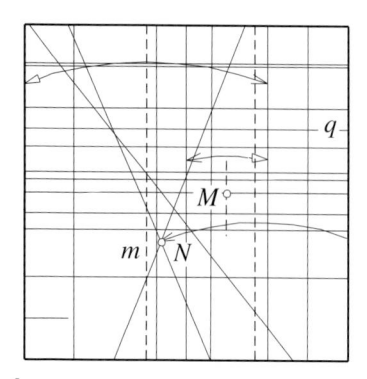

Chapter 8 — A Few More Polygons

9. fold edge to crease from step 1 and unfold (result is crease m); fold crease from step 1 to middle vertical crease marking point M on middle horizontal crease; unfold; fold right-hand edge vertically to point N where creases with slopes y_2 and y_3 intersect

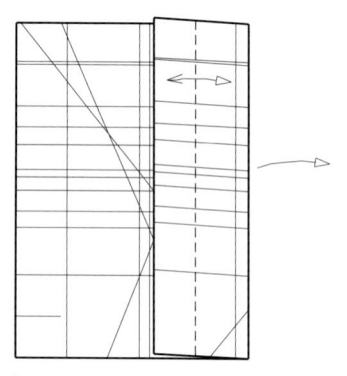

10. fold both layers vertically using crease as guideline; unfold

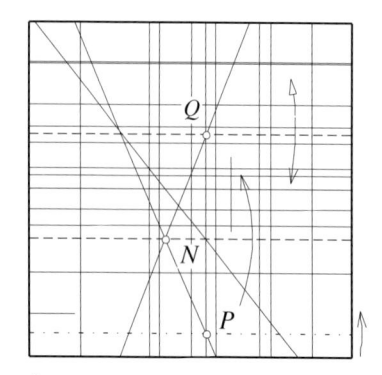

11. P is point where crease from step 10 intersects crease with slope y_3, and Q is point where this crease intersects crease with slope y_2; fold horizontally through Q and unfold; mountain-fold horizontally through P and valley-fold horizontally through N

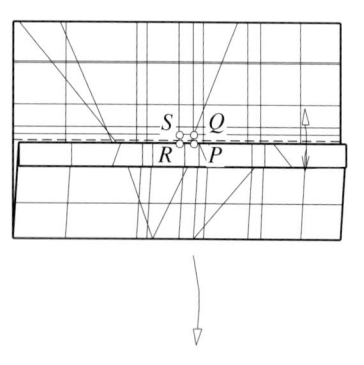

12. fold bottom layer horizontally through P, marking point R on middle vertical crease; S is point of intersection of middle vertical crease with horizontal crease through Q from step 11; unfold everything

28 The regular 19-gon

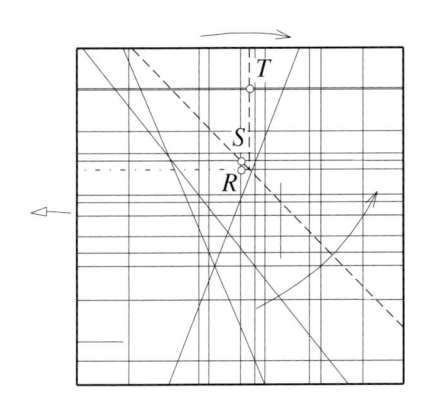

13 | fold at 45° such that crease goes through S and vertical crease comes to lie on horizontal crease; fold both layers vertically through R; point where resulting crease intersects top horizontal fold from step 6 is T; unfold

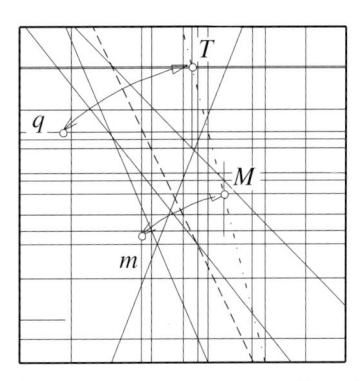

14 | fold T onto q (from step 8) and M onto m (from step 9) simultaneously and unfold

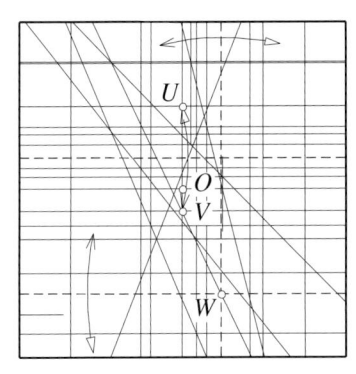

15 | U is mid-point of line joining center O of square to mid-point of top edge and V is point of intersection of vertical middle crease with fold from step 14; fold U to V; then fold at bottom using edge as guideline; W is point where resulting crease intersects crease from step 14; unfold everything; fold vertically through W and unfold

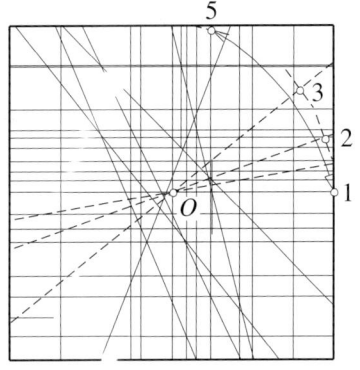

16 | 1 is mid-point of right-hand edge (first corner of 19-gon); fold 1 onto point 5 on last (vertical) crease from step 15, such that crease contains O; mark point 5 using edge as guideline and unfold; repeat process folding 1 onto 3, marking 3; unfold and repeat process again folding 1 onto 2, marking 2; unfold

187

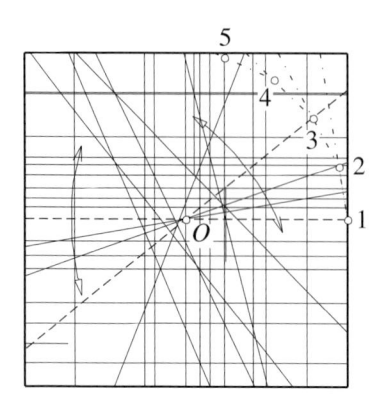

| 17 | mountain fold edges 1 2 and 2 3; refold crease joining 3 and O; fold edges 3 4 and 4 5 using 1 2 and 2 3 as guidelines; unfold crease 3O; fold bottom edge to top edge and fold edges 19 1, 18 19, 17 18 and 16 17 using 1 2, 2 3, 3 4 and 4 5 as guidelines; unfold horizontal fold through 1

| 18 | fold such that crease joins 5 and O; using edges of 19-gon already folded as guidelines yields all edges from 5 6 through 12 13; unfold first fold; repeat with fold joining 16 and O, yielding remaining edges; unfold O 16

| 19 | the finished 19-gon

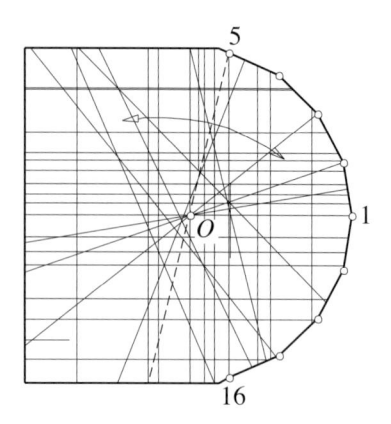

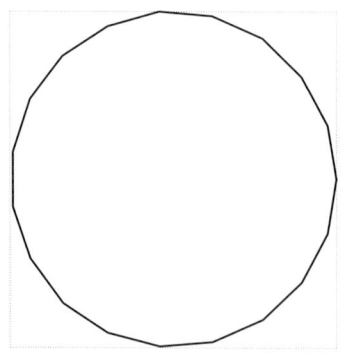

In steps 1 through 3 we assume that the folding square has edges of length 8, and that the origin is on the middle vertical crease of the square (as produced in fold 1 of step 1), and one-half unit from the top edge. Point A in step 2 then has the coordinates $\left(0, \frac{1}{2}\right)$, and crease a is represented by the equation $y = -\frac{1}{2}$. Point B has the coordinates $(-4, -3)$, and crease b is represented by the equation $x = 3$. We therefore have $B = F_1$, $b = \ell_1$, $A = F_2$ and $a = \ell_2$, and folding A onto a and B onto b simultaneously such that the resulting crease has a positive slope results in this crease having the slope y_2.

Unfortunately, we cannot use these positions of the foci and directrices to produce the

28 The regular 19-gon

creases with negative slopes y_1 and y_3. In step 3, we therefore shift the position of the origin to the mid-point of the folding square. (This does not, of course, affect the slopes of the creases.) While $b = \ell_1$ still holds, F_1 has now shifted to point D, F_2 to point C, and ℓ_2 to crease c. Folding D to b and C to c simultaneously then yields the creases with slopes y_1 and y_3. Folding y_1 is made easier by folding back vertically through b and horizontally through C, so that the points and creases can be better seen. No such trick is possible for folding the crease with slope y_3, unfortunately, since both C and the point on c onto which C is folded are pretty much in the middle of the line-segment joining D and the point on b onto which D is folded. This is therefore a rather difficult step to handle precisely.

Now that we have creases with slopes y_1, y_2 and y_3, we can go on to finding foci and directrices of the parabolas needed to determine f_1. Ultimately, in step 14, we will be able to actually fold a crease with slope f_1.

In order to accomplish this in a reasonably simple way, we now define new directions for our system of coordinates. (In order to differentiate the coordinate systems, we name this new system the f-system, and the coordinate system in which we determined y_1, y_2 and y_3 the y-system.) We assume that the x-axis in the f-system is oriented vertically with the positive orientation pointing down, and the the y-axis oriented horizontally with the positive orientation pointing to the right. The origin is assumed to be in the mid-point of the folding square, and we assume that the sides of the folding square are 4 units in length. Steps 4 through 13 are now all geared toward producing the foci and directrices necessary for folding the crease with slope f_1.

Point E in step 4 is the point of intersection of the creases with slopes y_1 and y_3 with respect to the y-system. Assuming that the sides of the folding square are 4 units in length (as required for the f-system), crease b is therefore one half unit from the right-hand edge of the paper, and we therefore see that the distance between points F and H in step 6 is $\frac{y_1-y_3}{2}$. The uppermost crease produced in step 6 is therefore represented by the equation $x = \frac{y_3-y_1}{2} - 1$ with respect to the f-system, since G is one unit from the top edge.

Furthermore, point L in step 7 is $\left|\frac{y_1+y_3}{2}\right|$ units from the the horizontal line through H, and therefore, since K is also one unit from the bottom edge, fold q produced in step 8 is $\left|\frac{y_1+y_3}{2}\right| + 1$ units from the bottom edge. Since y_1 and y_3 are both negative, this means that crease q is represented by the equation

$$x = \frac{y_1 + y_3}{2} + 1$$

in the f-system, and q is therefore the directrix ℓ_1 as required.

In step 9, point M has the coordinates $\left(0, \frac{1}{2}\right)$, and is therefore focus F_2 as required. Also, crease m is represented by the equation $y = -\frac{1}{2}$, and is therefore the directrix ℓ_2. Since point N is the point of intersection of the creases with slopes y_2 and y_3 and crease b is one half unit from the right-hand edge, the distance between points R and S in step 12 is $\frac{y_2+y_3}{2}$. In step 13, this distance is transferred to the direction of the y-axis in the f-system, and we see that point T has the coordinates

$$\left(\frac{y_3 - y_1}{2} - 1, \frac{y_2 + y_3}{2}\right).$$

T is therefore the required focus F_1, and folding T onto q and M onto m simultaneously such that the crease has a positive slope in the f-system therefore yields a crease with slope f_1. (This is done best by folding back TM first.)

We can now redefine the unit length for the final steps (since this does not affect the slopes), and choose the folding square to have sides of length 2. Since the crease generated in step 14 has the required slope $f_1 = 2 \cdot \cos \frac{8\pi}{19}$ and U in step 15 is one half unit from the top edge, point W as generated in step 15 is exactly $\cos \frac{8\pi}{19}$ units from the middle vertical fold. The angle $\angle 1O5$ as produced in step 16 is therefore exactly $\frac{8\pi}{19}$, and the remaining steps 16 through 18 simply complete the regular 19-gon.

Some Final Remarks

The world of origami mathematics in general and origami geometry in particular is now expanding rapidly. While the subject may have seemed like an esoteric intellectual playground just a few years ago, we now know that there is much to be gained from research in this area, both from the practical point of view of the applied mathematician and the abstract point of view of pure mathematics.

Several recent books, such as Robert J. Lang's amazing *Origami Design Secrets* [45], Toshikazu Kawasaki's *Roses, Mathematics and Origami* [41] or Kazuo Haga's *Origamics* [25] show the depth to which research in this area has already developed, and the papers in the *Proceedings of the Third International Meeting of Origami Science, Mathematics and Education - OSME^3* [66] and the forthcoming proceedings of 4OSME [67] give a good impression of the range of topics related to this one.

There are several obvious ways for future research to widen the topics treated in this book. Robert J. Lang's method for the quintisection of an acute angle (see his web-site [76]), which is based on Abe's trisection method (presented on page 33) shows that quintic equations can be solved in principle, if some additional folding method is allowed in addition to those presented in section 3. Specifically, folding points onto lines which are themselves being folded, that is, folding two dependent creases simultaneously in some appropriately defined way, certainly yields an extension of the constructions accessible by origami methods. More interesting results can be expected soon in this area.

Another area just starting to be dealt with in the literature is the intrinsic geometry of folding curves. There is a good reason for this: folding curves is not at all easy to do with any precision. It turns out that simply crumpling paper tends to produce many straight folds, but not curves. Perhaps the first paper to treat this subject in an interesting way is Jeannine Mosely's contribution to [66], *The Validity of the Orb, an Origami Model*. The methods of differential geometry used there seem to be one good way to attack this subject, and several papers presented at 4OSME appear to have used her ideas as a starting point.

I hope that this book will motivate more people to turn their attention to this fascinating and growing field of research.

Bibliography

[1] Roger C. Alperin, *A Mathematical Theory of Origami Constructions and Numbers*, New York Journal of Mathematics, No. 6, 2000, pp 119–133

[2] W. W. Rouse Ball, H. S. M. Coxeter, *Mathematical Recreations and Essays*, 13th edition, Dover Publications, New York, 1987

[3] Ludwig Bieberbach, *Theorie der Geometrischen Konstruktionen*, Verlag Birkhäuser, Basel, 1952

[4] Benjamin Bold, *Famous Problems of Geometry and How to Solve Them*, Dover Publications, Mineola NY, 1969

[5] Barry Cipra, *In the Fold: Origami meets Mathematics*, SIAM News, Vol. 34, No. 8, October 2001

[6] David Dureisseix, *Searching for optimal polygon*, unpublished manuscript, 1997

[7] David Dureisseix, *Searching for optimal polygon — application to the pentagon case*, unpublished manuscript, 1997

[8] David Dureisseix, *Searching for optimal polygon — remarks about a general construction and application to heptagon and nonagon*, unpublished manuscript, 1997

[9] Betsy Franco, *Unfolding Mathematics with Unit Origami*, Key Curriculum Press, Emeryville CA, 1999

[10] Hidetosi Fukagawa, *Japanese Temple Geometry Problems, San Gaku*, The Charles Babbage Research Centre, Winnipeg, 1989

[11] Tomoko Fuse, *Unit Origami*, Japan Publications, Tokyo, New York, 1990

[12] Martin Gardner, *The Golden Ratio*, Chapter 8 of *More Mathematical Puzzles and Diversions*, Penguin Books, New York, 1961, pp 69–81

[13] Martin Gardner, *Origami*, Chapter 16 of *More Mathematical Puzzles and Diversions*, Penguin Books, New York, 1961, pp 137–145

[14] Robert Geretschläger, *Euclidean Constructions and the Geometry of Origami*, Mathematics Magazine, Vol. 68, No. 5, December 1995, pp 357–371

[15] Robert Geretschläger, *Folding the Regular Heptagon*, Crux Mathematicorum with Mathematical Mayhem, Vol. 23, No. 2, March 1997, pp 81–88

[16] Robert Geretschläger, *Folding the Regular Nonagon*, Crux Mathematicorum with Mathematical Mayhem, Vol. 23, No. 4, May 1997, pp 210–217

[17] Robert Geretschläger, *Folding the Regular Triskaidekaagon*, unpublished manuscript, 1998

[18] Robert Geretschläger, *Folding the Regular 19-gon*, unpublished manuscript, 1998

[19] Robert Geretschläger, *Solving Quartic Equations in Origami*, unpublished manuscript, 1998

[20] Robert Geretschläger, *Geometric Constructions in Origami*, Japanese translation by Hidetoshi Fukagawa, Morikita Publishing, ISBN 4-627-01681-6, Tokyo, 2002

[21] Robert Geretschläger, *Just Like Young Gauss Playing with a Square: Folding the Regular 17-gon*, Proceedings of the Third International Meeting of Origami Science, Mathematics and Education — OSME[3], A. K. Peters, Natick, Massachusetts, 2002, pp 95–106

[22] Robert Geretschläger, *Folding Curves*, Proceedings of the Fourth International Meeting of Origami Science, Mathematics and Education — 4OSME, A. K. Peters, Natick, Massachusetts, to appear

[23] Rona Gurkewitz and Bennett Arnstein, *3-d Geometric Origami*, Dover Publications, New York, 1995

[24] Kazuo Haga, Article in ORU, Spring 1996, No. 12 issue, pp 60–64

[25] Kazuo Haga, *Origamics*, ISBN 4-535-78293-8, Tokyo, 2000

[26] Liang-shin Hahn, *Complex Numbers and Geometry*, Mathematical Association of America, Washington, 1994

[27] R. Harbin, *Origami, The Art of Paper Folding, Vols. 1–4*, Hodder Paperbacks, Norwich, 1968

[28] Johannes Hjelmslev, *Geometrische Experimente*, B. G. Teubner Verlag, Leipzig, 1914

[29] Ross Honsberger, *More Mathematical Morsels*, Mathematical Association of America, Washington, 1991

[30] Thomas Hull, *Project Origami*, A. K. Peters, Natick, Massachusetts, 2006

[31] K. Husimi, *Origami na Kikagaku*, Appendix to Saiensu (Japanese version of Scientific American), Oct. 1980

[32] Humiaki Huzita, Benedetto Scimemi, *The algebra of paper-folding (Origami)*, Proceedings of the First International Meeting of Origami Science and Technology, Ferarra, 1989, pp 215–222

[33] Roger A. Johnson, *Advanced Euclidean Geometry*, Houghton Miffin Co., London, 1929, reprinted by Dover Publications, New York, 1960

Bibliography

[34] Jacques Justin, *Resolution par le Pliage de l'Equation du Troisieme Degre et Applications Geometriques*, Proceedings of the First International Meeting of Origami Science and Technology, Ferarra, 1989, pp 251–261

[35] Kunihiko Kasahara, *Origami Omnibus*, Japan Publications, Tokyo, 1988

[36] Kunihiko Kasahara, Toshie Takahama, *Origami for the Connoisseur*, Japan Publications, Tokyo, 1987

[37] Kunihiko Kasahara, *Origami — figürlich und geometrisch*, Augustusverlag, Munich, 2000

[38] Kunihiko Kasahara, *Origami ohne Grenzen*, Augustusverlag, Munich, 2001

[39] Kunihiko Kasahara, *The Art and Wonder of Origami*, Quarry Books, Gloucester, 2004

[40] Miyuki Kawamura, *Polyhedra by Origami*, ISBN 4-535-78224-5, Tokyo, 1996

[41] Toshikazu Kawasaki, *Roses, Mathematics and Origami*, Morikita Publishing, Tokyo, 1998

[42] Felix Klein, *Elementarmathematik vom höheren Standpunkte aus, Bd. II*, Springer Verlag, Berlin, 1926

[43] Felix Klein, *Vorlesungen über ausgewählte Fragen der Elementargeometrie*

[44] Robert J. Lang, *The Complete Book of Origami*, Dover Publications, Mineola NY, 1988

[45] Robert J. Lang, *Origami Design Secrets*, A. K. Peters, Natick, Massachusetts, 2003

[46] Zsolt Lengvarsky, *Compound Platonic Polyhedra in origami*, Mathematics Magazine, Vol. 79, No. 3, June 2006, pp 190–198

[47] George Markowsky, *Misconceptions about the Golden Ratio*, The College Mathematics Journal, Vol. 23, Jan. 1992, pp 2–19

[48] George E. Martin, Geometric Constructions, Springer Verlag, Berlin, Heidelberg, New York, 1997

[49] H. Meschkowski, *Unsolved and Unsolvable Problems in Geometry*, Ungar Publications, New York, 1966

[50] Peter Messer, *Problem 1054*, Crux Mathematicorum, Vol. 12, No. 10, Dec. 1986

[51] Robert Morassi, *The Elusive Pentagon*, Proceedings of the First International Meeting of Origami Science and Technology, Ferarra, 1989

[52] Meenakshi Mukerji, *Marvelous Modular Origami*, A. K. Peters, Natick, Massachusetts, 2007

[53] Alton T. Olson, *Mathematics Through Paper Folding*, National Council of Teachers of Mathematics, Reston, VA, 1975

[54] Theoni Pappas, *Mathematical Scandals*, Wide World Publishing/Tetra, San Carlos, California, 1997

[55] Dan Pedoe, *Geometry, A Comprehensive Course*, Dover Publications, New York, 1988

[56] Margherita Piazzolla Beloch, *Sul metodo del ripiegamento della carta per la risoluzione problemi geometrici*, Periodico di Matematiche, Serie IV, 41, pp 104–108

[57] Margherita Piazzolla Beloch, *Sulla risoluzione dei problemi di terzo e quarto grado col metodo del ripiegamento della carta*, Scritti matematici offerti a Luigi Berzolari, 1936

[58] C. A. Rupp, On a Transformation by Paper Folding, American Mathematical Monthly, Vol. 31, Nov. 1924, pp 432–435

[59] Benedetto Scimemi, *Algebra and Geometry by Paper-Folding*, translation of *Algebra e Geometria piegando la carta*, Matematica: gioco ed apprendimento, a cura di B. d'Amore, ed. Apeiron, Bolgna, 1990

[60] Benedetto Scimemi, *Draw of a Regular Heptagon by the Folding*, Proceedings of the First International Meeting of Origami Science and Technology, Ferarra, 1989

[61] T. Sundara Row, *Geometric Exercises in Paper Folding*, Dover Publications, New York, 1966, Reprint of 1905 edition

[62] Dirk J. Struik, *A Concise History of Mathematics*, Dover Publications, New York, 1987

[63] B. L. van der Waerden, *Algebra I*, Springer Verlag, Berlin, Heidelberg, New York, 1971

Proceedings and Journals

[64] Proceedings of the First International Meeting of Origami Science and Technology, Ferarra, 1989

[65] Origami Science and Art — Proceedings of the Second International Meeting of Origami Science and Scientific Origami, Otsu, Japan, 1994

[66] Proceedings of the Third International Meeting of Origami Science, Mathematics and Education — $OSME^3$, A. K. Peters, Natick, Massachusetts, 2002

[67] Proceedings of the Fourth International Meeting of Origami Science, Mathematics and Education — 4OSME, A. K. Peters, Natick, Massachusetts, to appear

Bibliography

[68] Proceedings of COET 1991 — Conference of Origami in Education and Therapy, Birmingham, UK, ed. John Smith, British Origami Society, 1992

[69] Proceedings of COET 1995 — Second International Conference on Origami in Education and Therapy, New York, ed. V'Ann Cornelius, OrigamiUSA, 1995

[70] Symmetry: Culture and Science, Volume 5, Nos. 1 and 2, 1994

Websites

[71] Eric M. Andersen, Origami and Math: http://www.paperfolding.com/math/

[72] Alex Bateman, Origami Tessellations: htpp://www.sanger.ac.uk/Users/agb/Origami/Tessellation/

[73] British Origami Society web-site: http://www.britishorigami.org.uk

[74] David Eppstein, The Geometry Junkyard/Origami: http://www.ics.uci.edu/~eppstein/junkyard/origami.html

[75] Tom Hull: http://web.merrimack.edu/~thull/OrigamiMath.html

[76] Robert J. Lang: http://www.langorigami.com

[77] Meenakshi Mukerji, Origami — MM's Modular Mania: http://hom.comcast.net/~meenaks/origami/

[78] Jim Plank: http://www.cs.utk.edu/~plank/plank/pics/origami/origami.html

[79] Origami Tanteidan web-site: http://www.origami.gr.jp

[80] Origami-USA web-site: http://www.origami-usa.org

[81] Joseph Wu's Origami Page: http://origami.vancouver.bc.ca

[82] Helena Verrill, Origami Dissection Puzzles: http://www.math.lsu.edu/~verrill/origami/disect/

Index

13-gon, 164
14-gon, 148
16-gon, 124
17-gon, 172
19-gon, 180
$8k$-gon, 123

Abe, H., 33
algebra, origami and ~, 19
angle, trisecting an ~, 33

circle, squaring the ~, 28
construction
    geometric ~, 3
    origami ~, 53
cube root, 26
cubic equation, 30, 145

decagon, 140
Delian problem, 28
dividing a line segment, 53
dodecagon, 127

equation
    cubic ~, 30, 145
    fourth-degree ~, 37
    linear ~, 21
    quadratic ~, 23
    quartic ~, 37
equilateral triangle, 118
Euclidean procedure, 3

Ferrari, Ludovico, 37
Fibonacci numbers, 130
fourth-degree equation, 37

Gauss, Carl Friedrich, 172
geometric construction, 3
golden section, 129
grid, triangular ~, 120

Haga theorem, 62, 64
Haga, Kazuo, 62
heptagon, 145, 148, 152

hexagon, 125
Huzita, Humiaki, 4

Justin, Jacques, 36

Kawahata, Fumiaki, 58
Kawasaki, Toshikazu, 53

Lang, Robert J, 53
line segment, dividing a ~, 53
linear equation, 21

maximum polygon, 103
Messer, Peter, 29

n-gon, *see* regular polygon
nonagon, 159

octagon, 122
origami
    ~ and algebra, 19
    ~ construction, 53
    ~ paper, 103
    ~ procedure, 3

paper, origami ~, 103
parabola, 96
pentagon, 129, 133
Piazzolla Beloch, Margherita, 4
polygon, 103

quadratic equation, 23
quartic equation, 37

regular polygon, 103
Row, T. Sundara, 4

sangaku, 65
squaring the circle, 28

triangle, 115
    equilateral ~, 118
triangular grid, 120
trisecting an angle, 33
triskaidekagon, 164
triskaidekaphobia, 164